Mark C. Taylor

HIDING

Foreword by Jack Miles

Taylor, Mark C., 1945–
Hiding / Mark C. Taylor
p. cm. – (Religion and postmodernism)
Includes bibliographic references.
ISBN: 0–226–79159–9 (pbk.:alk.paper)
1. Surfaces (Philosophy) 2. Postmodernism.
3. Theology.
I. Title. II. Series.
B105.S85T39 1997
210–dc21
97–15648
CIP
The University of Chicago Press,
Chicago 60637
The University of Chicago Press, Ltd., London
© 1997 by The University of Chicago
Printed in Hong Kong
Design: 2x4

for Aaron

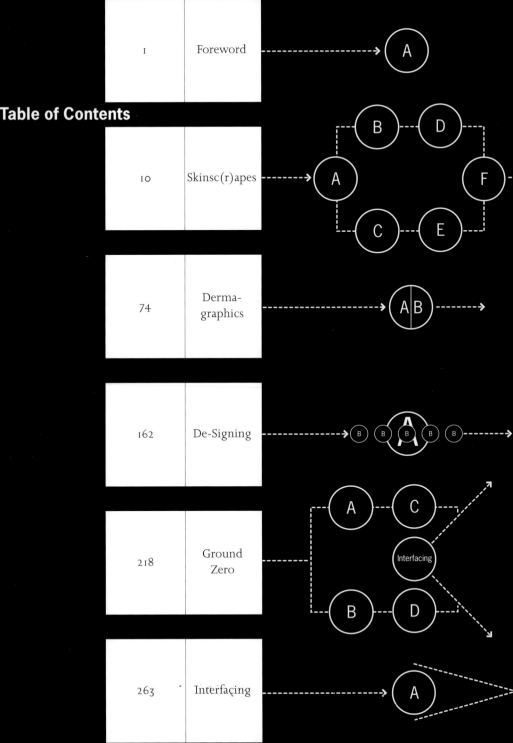

Table of Contents

How to Read This Book

A Note to the Reader from a Concerned Friend

Jack Miles

To read this book right, you have to read it wrong. Reading a book wrong is getting lost in what is superficial or merely charming about it – its interesting examples, its striking illustrations, its literary style, the way the print looks on the page, and so forth – and failing to come to grips with its central argument. But that's just the right way to read this book. Its surface fascinations are considerable. Enjoy them. Don't try to link them into a thesis that you can accept or rebut. Don't read *Hiding* as a book, in short. Instead, take it as a trip. For most serious works of nonfiction, that would be a mistake. For this one, it won't be.

To read *Hiding* by coming to grips with its central argument would be to misread it because Mark C. Taylor, its author, is not trying to come to grips with you. You can't wrestle with a man who won't wrestle back, and Taylor won't. I'll try to say why in a moment, but let me remind you first how often argumentation does indeed become a kind of mental wrestling match. The attacker, the author, tries to pin the defender, the reader, with his arguments. If he succeeds, the reader says, "OK, you got me, you're right, *I give up.*" Our language is full of buried metaphors alluding to this struggle. "I am *convinced,*" we say, using an English word derived ultimately from the Latin word *vincere,* "to conquer." "Your arguments are *cogent,*" we say, using an English word derived from the Latin *cogere,* "to force." If your arguments are not cogent, then I can *refute* them, from the Latin *refutare,* "to drive back."

But Taylor, as I say, doesn't want to conquer his readers. He doesn't want to bring us round to his views by force. It isn't that he is kinder or gentler or more forbearing or more polite than the next author. It is because his guiding conviction is that reality cannot be coerced into a form that would permit him or anyone to derive a cogent, convincing, coercive argument from it. When we try to do that with reality, he says, we turn it into illusion. To those who might reply, "But if we *can't* do that with reality, then reality might as well be illusion," he says, "Yes, and...?" Life can be lived, he implies, without the usual sturdy certainty that the world is really *there.*

One name for this conviction of his is *nihilism*, from the Latin *nihil*, "nothing." A kinder name for it is *vision*. In popular parlance the nihilist is the ultimate, universal aggressor, the enemy not just of religious faith but of any and every claim of truth. But as Taylor knows and Buddhism shows us, nothingness and emptiness can function as guiding concepts within a religious vision that eludes or transcends conventional demonstrations of truth or falsehood. It is no ordinary aggressor, surely, who disarms himself before he disarms you. The right way to read this book, I suggest, is to allow yourself to be disarmed by its disarmed author. Try not to fight with him, he's not fighting with you. Don't accept or reject his book as an argument, see it as a vision or, to repeat, take it as a trip.

A trip may change your mind, after all. In the 1960s, the word *trip* became American slang for the mind-change that mind-altering drugs were bringing about. In subsequent usage, *trip* has come to mean, by implied comparison with the drug experience, any highly stimulating or intense experience. However, the original term of comparison remains the voyage experience. A voyage is not an argument. It may have a destination, it does not have a point. And it may not even have a destination: a trip to nowhere is still a trip and may be the most rewarding kind of trip, for it truly begins with the first step: every part of it counts.

Taylor and I met as graduate students at Harvard University in the late 1960s when the counterculture was at flood tide. What we both took from that extraordinary American moment is what American academic life itself, in varying measures, has taken; namely, an unshakeable suspicion that, to borrow a Spanish proverb, *mas enseña la vida que la universidad*: life teaches more than the university.

At the beginning of the decade, the imperial demands of "the discipline" – words always spoken with a slightly minatory air – were unchallenged. By the end of the decade, there was a restive and ubiquitous challenger: "interdisciplinary" study had become a new imperative. Had it arisen spontaneously, this new imperative, as professors in one discipline began impulsively knocking on the doors of professors in the discipline next door? Anyone who knows professors knows how seldom they do this. No, the mail from one door to the next in *la universidad* is typically carried first by *la vida*, and so it was in the 1960s. Interdisciplinary study permitted academics to expand and modify the vessels of on-campus, schooled reflection to contain social, political, cultural, and technological subject matter that, encountered first off campus, seemed too important and too intellectually fertile to ignore.

My own response to the new interdisciplinary imperative was to obey it to an extreme. Though I completed my doctorate, I became in short order that which the ancients of "the discipline" most abhorred: a journalist. But I became a journalist who, let it be admitted, was always trying to make the newspaper behave more like a university. Taylor, who remained in academe, did the same work from his side of the border: he tried to make the university behave like a newspaper. I wanted an impossibly serious and analytic newspaper. He wanted an impossibly receptive and inquisitive university. Thirty years after graduation, I published *God: A Biography*, a book that, though it won the Pulitzer Prize, neither journalism nor academe knows quite what to do with. *Hiding* is the comparable effort from my penpal. Readers, in their disorganized individuality, will respond to it warmly. Institutions, I predict, will have trouble with it.

There is a pleasure principle of a sort at work here. I once waited for Taylor for two hours on Harvard Square without a book or magazine or anything to divert my attention from the people walking through the square. It was easy to tell those who had a destination from those who did not. Those who had a destination were, in particular, white men in their thirties and forties, Harvard professors perhaps, frowning slightly, carrying briefcases, walking quickly, nervously, as if irritated that they were not already where they intended to go. They met no one's eyes and were otherwise blind to what they walked past. Those who had no destination were, in particular, black men in their forties and fifties, possibly unemployed, carrying nothing, walking a lot more slowly. They met the eyes of anyone who would look back (I remember, because they met mine). They took everything in.

Mark Taylor may be the most focused thinker I know, and yet he would ever blur his own focus, forget his original destination, take in the scene. This is a quintessential sixties habit that can be a weakness or a strength. He makes it a strength. The trip on which he invites his readers is a trip that, so to speak, has a destination even if you never arrive. For twenty-five years he has been on that kind of trip, taking in the scene, assimilating everything that came his way, putting it all together. If nothing else, *Hiding* is a fabulous travelogue.

No other philosopher now writing moves so deftly through theology, literature, literary criticism, art, architecture, biochemistry, neurophysiology, fashion, and technology. In his twenties, as a philosopher of religion, Taylor read the eternal Germans – Kant, Hegel, and Nietzsche – and the Dane Kierkegaard as an anti-Hegel. In his thirties and forties, as a philosopher of language, he read the fashionable French – Michel Foucault, Jacques Derrida, Hélène Cixous, Julia Kristeva, Michel de Certeau – and brought their insights to bear on contemporary theology with startling originality. During this period, Taylor also ventured into twentieth-century art and architecture in a series of remarkable essays and books. Now in his fifties, he seems to have drawn the conclusion about his own country that many foreign observers draw; namely, that what the Americans say is rarely as provocative as what they do. He has become a philosopher of culture who functions not only as a penetrating intellectual reporter but also as an innovative practitioner who is helping to lead others into the new worlds opened by new technologies.

God – the God of Genesis, the God of the West – is an artist rather than a philosopher. He does not find the world and try to understand it, as a philosopher does. He creates the world and tries through it to understand himself, as an artist does. Taylor – more an artist than a philosopher of religion – is thoroughly Western in his conviction that there is no escaping creativity: nothing is given, everything is made. For him, the average scientist is just an artist who will not see his own fingerprints on his work. Consistently, the synthesis that he offers in *Hiding*, the banquet he spreads here from all he has assembled over the past twenty-five years, has about it more art than philosophy. But then, as a philosopher, Taylor believes that he has no choice but to be an artist.

As omnivorous as Hegel in his cultural appetite and akin to Hegel in the way he collapses any final distinction between the spiritual and the real, Taylor stands as a powerfully original and authentically American exponent of a philosophical tradition that most Americans find deeply antipathetic. In the United States and in the rest of the English-speaking world, the triumph of science as implicit philosophy rather than as just the theoretical dimension of technology has been virtually complete. In the late twentieth century, as everyone knows, science speaks English: the language of international scientific gatherings is overwhelmingly English. But by the same token we may well say that the English (and the Americans and the other English speakers) "speak science." The assumptions of science define the whole of our culture, and central among these is the assumption that ultimate reality is one great thing which may be analyzed into many smaller things, down to its ultimate constituents. These constituents are themselves assumed to be real, and so are the relationships among them. They are external, "out there." Analyzing them is assumed to be the proper object not just of science but of thought itself.

So it happens that the school of philosophy dominant for nearly a century in the English-speaking world is the "analytic" school begun by the mathematician Bertrand Russell, who took scientific thinking to be the paradigm of all thinking.

To any suggestion that reality has no ultimate, scientifically analyzable constituents and/or that the relationships among its alleged constituents are inseparable from the minds of the scientists themselves, the reply not just from most scientists but from most of the English-speaking world would invoke technology, and that with no little indignation. If scientists were making it all up, so the refutation would go, could they put a man on the moon?

Well, could they? And what if they could? Then what? The idealist, originally German tradition out of which Taylor works would reply to the moon question by saying that the fact that scientists have put a man on the moon does not prove that either the man or the moon exists; it merely proves, tautologically, that scientists have put a man on the moon.

Crazy? Maybe, but in the words of the Bible (Proverbs 6:6), "Go to the ant." The ant produces prodigies of micro-engineering, technological miracles that, given the ant's limitations, bear fair comparison to our putting one of our own species on the moon. But do those tiny tunnels prove to the ant that the Earth really exists? No, they do not. The ant, obviously, has no concept of the Earth or of existence. Now, for a thinker like Taylor, that very fact – the fact that that the ant lacks these concepts and is yet able to do so much – should put our own concepts into perspective. It may be necessary for our species, when it undertakes its own kind of technology, to employ concepts such as *existence*. But another species, lower or higher, may dispense with our concepts; and as for ultimate reality, it may escape us as completely as Earth escapes the ant. How would we know? To state the obvious, we don't know what we don't know.

The assumption in the scientific worldview dominant in the English-speaking world and in the analytical philosophy most closely akin to that worldview is that though science does not yet know everything, it has in place a reliable framework and is patiently filling in the blanks. The assumption in Taylor's worldview and in the idealist philosophy that lies behind it is that the framework around science as around all the products of the human mind is the human mind itself and that the relationship of this framework to ultimate reality can never be known. All that we can know is that we are ourselves and that we cannot be other than we are or make anything that will not bear the marks of our own making. *Existence* is just another human word.

A scientist who did not believe that either the man or the moon existed could still go through all the empirical steps necessary to put the one on the other, for science as philosophy may fall and yet leave science as science standing. The tradition in which Taylor writes insists that the limitation of the human mind is such that in order to say anything, it must leave everything else out. Conversely (it insists again), the besetting temptation of the human mind is to claim for some one of its products – physics, for example – that this one product has left nothing out and so must be understood to include everything. To make or imply such a claim, Taylor believes, is not to capture reality but to flee it. This mistake, the error that he calls "totalization," is what he alludes to when he says at the beginning of his final chapter, a chapter that evaginates from the one that precedes it as an organ from a developing embryo: "After (the) all has been said and done, the question that remains is not 'What is virtual reality?' but 'What is not virtual reality?'"

The embryological emergence of the ultimate from the penultimate chapter of Hiding is by design – specifically, by the remarkable design of Michael Rock and Susan Sellers of 2 x 4 Studio. Their intent, clearly, is to make the design of the final chapter evoke the content of the first. The final chapter climaxes with Taylor's ten rules for "nontotalizing structures that function as a whole" or, if you will, ten rules for worldwide webs. The first chapter begins with his description of how the human embryo, all skin at the start, becomes a human body that beneath the surface . . . is still skin, skin all the way in. Near the very beginning of that first chapter, we read of the developing embryo:

> The endoderm generates the blood, internal organs, and all interior linings; the mesoderm produces the skeleton, connective tissue, muscles, and the urogenital and vascular systems; and the ectoderm engenders nerves, hair, nails, and the epidermis. Since the organism as a whole is formed by a complex of dermal layers, the body is, in effect, nothing but layers of skin in which interiority and exteriority are thoroughly convoluted.

Near the end, just before the mentioned rules for nontotalizing structures that function as a whole, we read:

> Such a structure would be neither a universal grid organizing opposites nor a dialectical system synthesizing opposites but a seamy web in which what comes together is held apart and what is held apart comes together. This web is neither subjective nor objective and yet is the matrix in which all subjects and objects are formed, deformed, and reformed. In the postmodern culture of simulacra, we are gradually coming to realize that complex communication webs and information networks, which function holistically but not totalistically, are the milieu in which everything arises and passes away. These webs and networks are characterized by a distinctive logic that distinguishes them from classical structures and dialectical systems.

Several years before the rest of his countrymen took notice, Taylor was pointing out that cybernetically precocious Finland, with sixty-two internet hosts per thousand people (the American average is thirty-one, the German seven), had something to teach the rest of the world. In the fall of 1992, he and his Finnish colleague, Esa Saarinen, used the most advanced telecommunications technology to create a trans-Atlantic, real-time, interactive classroom. This unprecedented undertaking, which is recorded in *Imagologies: Media Philosophy*, resulted in Taylor's being named the 1995 Outstanding College Professor of the Year by the Carnegie Foundation. Relentlessly experimental, Taylor runs to meet the cutting edge with a knife sharpener.

Taylor does not argue conventionally, competitively, coercively from his first picture of skin (in fact, a gallery of amazing pictures of skin) to his closing vision of distributed intelligence. He does not offer the first as premise and the last as conclusion. What he offers, in sum, is not demonstration but verisimilitude. Artist that he is, he aims not to compel but to seduce. The response he awaits is not agreement but surrender and aesthetic delight. He presents the eery isomorphisms and then stands back with a half-smile to watch us react.

If his is also a paradoxically religious vision, it is such by foregrounding the similarity between aesthetic climax and religious conversion. A Buddhist proverb says that "the Tathagata [the Buddha] makes no hypotheses." The point of all koans is that there is no point to a koan, or to Buddhism itself. Obviously, to *argue* that all is illusion is to concede by the very act of arguing that not *all* is illusion, for argument supposes structure, coherence, and a distinction between reality and illusion. This is why the Buddhist master does not indoctrinate the novice by argument but suggests by hint as in the famous Buddhist gesture of the finger pointing at the moon. Taylor advances his own vision by similar tactical abstentions.

The latest epigones of idealist philosophy – the deconstructionists and poststructuralists and postmodernists – have all seemed to me to make a similar kind of gesture and call for a similar kind of response. Like Buddhists, but unfortunately without the elegant restraint and perfect self-consciousness of Buddhism, they blithely dismiss rather than carefully refute their opponents' views and blandly assert rather than patiently argue their own. One cannot agree with them, for mere agreement is not sought, one can only espouse them – marry them – and I have never been inclined to do so. And yet Taylor, who knows all that they know, touches me as they do not, for he takes their ideas, and the ideas that lie, historically, behind their ideas, and applies them – better, fits them – to an astounding array of subjects in which I am already interested. I find myself, after a time, if not converted, then at least surrounded. The experience is both unsettling and rewarding.

I have called Taylor a philosopher-artist. I might also describe him as a particularly artistic and extraordinarily wide-ranging species of critic, a critic at once of art and architecture, of philosophy and science, of literature and culture. Like any criticism, his is parasitic on the works criticized, but it is so in a uniquely illuminating way. By being parasitic simultaneously on so many wildly different works, Taylor manages to make that which infects them all, namely his own parasitic reading of them, seem infectious indeed, a wildly spreading virus. You don't refute a virus. You either catch it or you don't. I haven't caught it yet, but I know I am susceptible. I know what it would feel like. Or, to change the metaphor to one that for Taylor is scarcely a metaphor at all, you don't refute a fashion. You either adopt it or you don't. Again, I haven't adopted it, but I know I could. I can see myself wearing it.

In the meantime, I relate to the spectacular intellectual show that Taylor puts on just as I urged you to relate to it in the opening paragraph of this brief foreword: I don't read it as a book, I take it as a trip. No one but Taylor can cite Friedrich Nietzsche's most blushingly biblical passage,

> The madman jumped into their midst and pierced them with his eyes. "Whither is God?" he cried; "I will tell you. *We have killed him* – you and I. All of us are his murderers. But how did we do this? How could we drink up the sea? Who gave us the sponge to wipe away the entire horizon? What were we doing when we unchained this earth from its sun? Whither are we moving? Away from suns? Are we not plunging continually? Backward, sideward, forward, in all directions? Is there still any up or down? Are we not erring as through an infinite nothing? Do we not need to light lanterns in the morning? Do we hear nothing as yet of the noise of the gravediggers who are burying God? Do we smell nothing? God is dead. God remains dead. And we have killed him.

and then go on to say:

> This is a remarkably apt description of the experience of cyberspace where all reality seems to be virtual. Nietzsche's telling insight grew out of intellectual and cultural developments that had been unfolding for more than a century. Though rarely recognized, the terms of cultural debate in the modern western world were set during the pivotal decade of the 1790s in the small German town of Jena. The artists, poets, philosophers, and theologians gathered in Jena defined the philosophical and theological agenda for the nineteenth century and articulated what would become the guiding principles of twentieth-century art and practice.

After a leap like that, I find myself writing in the margin ??!!! But whether I am quite prepared to leap along with Taylor at any given moment or not, there is again and again in this work an intellectual daring that is its own reward. As we say in California, Taylor takes it to the limit, pedal to the metal, straight out across the burning sands. His designers take the book-as-machine – the ink-on-paper codex as a text-storage unit – to its physical limit. He himself takes a set of two-hundred-year-old ideas to their intellectual limit and finds that they carry him to corners of our science-shaped culture that no other vehicle can reach. Sit back, reader – no, buckle down: You're in for a wild ride.

Skinsc(r)apes

In the end, it all comes down to a question
of skin. And bones. The question of skin and
bones is the question of hiding and seeking.
And the question of hiding and seeking
is the question of detection. Is detection any
longer possible? Who is the detective?
What is detected? Is there anything left to
hide? Is there any longer a place to
hide? Can anyone continue to hide? Does
skin hide anything or is everything nothing
but skin? "Skin rubbing at skin, skin,
skin, skin, skin..."

When nothing remains...nothing but skin and bones, when bones appear to be nothing...nothing but layers of skin, what once was called "reality" becomes not only unbearably light but impossibly thin. At this point...in this point, the body is deprived of its substance and appears to be on the verge of disappearing. The missing body sets in motion the detective story – in all of its (dis)guises.

In the beginning, it is a question of skin. Not yet a question of bones but of skin – dermal layers that hide nothing...nothing but other dermal layers. Humpty-Dumpty need not have fallen to be faulted, for every fertilized egg is always already divided between vegetal and animal poles. The process of embryonic development involves cellular division and further differentiation. Through a quasi-cybernetic process governed by preprogrammed DNA, the pluripotentiality of the ovum is limited in ways that allow the articulation of different organic

Skin-coveredness – All people who have depth find happiness in being for once like flying fish, playing on the peaks

structures and functions. Cells multiply by division to create a hollow ball called a blastomere. This sphere eventually invaginates to form a lined pocket comprising two layers known as the endoderm and ectoderm, which, in turn, partially peel away to generate a third surface named the mesoderm. The mature organism develops from these three dermal layers. The endoderm forms the blood, internal organs, and all interior linings; the mesoderm produces the skeleton, connective tissue, muscles, and the urogenital and vascular systems; and the ectoderm engenders nerves, hair, nails, and the epidermis. Since the organism as a whole is formed by a complex of dermal layers, the body is, in effect, nothing but strata of skin in which interiority and exteriority are thoroughly convoluted.

The skin, which is not a simple covering or container but is the body's largest organ, is internally differentiated into the epidermis and the dermis. As such, the skin is forever doubled and hence unavoidably duplicitous. Hide hides hide, which hides nothing...nothing but other hides. Not all hides, however, are the same. The basal cells of the epidermis, which are internally differentiated, are the progenitors of other epidermal cells. As new cells form, old cells die and drift away. The very mechanism of differentiation through which life emerges also leads to death. When epidermal cells become radically differentiated and migrate to the dermis, their nuclei are destroyed and the cells die. The outermost layer of the body consists of proteinaceous debris that is dead. Death, like life, is not a momentary event but is an ongoing process whose traces line the body. At the point where I make contact with the world, I am always already dead.

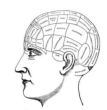

And then a question of bones. Or, more precisely, a question of skin and bones. What is the relation of skin to bone and bone to skin? If the question of skin and bones is the question of hiding and seeking, and if the question of hiding and seeking is the question of detection, then might the question of skin and bones be the question of the possibility and/or the impossibility of knowledge and self-knowledge? What if, upon investigation, the question of skin and bones turns out to be nothing... nothing less than the question of reason?

In 1806 and 1807, Franz Joseph Gall, the German physician who first formulated

of waves; what they consider best in things is that they have a surface: their skin-coveredness – sit venia verbo.

the theory of the cerebral localization of mental and characterological functions, and his erstwhile student Johann Christoph Spurzheim delivered lectures on phrenology in Karlsruhe, Germany. Karlsruhe was one stop on a five-year lecture tour that took Gall and Spurzheim throughout Europe. Though often dismissed as more nescience than science, in its day phrenology enjoyed greater credibility than the emerging fields of geology and botany. By the 1830s–1840s, phrenology

had spread to America. In 1843, a series of forty lectures on phrenology in Boston attracted as many as three thousand enthusiastic supporters. In an effort to develop an account of the interaction between physical and mental reality, Gall identified thirty-seven independent faculties of the mind, which he associated with different regions of the brain. The development of mental faculties, he argued, determines the size and shape of the skull. Moreover, the

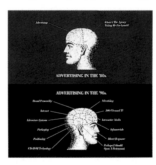

functioning of the mind is directly influenced by the condition of the body. The correspondence between the mental and the physical makes it possible to detect the depths of the mind by reading inscriptions on the surface of the skull.

In his popularization of Gall's views, Spurzheim emphasized the practical more than the theoretical aspects of phrenology. His reflections on education, hygiene, mental illness, criminology, and penology provoked great interest and exercised considerable influence throughout a broad cross section of society.

While Gall and Spurzheim were lecturing in Karlsruhe, Hegel was in Jena writing his most important work: *Phenomenology of Spirit*. Designed as the introduction to his system, the *Phenomenology* charts the course of the experience of consciousness as it progresses from the most rudimentary form of awareness (i.e., sense certainty) to "absolute knowledge." Hegel initially intended the *Phenomenology* as a response to contradictions in Kant's critical philosophy, but the work quickly exceeded the limits of epistemology to encompass the evolution of society and culture as a whole. According to its original program, the *Phenomenology* was to consist of three parts: consciousness, self-consciousness, and their synthesis in reason. In expanding his argument, Hegel maintains this basic structure in the final version of the work. One of the most puzzling aspects of the *Phenomenology* for present-day readers is the pivotal role that phrenology plays in the argument. The tendency of critics to dismiss Hegel's reading of phrenology as a historical curiosity not only obscures its place in his overall analysis but ignores the broader issues raised by the question of skin and bones.

In Hegel's grand philosophical scheme, reason unites consciousness and self-consciousness in such a way that knowledge is possible and truth is knowable. In the course of reason's development, consciousness reappears as "observing reason," and self-consciousness returns as "the actualization of rational self-consciousness through itself." Hegel's interpretation of phrenology marks the transition from observing to acting reason. The movement from consciousness through self-consciousness to reason involves overcoming the apparent opposition of subject and object by means of cognitive reflection and volitional action. Through the interrelated processes of sense-intuition, perception, and understanding, the knowing subject discovers itself in the known object. Consciousness of the object reveals itself as self-consciousness of the subject. Self-consciousness, in turn, necessarily involves consciousness of self as object. In other words, self-consciousness is impossible apart from self-objectification. While consciousness entails the subjectification of objectivity, self-consciousness implies the objectification of subjectivity. Reason is the dialectical union of consciousness and self-consciousness in which subject and object, or self and world, become one.

Phrenology embodies the truth of reason in skin and bones. In the third and concluding section of the chapter devoted to observing reason, entitled "Observation of the Relation of Self-Consciousness to Its Immediate Actuality: Physiognomy and Phrenology," Hegel maintains that "since the individual is... only what he has done, his body is also the expression of himself, which he himself has *produced*; it is at the same time a sign, which has not remained an *immediate* fact, but something through which the individual only makes known what he really is, when he sets his original nature to work." Inasmuch as the outer is an *expression* of the inner, the body is a sign that can be deciphered by those who know the code. For the canny detective, surfaces harbor clues of depths that render seemingly senseless appearances surprisingly intelligible. This is the central insight captured, albeit partially and inadequately, in the doctrine of phrenology.

Consciousness and self-consciousness, Hegel argues, meet in a bone that is the incarnation of spirit.

> It is not the function of observation to seek to determine this relation, for in any case it is not the brain, *qua a physical part*, which stands out on the side, but the brain qua the being of the *self-conscious* individuality. This latter as a lasting character and spontaneous conscious activity exists *for* itself and *within* itself. Over against this being-for-and-within-itself stand its actuality and its existence-for-another. The being-for-and-within-itself is the essence and the subject that has a being in the brain; this being is *subsumed under the subject*, and gets its value only through its indwelling significance. But the other aspect of self-conscious individuality, the aspect of its outer existence, its *being qua* independent and subject, or qua "thing," viz. a bone: the *actuality and existence of man is his skull-bone*. This is how the relationship and the two sides of this relation are understood by the consciousness observing them. Observation has to deal with the more determinate relation of these aspects. The skull-bone does have in general the significance of being the immediate actuality of spirit.

As "the immediate actuality of spirit," the skull bone, as read by the phrenologist, purports to disclose person (i.e., subject) in thing (i.e., object). This coincidence of subjectivity and objectivity anticipates "the general rational principle that the outer is the *expression of the inner*," which constitutes the very foundation of Hegel's speculative enterprise. If inwardness manifests itself outwardly, then surfaces are always signs (*Zeichen*) that point (*zeigen*) beyond themselves. For Hegel, the play of signs is neither arbitrary nor endless but necessarily grounded in the logical idea that forms the substance of reality. According to the principles of absolute idealism, logic is not merely the form of subjective thought but is also the structure of objective reality. By peeling away the skin of the world, Hegel's speculative gaze renders transparent the skeletal essence of every thing and every body. When fully deployed, Hegelian philosophy involves nothing less and nothing more than a thoroughgoing explication of phrenology.

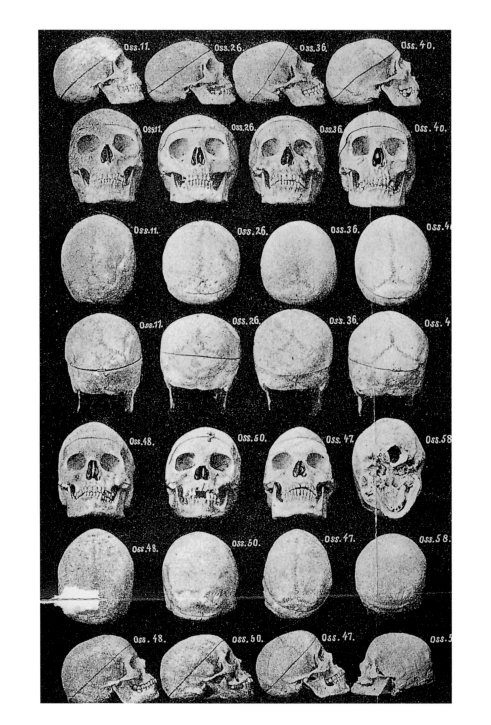

Though seemingly a ghost from the distant past, the specter of phrenology continues to haunt human reflection. If comprehended speculatively,
phrenology serves as a figure for the understanding of understanding. As the word
itself implies, to understand is to grasp that which stands under. True knowledge,
it seems, is never superficial or insubstantial but appears when surface gives way
to depth. The search for knowledge always involves something like a game of
hide-and-seek in which every investigator is a private eye and every investigation
becomes a detective story.

But a good detective story never turns out as expected. Even though the
solution should have been obvious from the beginning, the ending is always surprising. Perhaps the most startling conclusion emerges when the detective story
itself is subjected to investigation. As the detective story bends back on itself, it
appears to undo itself in the process of its own telling. Through an unexpected
reversal, the condition of the possibility of dis-guising turns out to be the condition
of the impossibility of detection. The drama of investigation is set in motion by tensions between surface/depth, outer/inner, appearance/reality, pretext/text, and so
forth. The terms of such binary oppositions are not equivalent but stand in a hierarchical relation in which the latter is consistently privileged over the former. Thus,
the truth of every surface is found in the depths, the significance of outwardness is
discovered in inwardness, the reality of appearances is revealed through essences,
and the meaning of any pretext is discerned in the text proper. For knowledge to be
possible, the world must be a "city of glass" in which appearances are transparent.
Speculative philosophy lays bare the logic by which such transparency emerges.
Every detective presupposes, in Hegel's apt phrase, that "reason is in the world." Far
from a matter of chance, reason is essential and the essence of essence is to appear.
Essence, in other words, becomes itself in and through its own appearance. When
properly understood, appearances are not merely apparent but are essentially reasonable. This point can be reformulated in terms of the basic axiom of phrenology:
since outwardness (i.e., the body or, more precisely, the skull bone) is the expression of inwardness (i.e., mind or spirit – Geist), the outer is at the same time the
inner. The inner is the outer and the outer is the inner. This dialectical identity of
opposites is what makes knowledge possible.

But Hegel and those who directly or indirectly follow the course he
charts resist drawing the most important conclusion to which their investigations
inevitably lead. The dialectical reversibility of opposites subverts the very hierarchy
upon which detection depends and thereby renders meaning undecidable. If the

inner is the outer and the outer is the inner, then not only are appearances essential, but *essences are apparent*. The far-reaching ramifications of this conclusion become clear if we return to the strange case of phrenology. For the phrenologist, we have discov-

The biggest fable of all is the fable of knowledge. One would like to know what things-in-themselves are; but behold, there are no things-in-themselves!

ered, the body is a sign whose significance can be discerned by stripping away the surface to uncover the depths. To read the writing of the body, the lines of skin must be traced to the underlying contours of bone. Yet even the awareness of this ossified infrastructure is insufficiently profound. Only when the body is under-stood as being finally grounded in spirit does knowledge become secure.

But what is the status of this ground that is supposed to be a stable foundation? If the principle of dialectical reversibility is applied to the binary surface/depth, then surface is depth and depth is surface. Upon closer investigation, what appears at one level to be depth supporting surface turns out to be another surface. In phrenological terms, bone and even mind are invaginated layers of skin. Peel away skin and you always find more skin: … ectoderm… mesoderm… endoderm… mesoderm… ectoderm…

"Skin rubbing at skin"… Hides hiding hides hiding… If depth is but another surface, nothing is profound… *nothing is profound*. This does not mean that everything is simply superficial; to the contrary, in the absence of depth, every-

We no longer believe that truth remains truth when the veils are withdrawn; we have lived too much to believe this.

thing becomes endlessly complex. In the city of glass, where (the) all has become impossibly thin, nothing is ever what it seems.

If, however, nothing is profound, is it any longer possible to write detective stories? Who would be the detective? What would be detected? Would there be anything left to hide? Would there be any place to hide? Could anyone continue to hide? What if someone were to write a detective story in the city of glass by writing about hides, which are, of course, nothing but skin?

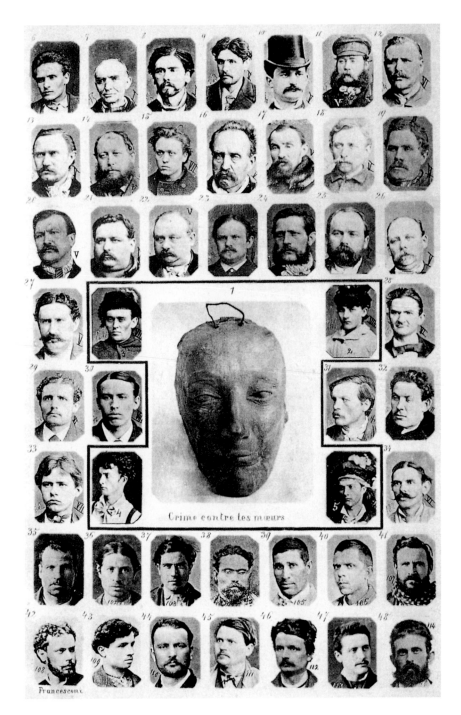

Crime contre les mœurs

The neon glow of **SKINSCAPE'S** above pavement level, and with a recalcitrant t flicker on the"C," gradually fills the screen.

It begins not with one but with two scenes – two scenes that mirror each other in such a way that they double again to create four narrative strands, which never become one. Two scenes and the traffic, transition, translation, and transference between them: above ground/underground, surface/depth, hospital/crypt. 'A railed flight of stone steps twists down from the pavement to a wide basement. A neon sign above the door says SKINSCAPE'S.' Skinscapes: layer upon layer, "skin rubbing at skin, skin, skin, skin, skin."

Above ground, a present-day hospital ward with the empty bed of an absent patient named P. E. Marlow. Under ground, a nightclub "underlit, (an) almost crypt-like series of arches, low at the ceiling." As Mark Binney descends into Skinscape's, he gives a panhandler a coin wrapped in silver paper with a message written on it. Depth and surface are linked by music: "'I've Got You Under My Skin' swells from SKINSCAPE'S neon to the bed, in sugary syncopation." The action switches back and forth between the hospital and the bar. When Marlow first appears, his image is hideous. "Marlow is glowering morosely, crumpled into himself, and his face is badly disfigured with a raggedly acute psoriasis, which looks as though boiling oil has been thrown over him. He is wearing a fully sleeved white X-ray smock. Very close, so that we know or hear his thoughts – and recognize the voice." Listening to Marlow's thoughts in

And then again a question of skin. It all starts innocently enough. Or so it seems. In the beginning, there is nothing but a pinhead-sized lesion that is virtually undetectable. Before the beginning, there is the code – the code in which the story of the skin is always already written. Whether the surface appears to be "material" or "mental," there is no such thing as a clean slate. The pinpoint slowly spreads until it becomes easily detectable as a reddish patch surrounding layer upon layer of dead skin. If not controlled or contained, the spot expands until it envelops the entire body. For those who bear these marks, the sign is both visible and tactile. The lesions itch but scratching brings no relief. As one layer is peeled away, another appears until the sore starts to bleed like a stigma that can never be wiped away. Whether these stigmata are a blessing or a curse remains forever uncertain.

Psoriasis (from psorian, to have the itch, by way of psen, to rub, scratch) has been recognized at least as long as medicine has been practiced. The earliest description of psoriasis appears in the Corpus Hippocraticum, which was compiled in Alexandria one hundred years after

Was my creativity, my restless need to produce, but a parody of my skin's embarrassing overproduction?

Indeed, what forces us to supp

the voice-over that floats between the scenes, it quickly becomes clear that the layers of the narrative apparently are not equivalent: "Back to reality, and the hospital, as Marlow, in his wheelchair 'composes' the story." While confined to the hospital to receive treatment for psoriatic arthritis, Marlow is fashioning what is ostensibly a detective story. Since his hands are crippled by psoriasis, he cannot write what he thinks. The underground figures apparently are materializations of his thoughts. The hospital ward seems to be the world of "reality" and Skinscape's a world of illusion. But no sooner has the distinction between reality and illusion been drawn than it is erased: "The bar at Skinscape's reasserts its occupation of the screen." From the beginning, everything — even the "real" world of the hospital — transpires on the surface of screens.

When Dennis Potter's *Singing Detective* was telecast in Britain on the BBC in 1986 and in the United States on PBS in 1988, the response was overwhelmingly positive. What impressed critics as much as the specifics of the play was Potter's conviction that television need not be limited to the banalities of "low" culture but could be a vehicle for "serious" drama. In a *New York Times* essay entitled "The Potter Legacy: Faith in Quality TV" published on the occasion of his death on June 7, 1994, John J. O'Connor wrote: "Dennis Potter died this week. And so did a powerful voice cantankerously insisting that television, which he always praised as the most democratic medium, could be far more than a tireless purveyor of fluffy diversions." The *New York Times* obituary anticipated O'Connor's point: "Mr. Potter wrote novels and screenplays, but it was in television, which he referred to as the greatest of all media' because of its accessibility, that he preferred to work. He took audacious liberties with television drama, infusing it with new life by turning its conventions upside down." In all the words of praise, the precise nature of Potter's faith in television and the exact way in which he turned the "medium's conventions upside down" were left unexplained.

The contribution of Potter's art is not limited to the treatment of themes

ose that there is an essential opposition between "true" and "false"? Is it not sufficient to assume degrees of apparentness and, as it were, lighter and darker

traditionally reserved for high culture in a medium that is increasingly consumed by cartoons, soap operas, sitcoms, and infomercials. The questions he raises are much more searching and disturbing than his most ardent supporters tend to realize. Far from simply adapting traditional drama to an untraditional medium, Potter's programs fold back on themselves not once but at least twice to examine questions that televisual and telephonic media raise about the relation between fact and fiction, reality and illusion, truth and appearance, history and story, and surface and depth. When read in the context of contemporary electronic technology

Against positivism, which halts at phenomena – "There are only facts" – I would say:

and media culture, *The Singing Detective* becomes a story about the possibility or impossibility of detection in a world where all "reality" is rapidly becoming virtual reality.

The point of Potter's televisual drama is not hidden in the depths of his work but is, from the outset, clearly displayed on the surface of the text: "A neon sign above the door says SKINSCAPE'S. "A sign... a neon sign... a sign that is a matter of light... a sign whose matter is lite. This sign is, in effect, a sign for all of Potter's signs, which have become light... unbearably light. In the televisual and telephonic era, words are always already processed and screens reveal nothing... nothing beyond screens. The screen, in other words, has become (the) terminal, thereby transforming every place into a skinscape.

On the screen of a word processor, a bright glow of letters softly blip-blips across the monitor — *the other, natural noises increase as the struggling, grunting policeman slowly pulls up on the deck of the launch the naked drowned body of a beautif-*

Like a purloined letter placed on the mantel for all to read, P. (O.) E.

the death of Hippocrates (c. 377 B.C.E.) Hippocrates' practice of using both psora and lepra to describe conditions that can be psoriatic led to the common confusion of psoriasis and leprosy, which persisted until 1908. As a result of this misunderstanding, it was not uncommon for people with psoriasis to be declared dead by the church and burned at the stake. While considerable progress has been made in understanding the etiology of psoriasis, its cause is still obscure and a cure remains elusive.

Psoriasis, like AIDS and diabetes, is an autoimmune disease.

Though commonly regarded as a sack enclosing the body's organs, the skin, I have noted, is actually quite complex and is the body's largest organ. The skin of the average person measures about two square yards and weighs approximately nine pounds. Among its many functions, the skin serves as the body's first line of defense against invasion by foreign agents known as antigens. The immunological system functions as something like a central intelligence agency whose efficacy depends on the ceaseless detective work of an army of agents and counteragents. When detection either becomes impossible or

shadows and shades of appearance – different "values," to use the language of painters? Why couldn't the world that concerns us – be a fiction?

Marlow's letters are obscure because they are so obvious. By repeatedly seeking what hides, we tend to forget how to read the surfaces on and between which life is lived.

The four layers of text are not woven together to form a continuous narrative. Lying in a "real" hospital bed writing or rewriting a screenplay for his detective story entitled *The Singing Detective*, which a rather dimwitted fellow patient

No, facts is precisely what there is not, only interpretations.

is simultaneously reading, Marlow is besieged by nightmare visions and suffers hallucinations brought on by severe psoriasis. As the story doubles and redoubles, characters drift in and out of different layers of the text. Lines from one narrative are quoted in another as the same scenes are repeated in different contexts. In the television rendering of the screenplay, the identity of characters is further obscured by actors who play multiple roles. Sound compounds the confusion of images. Voice-overs and lip-syncing make it impossible to be sure who is speaking or in what world conversations take place. The story or stories fold more than unfold to create what amounts to a hypertext whose cards are stacked against the traditional detective. Never integrated, layers of the text are connected by "hot" images, words, and sounds: hideous skin, burning eyes, illicit intercourse...; "shit," "oink," "shagging," "Reykjavik,"...; "I've Got You under My Skin," "Peg o' My Heart," "Dry Bones," "You Always Hurt the One You Love,"... The most telling point of intersection, however, is a strange "click" or "click-clack" that returns repeatedly at all levels of the work in the sound of wheelchairs, trains, clocks, and shoes. Every time something clicks, a chain of associations is activated that allows the reader/viewer to shift between and among discontinuous textual strata.

By clicking on "click," the space of the text becomes hypertextual. More complex than Alice's looking-glass world, Potter's screen opens windows that open other windows.

click

The neon glow of SKINSCAPE'S, above pavement level, and with a recalcitrant flicker on the "C," gradually fills the screen, as —

MARLOW: **(Voice over)** And so the man went down the hole,

In the negative point of this dream, I am sitting on a white bowl and

my excrement overflows, unstoppably, unwipably, engulfing my feet, my thighs, in patches I try to scrape.

I awaken and am relieved to be in bed, between clean sheets.

Then I look at my arms in the half-light of dawn and an ineluctable horror sweeps over me.

This is real. This skin is me, I can't get out.

like Alice. But there were no bunny rabbits there. It wasn't that sort of a hole. It was a rat-hole... **(Voice over)** Into the rat-hole. Down, down, down. And the one thing you don't want to do when you find yourself in one of those is to underestimate the rats in residence.

click

The "squeaking" and "gnawing" of this cast of characters echoes another rodent that seems less repulsive but is no more innocent than the rats who act out his screenplay. The clicking that circulates throughout the work is the sound of a mouse opening files of cases no detective can solve.

In detective stories, it is always a question of a body – usually a missing body. Where is it? Who is it? Who dunit? Marlow's *Singing Detective,* set in 1945 London, is pervaded by a film noir atmosphere. Characters bordering on parody roam through misty darkness, dropping hints of intelligence and counterintel-ligence activities that seem to involve covert trafficking in the sale or exchange of Nazi war criminals. The story within the story begins with the discovery of the body of a beautiful young woman floating in a river whose "dark water" recalls the per-ilous journey of Marlow's namesake, and whose "oily black" consistency, which "looks as though it's made of tar," resembles medicine applied to psoriatic lesions. To fathom the depths of this river is to discover the profun-dity of skin.

The detective story is set in motion by the problem of the identity of the body and the questions of how and why death occurred. From the beginning, the narrative lines are tan-gled. As the police pull the naked body from the river, "dream-like" figures from the "real" world of the hospital watch from a nearby bridge. With the voices of Mark Binney and a Skinscape's call girl in the background, Marlow, "1945-style, without psoriasis or seized joints," appears on the scene. No sooner has Marlow's face come into focus than it fades into the disfigured visage of the "real" Marlow. Badgering a fellow patient for a cigarette, Marlow cries out: "I'm *skin,* Ali. Skin! How many times!"

While it remains uncertain whether the body is real or illusory, the "intent, silent, accusing" stares of the phantom spectators leave no doubt that the

goes awry, lines of communication are snapped, feedback mechanisms break down, and the body misinterprets itself as an other. One of the consequences of this lack of self-recognition is that the reproduction of the skin becomes excessive. The skin, as it were, goes mad.

The precise mechanisms of these processes are gradually becom-ing clear. The Langerhans cells, which are produced in the pancreas, circulate through the blood to the epidermis, where they play a critical role in immune response. These cells are genetically programmed to detect invaders by decoding or reading the structure of protein molecules on the surface of anti-gens. When the body comes into contact with a foreign agent, the Langerhans cells react by presenting the antigen to lymphocytes or T-cells, which are responsible for destroying antigens. This operation sets in motion the body's immune response. For this response to be effective, the Langerhans cells must read the invaders correctly and communicate information clearly to the T-cells. The lymphocytes, in turn, must understand what the Langerhans cells are telling them and react by consuming or otherwise neutralizing the foreign death was not from "natural" causes. The mystery to be solved is the identity of the victim as well as the murderer. Marlow, appearing as a detective named Marlow in the detective story he is writing while lying in the hospital, observes: "The thing is – It's always the least likely character who turns out to be the killer. Got to obey the rules **(Blows smoke.)** The least likely. **(A twisted grin, a sidelong look.)** This must be him. This must be the one Old Noddy here. Defin-ite-ly. Noddy did it. You hear that, Nicola? You get that?...Well – it can't me, that's for sure. It can't be me. I didn't do it." But, for the reader, it is precisely Marlow who is the prime suspect in the murder of the woman. As the subject and object of his own investigation, Marlow's detective story becomes a narrative of self-examination in which ostensibly interior and exterior worlds repeatedly pass into each other until inside is outside and outside is inside. Appropriating the psychoanalytic strategy of denegation for literary ends, Potter allows Marlow to affirm by negating. When "no" means "yes," "It can't be me. I didn't do it" must be translated: "It must be me. I did it." Marlow suspects that he is the criminal he is seeking and that psoriasis is the sign of his guilt. But he must write his detective story to try to confirm his suspicion.

The psychoanalyst is a detective; his or her cases are detective stories. In the eyes of the analyst, surfaces are never self-explanatory but are always symptomatic of the psychic underground. There is a temporal as well as a spatial dimension to psychoanalysis. While the present is confined to the surface, the past lurks in the depths. Since the psychoanalyst reads surface in terms of depth, he understands the present in terms of the past. When exploring the cryptic mysteries of the mind and body, to dig down is to go back – back to the beginning from which the present state of affairs has developed. To unearth the causes of mental and certain physical diseases, it is necessary to strip away the accumulated strata of the past like so many layers of dead skin. When therapy is successful, the subtext of the patient's life becomes legible and thus his or her personal story becomes comprehensible. Though its variations are infinite, the plot the detective uncovers is always the same. In one way or another, every case is a murder case that must be traced back to a primal scene where a crime occurred. The crime is inevitably a crime of passion involving eros and thanatos. The mystery is solved when the missing body is recovered, its identity established, the murderer named, and his motives explained. For the psychoanalyst, the body is always the body of the father (or his representative), the murderer is always the son, and the motive is always jealousy.

If symptoms – mental and physical – are read as signifiers that point

The "apparent" world is the only one:

beyond themselves, then the body of the father can be understood as the signified that grounds signs and secures their meaning. Though rarely acknowledged, psychoanalysis inverts theology by transferring the locus of truth from heights to depths. The gods do not die but go underground where they assume pseudonyms in order to continue to exercise their control. In this way, meaning is preserved even when the gods seem to be absent. If, however, the gods do not merely don disguises but die both as mind and as body, then meaning, in all of its guises, becomes questionable. When the body (or its representatives) disappears, signs lose their foundation and are left to float freely on a sea that cannot be fathomed. At this point, the detective story becomes either impossible or unending because no solution can be found.

The story of psychoanalysis unravels in its very telling and, therefore, must be significantly revised. As Freud struggled to plumb the depths of the mind, he was eventually forced to admit that the primal scene, which he had supposed could explain everything, never took place but was a fantasy rather than an actual historical event. This recognition cast Freud into a prolonged period of despair. Since he remained committed to the principles of nineteenth-century positivism and realized all too well that the acceptance of his theories by the medical and scientific communities required at the very least their empirical verifiability, he was initially convinced that the nonoccurrence of the primal scene invalidated his entire analytic enterprise. But the longer Freud pondered these startling and discouraging revelations, the less persuaded of their devastating consequences he became. Whether this change of mind was a matter of conviction or convenience we will never know. Nonetheless, Freud salvaged his theory by rewriting fact as fiction. In the final analysis, he argued, it does not matter whether or not the primal scene "really" took place;

agents. Any failure of communication leaves the body vulnerable to attack by either aliens or itself.

Psoriasis involves precisely such a breakdown in the circuit of communication. T-cells escape from the blood vessels and migrate to the dermis, where they produce protein substances known as interleukins. For reasons that remain unknown, these interleukins trigger an excessive production of epidural cells. The hyperstimulation of epidural cells is not precisely an "abnormal" process but a "normal" one that becomes uncontrollable. As a quasi-cybernetic or self-regulating system, the body depends on complex feedback networks. In psoriasis, as in most forms of cancer, a biochemical governor malfunctions or falls asleep at the switch. It is as if the switch regulating the production of epidural cells is turned on but cannot be turned off. Consequently, cells proliferate uncontrollably. When understood in this way, psoriasis appears to be a disease of speed and excess.

While so-called normal skin reproduces every fourteen to eighteen days, psoriatic skin reproduces every three days. This rapid rate of propagation

: the "true" world is merely added by a lie.

what is crucial is that the patient *believes* the transgressions occurred. In Freud's revised scheme, the difference between historical fact and psychic fantasy is a difference that makes no difference. In the vast majority of cases, Freud acknowl-

Legible, from *legere*, to read. "Leg: gather, set in order; consider, choose; then read, speak." Greek,

edged, the primal seduction in all probability never happened. Yet everything that follows unfolds *as* if it had taken place. With the mere flick of the pen, Freud changed everything by changing nothing. If the primal scene is never staged either in the life of the individual or in the history of the race, then personal as well as sociocultural development is the aftereffect of an event that was a nonevent. The nonevent that sets history in motion is a fictive construction fabricated for explanatory purposes. If the explanation is therapeutically effective, it does not matter whether it is what was once called "true."

The implications of the Freudian "solution" reach far beyond the bounds of psychoanalysis. Once again it comes down to a question of skin and bones. Though Freudianism and Hegelianism are usually regarded as polar opposites, they share more than is generally realized. Freud and Hegel agree that suprastructures must always be interpreted in terms of infrastructures that lie within or beneath superficial appearances. As we have seen, while Hegel insists that the inner is the outer and the outer is the inner and maintains that appearances are essential, he resists the no less necessary conclusion that essences are apparent. The logos, which renders every body and every thing legible, is dis-covered not fabricated, un-covered not invented, un-earthed not constructed. Or so it seems. Though longing for something like Hegelian certitude, Freud dares to venture where Hegel fears to tread. Since the originary event is a nonevent or, more precisely, a fictive event, the substance of "reality" is fantasy. The real, in other words, is illusion. If reality is illusory, then the difference between skin and bone, appearance and essence, outer and inner, and surface and depth is a difference that makes no difference. The erasure of this difference does not, however, result in the collapse of opposites into identity but issues in the reversibility of differences, which leaves everything unstable and infinitely complex. When surface is depth and depth is surface, solutions become dissolutions in which (the) all is undecidable. To approach surface through depth is not to interpret fiction through fact but to read one story through a different story. In this labyrinth of signs, nothing is dis-guised because every body is disguised.

Through its revision, the Freudian corpus becomes a virtual pretext of/for Wallace Stevens's "Notes toward Supreme Fiction," which, in turn, reworks the insights of Nietzsche, whose writings Freud would not read because of his insurmountable anxiety of influence. Stevens summarizes the insight that makes the continuation of the analytic process possible and its end impossible: "The final

logos....Dunlop's *Encyclopedia of Facts* (1969) lists 362 words ending (o)logy (meaning mainly the study of), including analogy, biology, geology, psychology, bac

belief is to believe in a fiction, which you know to be a fiction, there being nothing else. The exquisite truth is to know that it is a fiction and that you believe in it willingly." This conclusion is, of course, inconclusive because it leaves everything open-ended. Instead of solving the mystery of life, Freud's detective story dissolves in a forest of signs.

Four layers become more and more twisted in the very effort to untangle them: reality, illusion, fiction, history. Marlow (and/or Potter – it is never clear where one ends and the other begins) not only suffers and writes but also dreams, hallucinates, and remembers (it is never clear where one ends and the other begins). Memories, dreams, and reflections transport him from the city and adulthood to the forest and childhood. He seeks the answers to his present in his past. The story is, as always, the story of the mother and the father, and the history of their transgression. But there is an unexpected twist in Marlow's story. Though the structure of the plot is predictable, the principal characters switch roles. In this murder mystery, the body of the mother displaces the body of the father.

Throughout *The Singing Detective*, the scene switches not only between the "real" world of the hospital and the fictive world of the novel and screenplay but also between Philip's hallucinations in the present and his dreams and memories of the past. Philip grew up in a rural village where his father and grandfather were miners who worked in the depths of mother earth. Though a rather dull person, Philip's father sought relief from the boredom and monotony of his bleak world by

inhibits the peeling away of outer layers and leads to a buildup of dead skin. As the hide thickens, itching increases. But rubbing and scratching bring no relief; the more one scratches, the more the sores itch. Skin rubbing at skin – plaques and scales flake off only to expose more and more layers of skin.

Since skin is never merely skin-deep, the effects of psoriasis are not limited to the outermost surface of the body. Inasmuch as bone and connective tissue are generated from the mesoderm, skin and bones can both be affected by the same disease. In addition to suffering superficial lesions, approximately 5 – 8% of the people who have psoriasis develop what is known as psoriatic arthritis. Though it sometimes affects the spine and lower extremities, psoriatic arthritis more often involves upper limbs. The hands are particularly vulnerable and in severe cases can become deformed and even crippled.

While always indicating a genetic predisposition, psoriasis never develops without some kind of initial trauma. The most common causes of onset are cutaneous injuries and infections. But not all the traumas that trigger psoriasis are physical. There is a well-established but inadequately singing in local pubs. Philip's mother, Betty, who is considerably more intelligent and sensitive, finds that the occasional opportunity to accompany her husband in his performances cannot fill the emptiness of her life. In a desperate effort to escape

bacteriology, embryology, dermatology, phrenology, and my apology for not giving the rest.

the prison her world has become, Betty seduces a friend of her husband, who is the father of one of Philip's classmates. When her transgression increases rather than relieves the tensions in her life, Betty flees to London with her son. Though promising Philip that his father will soon join them, she realizes the family will never be reunited.

For the young Philip, the country is less a prison than an idyllic garden. While enduring typical childhood problems and adolescent conflicts and being harassed by a less-than-understanding teacher, Philip delights in roaming the forest for hours on end. He takes special pleasure in surveying his sylvan fantasyland from a treetop perch. One day, however, this ideal world suddenly comes crashing down. While contemplating the leafy green canopy beneath him, Philip hears the voices of his mother and the father of his friend Mark Binney. Waiting until they pass, Philip climbs down the tree and follows the couple deeper into the woods. Sneaking through tall grass and bushes, he watches an event no words can describe. With the scene approaching climax, physical frenzy mirrors visual and psychological confusion. Philip's mind spins as the worlds of reality, illusion, fiction, and history crisscross. As the metaphorical death of the lovers becomes the real death of a hospital patient named George, and the face of Philip's mother becomes indistinguishable from the face of his former wife, Nicola, who, in his delirium, Marlow is convinced is trying to purloin the screenplay he is rewriting.

Baffled and perplexed, Philip says nothing about the episode to his mother until their critical confrontation, which, significantly, takes place in the London Underground. While he pleads with his mother to return to the country, Betty Marlow notices Philip's first psoriatic lesion on his forearm. In the complex feedback loops that link mind and body, profound psychic traumas are readable on the surface of the skin. After it becomes clear that they are never leaving the city, Philip demands to know when his father will join him. His mother responds by uttering words he has long dreaded: "He's not!" Hardly surprised, Philip is nonetheless shocked and charges: "'It is coz of what thik bloke did to you in the woods. In thik dell. Is it?' She freezes."

MRS. MARLOW: Philip — ?

PHILIP: Doing that stuff. With thik Mr. Binney. With Raymond Binney. Mark's dad…

MRS. MARLOW: What stuff? What stuff do you mean — ?

PHILIP: Him on top of tha! Rolling on top of tha!

MRS. MARLOW: (Mock incredulity) What?…

PHILIP: Shagging.

When his mother instinctively slaps him hard across the face, Philip turns and runs through the underground while "You Always Hurt the One You Love" is playing. Whether the scene of seduction was "real" or illusory, the encounter between Philip and his mother has a lasting effect. The body floating in the river appears to have been his mother's corpse. In this reversed oedipal drama, the death of the mother allows father and son to be reunited. Getting his wish and returning to the country, Philip seals his "crime" with a lie by telling his father that his mother had died peacefully.

In his struggle to understand his present by unraveling his past, Marlow finally consents to a visit with the hospital psychiatrist, Dr. Gibbon. Determined to track down every clue that might help to solve the case, Gibbon is reading *The Singing Detective*. A reluctant, even hostile, patient, Marlow begins a particularly telling session by musing: "The rain, it falls. The sun, it shines. The wind blows. And that's what it's like. You're buffeted by this, by that, and it is nothing to do with you. Someone you love dies, or leaves. You get ill or you get better. You grow old and you remember, or you forget. And all the time, everywhere, there is this canopy stretching over you — "

GIBBON: (Determined to interrupt) What canopy?…

MARLOW: Things as-they-are…. Fate. Fate. Impersonal. Irrational. Disinterested. The rain falls. The sun shines. The wind

understood psychosomatic aspect of psoriasis. The immune system appears to mediate exteriority and interiority, surface and depth, and body and mind. The Langerhans cells that start the immunological reaction are stimulated by certain mental processes. The trace of psychological processes on the skin is not, however, limited to the originary trauma. Clinical studies suggest that, in 30–40% of the adults and 90% of the children who suffer from psoriasis, symptoms are exacerbated by stress. Cognitive processes that take place in the brain and are transmitted through the nerves influence the activity of T-cells and in this way modulate the immune response. Since thought is written on the body, the skin seems to be less a covering that hides than a transparent membrane that hides nothing.

The skin-mind relation is far from unidirectional. As mind is inscribed on skin, so skin influences mind. In extreme cases, psoriasis causes delusions by greatly increasing the flow of blood in the dermis. When the blood rushes to the skin, body heat swiftly dissipates, leaving the inside of the body chilled and the surface overheated. Rapidly fluctuating body temperature interrupts

blows. A bus mounts a pavement and kills a child. And —
Then, suddenly, with a savagery that implies the opposite of what he is saying.
      — I believe in no systems, no ideologies, no religion, nothing like that.
I simply think — Oh, it's very very boring, this. Very —
                 I just think that from time to time, and at random,
you are visited by what you cannot know cannot predict cannot control cannot
    change cannot understand and cannot cannot cannot escape
           — Fate. (Little shrug.) Why not? S'good old word.

Gibbon responds by observing that Marlow's skin is improving and inquires:
"But — do you still feel so — (Carefully choosing a word) disappointed? In things as
they are."

    MARLOW: Not a bit. *Things* as they are, are no concern of mine.
                GIBBON: You object to the word "things"?
    MARLOW: Oh, there are lots and lots of words I object to.
      Sensing a possible opening, Gibbon challenges Marlow to a word game
      that involves free and instantaneous association.
        Initially hesitant, Marlow finally agrees but with an important proviso.
GIBBON: If we are going to do this —
    MARLOW: — We have to agree in advance that it is meaningless.
                   GIBBON: Oh, quite.
       MARLOW: Has no diagnostic value.
    GIBBON: Fine.

With the "click-clock-clack" of Gibbon's shoes punctuating the exchange, words
"Interpretation," the introduction of meaning—not "explanation." ...There are not facts, everything is in flux, incomprehensible, elusive...
fly back and forth furiously:...doctor/charlatan...money/shit... fish/Jesus... God/
doctor... dream/wake... sleep/lie... politician/lie... tale/lie... writer/liar... sen-
tence/prison... As it quickly becomes obvious that none of this is meaningless or
that all of it is meaningful in its meaninglessness, Marlow becomes ever
more uneasy.

    MARLOW: (Shout) Stop!
A little pause. They look at each other. Then —

        A game.

GIBBON: Do you think so?...

    MARLOW: That's what you called it. And we agreed – No diagnostic value.

    GIBBON: Oh, none at all. None whatsoever.

MARLOW: I mean – it's words. Just –

      GIBBON: Just words.

Words... just words... sentence... prison... sentence. Feeling himself trapped, Marlow declares that this will be his last visit to Gibbon. And then, as if to remind the reader/viewer of what he or she knows but tends to forget, the "real" world fades as the window of the hospital is transformed into the window of the screen....Windows **(click)** opening to other Windows **(click)**...

> Words blip their faintly glowing track across the screen of the word processor.

Over now. Finished. He's dead. Out of it.
A pause in the progression. And then, underneath, in capitals –

THE EN

But neither the play nor the game is over; in the telephonic and televisual age – and perhaps long before – analysis is interminable. The screenplay is a wordplay; for Philip, as for his mother, there is no possibility of escape from the forest (of words) short of death. "MARLOW: (With satisfaction) There is no way out. Not through the bars. They never get out. Period." Period. Potter's point is not limited to the words printed on the page or flickering on the screen. *The Singing Detective* is not only a narrative that is at the same time a metanarrative about writing; Potter's words fade from the page to expose worlds in which every body and every thing is screened. "Minute by minute," Marlow avers, "we make the world. We make our own world." Language, to borrow a phrase from Heidegger, is "the house of being." But just because we

"normal" mental operations and causes hallucinations. If this condition is not quickly controlled, it can result in death.

Once the body turns on itself, its war with itself never ends. There is no cure for psoriasis. Therapies designed to relieve symptoms temporarily range from topical to systemic. In virtually every case, however, the treatment poses a threat of debilitating or deadly side effects.

In the most widely accepted therapies, keratolytics are used to strip away layers of dead skin, and corticosteroids are either applied to the skin or injected beneath the surface of individual plaques. Though often offering short-term relief, the use of cortisone and steroids can have serious long-term consequences. Since the body absorbs chemicals applied to its surface, the greater the area of skin treated, the more likely are complications. One of the most common and least disruptive treatments is the repeated use of coal tar creams, ointments, and shampoos. Such topical therapies usually require local or whole-body occlusion. A plastic wrap provides a supplemental layer of "artificial" skin, which enhances the capacity of chemicals to penetrate the build this house does not mean we are masters of it. Like some robotic machine, language always threatens to turn against those who fabricate it. Trying to explain to his physiotherapist what his psychotherapist cannot understand, Marlow reflects: "Suppose they get together, and ganged up on us when we weren't looking?"

> PHYSIOTHERAPIST: Who?
>
> MARLOW: Words. The little devils. Words.

Devils though they be, there is no avoiding words. If "we make our world," then the so-called real world is no more and no less real than so-called fictive worlds. It is not until the end of the play that Potter makes this point explicitly: "Marlow and Nicola stand as before examining each other, but in the middle of a now totally empty ward. A place in the mind." When even the "real" hospital ward is "a place in the mind," the "real" world appears to be a fiction we construct to convince ourselves that not everything is fictive.

Skinsc(r)apes: Layer upon layer... Skin rubbing at skin... Hide hiding hide. Potter's/Marlow's psoriasis is not an inconsequential detail unrelated to the

To move *over* existence! That's it! That would be something!

stories he tells. To the contrary, *The Singing Detective* is about skin – nothing but skin because there is nothing... nothing but skin. Far from an abnormality, psoriasis actually figures the human condition, for, in a certain sense, we all suffer skin disease. Peel away one layer and nothing appears... nothing but another layer. As info-tele-technology fast forwards the play of surfaces, the rate of superficial production and reproduction reaches a fever pitch until everything becomes obscure in its very transparency.

At this point, the detective story – in all of its versions – breaks down. Words... devilish words turn on their authors. Two mysterious characters from Marlow's detective story "storm the reality studio" of the hospital to turn everything upside down and inside out.

> NURSE MILLS: Who are you? What do you want here?
>
> FIRST MYSTERIOUS MAN: Those are exactly the right questions...
>
> MARLOW: Am I hot? Is it because I am or – ?
>
> (Suddenly) I don't know you. I have no idea who you are or what you want.
>
> FIRST MYSTERIOUS MAN: Ho, I see. Disowning us now, are you?
>
> SECOND MYSTERIOUS MAN: Bloody orphans, are we?

NURSE MILLS: I'm sorry. I'm grateful for your help – but I must ask you to leave…

SECOND MYSTERIOUS MAN: And what for?

FIRST MYSTERIOUS MAN: We're never told.

SECOND MYSTERIOUS MAN: Our roles are unclear.

FIRST MYSTERIOUS MAN: No names, even. No bloody handles…

MARLOW: (Croak) Nurse? Nurse – !…

FIRST MYSTERIOUS MAN: (Reasonable tone) Where are you going?

MARLOW: Home.

SECOND MYSTERIOUS MAN: But that's off the page, ennit?…

FIRST MYSTERIOUS MAN: You're going nowhere, sunshine. Not until we settle this…

MARLOW: S-settle what – ?

FIRST MYSTERIOUS MAN: Who we are. What we are.

SECOND MYSTERIOUS MAN: That's right. That's absolutely right. Who are we? What are we? When every body and every thing hides on surfaces that harbor no depths, these mysteries cannot be solved. The problem, Potter implies, is not the absence of solutions but the persistent longing for them. In the "real" world of the hospital, Nicola, who seems to be trying to dupe Marlow, implores: "Write about something new, Philip. You should write something else."

epidermis. Such "skin" grafts range in size from a few square inches to "sauna" suits that cover the entire body. Occlusion must be maintained overnight or for a minimum of six hours.

In addition to chemical remedies, ultraviolet light has long been recognized as effective in treating psoriasis. The therapeutic effect of sunlight helps to explain the geographical distribution of this disease. While occurring universally, psoriasis is considerably more common in northern climates than in southern (e.g., 2.3–2.5% in Scandinavia versus 0.97% in South America). In recent years, artificial phototherapy has become much more sophisticated.

The benefits of such treatments must always be weighed against possible side effects. As is becoming increasingly evident, exposure to ultraviolet light can be carcinogenic. If phototherapy becomes an integral part of the treatment regime, the "cure" for psoriasis might be skin cancer. As Plato suggested long ago, every pharmakon is duplicitous: medicine is also poison – gift is inevitably Gift. Cure is, therefore, impossible.

Disease always singles out but never more so than when it is written

MARLOW: Oh? Like what?

Nicola: Like this – what has happened to you. Like real things.

MARLOW: Pooh.

NICOLA: Use your talent, Philip.

MARLOW: Bugger that!

NICOLA: Write about real things in a realistic way – real people, real joys, real pains – Not these silly detective stories. Something more relevant.

      MARLOW: (With contempt) Solutions.

    NICOLA: What – ?

    MARLOW: All solutions, and no clues. That's what the dumb-heads want. That's the bloody Novel – He said, she said, and descriptions of the sky –

      I'd rather it was the other way around. All clues. No solutions.

I also foresee that when I weaken, when I am at last too ill for all these demanding and perilous palliatives,

That's the way things are. Plenty of clues. No solutions.

Plenty of clues. No solutions. If every text is a pretext for another text, meaning does not so much disappear as endlessly proliferate. "FIRST MYSTERIOUS MAN: But it's a clue. Everything – all things mean something. All things point." When "everything – all things mean something," "everything seems too full of significance, but puzzlingly so." The puzzle is not the lack of meaning but its excess.

    As the end of the show approaches, Marlow silently muses, "I think I've cracked the case, folks"; he then proceeds to leave the hospital with Nicola. A few lines later, *The Singing Detective* ends with an edited instant replay of Marlow's life in the forest. The young Philip declares: "When I grow up, I be going to be a detective. And then, unexpectedly, he grins. All the while, along the corridor to freedom, Marlow struggles on, leaning on Nicola. They disappear from view. The empty corridor is resonant with the birdsong and the sound of the wind in the leaves." But not everything is resolved; questions remain: What does it mean to crack a case? And, What bird is singing? "To crack" can, of course, mean both to solve and to destroy – as when one cracks an egg which, like Humpty-Dumpty, cannot be put back together again. But not only eggs crack; as the singing bird suggests, sometimes people do. We have heard this bird's song before. Philip's concluding declaration of his intention to become a detective repeats words uttered much earlier during one of his feverish dreams.

    Faintly greenish letters blip-blip on the word processor screen, which has the suggestion, or the merest hint of, the subdued grey reflection of a shimmering tree in its glass.

    H-e-l-p.

The letters slowly fade on the foliage of the special tree. Philip, the boy, is once again securely lodged in the saddle-like cleft of the upper branches of the tall old oak, able to stare out over gently moving, undulating acres of green, most of the trees being at a lesser height. He turns his head very deliberately to look straight at us, challengingly.

PHILIP: When I grow up I be going to be the first man to live for ever and ever. In my opinion, you don't have to die. Not unless you want to....

When I grow up, I be going to be – a detective.... I'll find out. I'll find out. I'll find out things! I'll find out. I'll find out who did it!

psoriasis like a fire smoldering in damp peat will break out and spread triumphantly; in my dying I will become hideous, I will become what I am.

Silence. Except for the insistent birds. Then, startlingly near, and distinct, a cuckoo begins its throaty, traditionally mocking call, *Cuck-oo! Cuck-oo!*

The leafy green that is our fate is the canopy of words and images floating freely on the screen. Our Windows on reality are a terminal display. In a gesture that virtually denegates denegation, Philip negates by affirming. When "yes" means "no," "I'll find things out. I'll find out. I'll find out who did it!" must be translated: "I won't find things out. I won't find out. I won't find out who did it."

Potter does not refuse "to write about real things in a realistic way" but struggles to write "realistically" in an age in which reality is no longer realistic. He calls this "realism" "non-naturalism." Non-naturalism, he explains, "can subvert. It doesn't necessarily show, or tell, even, but it pulls you in and then turns you inside-out. It's not exactly making you think, but it's making you feel. It is around you, it's sensory, it's virtual reality, it's having a helmet on your head, it's cybernetic space – that's non-naturalism!" To try to solve the mystery by rediscovering the body in cyberspace is cuckoo... as cuckoo as believing in phrenology or thinking that psoriasis can be cured.

on the skin. Seemingly superficial stigmata become profound as they work their way into the recesses of the mind. As we have been led to suspect, the relation between psyche and soma is strangely reversible. While mental mis-fires mar the skin, a hide-ous skin deranges the mind. In an effort to avoid detection, individuals who are stigmatized devise elaborate strategies of hid-ing. Apparel becomes disguise as clothing, makeup, wigs, and hair are trans-formed into masks that allow one to face the world. In a certain sense, how-ever, these dis-guises extend the dis-ease they are fabricated to conceal. Layer upon layer, skin upon skin, hide upon hide, until nothing is left...nothing but hiding.

Not all disguises, of course, are material; some are mental, even verbal. Words, stories, and plays can also be masks that are supposed to screen. But masks never simply mask. To screen can be either to hide or to display. If hides hide nothing...nothing but other hides, then hiding is actually a complex display in which every wordplay is a duplicitous screenplay.

Phrenology is no longer to be laughed at. It is no longer laughed at by men of common understanding. It has assumed the majesty of a science; and, as a science, ranks among the most important which can engage the attention of thinking beings – this too, whether we consider it merely as an object of speculative inquiry, or as involving consequences of the highest practical magnitude.... In regard to the uses of Phrenology – its most direct, and, perhaps, most salutary, is that of self-examination and self-knowledge. It is contended that, with proper caution, and well-directed inquiry, individuals may obtain, through the science, a perfectly accurate estimate of their own moral capabilities – and, thus instructed, will be the better fitted for decision in regard to a choice of offices and duties in life.... "By appealing to Nature herself, it can scarcely be doubted that certain forms of the head denote particular talents or dispositions; and anatomists find that the surface of the brain presents the same appearance in shape which the skull exhibits during life." *Edgar Allan Poe*

In 1960, a Harvard-educated professor of religion teaching at Columbia University published a richly suggestive book about the impact of the discovery of America on European utopian thought. Peter Stillman's *Garden and the Tower: Early Versions of the New World* is divided into two parts: "The Myth of Paradise" and "The Myth of Babel." Taking as his point of departure Christopher Columbus's declaration "For I believe that the earthly Paradise lies here, which no one can enter except by God's leave," Stillman proceeds to explore the ways in which the so-called New World was commonly associated with a second garden of Eden where the kingdom of God would be reestablished. Reviewing contrasting accounts of Indians as "prelapsarian innocents" and "savage beasts," Stillman maintains that the Native Americans were uncorrupted by ills plaguing European society. The question, he insists, is to explain how and why the "fall" from innocence to evil occurs.

In an effort to answer this age-old question, Stillman develops an imaginative rereading of Milton's *Paradise Lost*. What distinguishes Stillman's study is his contention that the force of Milton's work lies not only in the substance of the argument but in the duplicitous style of the language. In *Areopagitica*, Milton writes: "It was from out the rind of one apple tasted, that the knowledge of good and evil, as two twins cleaving together, leaped forth into the world." In interpreting these lines, Stillman concentrates on the word cleaving, which, he points out, can mean both "joining together" and "breaking apart." Like an accomplished detective carefully sifting clues, Stillman gradually develops evidence to support his conclusion that for Milton the fall is a *linguistic* event. The duplicity of language simultaneously reflects and promotes the corruption of humanity.

Adam's one task in the Garden had been to invent language, to give each creature and thing its name. In that state of innocence, his tongue had gone straight to the quick of the world. His words had not been merely appended to the things he saw, they had revealed their essences, had literally brought them to life. A thing and its name were interchangeable. After the fall, this was no longer true. Names became detached from things; words devolved into a collection of arbitrary signs; language had been severed from God. The story of the Garden, therefore, records not only the fall of man, but the fall of language.

Far from being a transparent skin, language is tainted by the fall. Stillman seals his case by reading the biblical

DIAGRAM SHOWING THE ESSENTIAL PARTS.

Side View.

On June 24, 1881, Francis Galton, explorer, anthropologist, and founder of eugenics, delivered a paper, "Composite Portraiture," to the British Photographic Society, in which he described a new apparatus he had devised for producing his signature photographs. The technique that Galton developed consists of layering image upon image until a new and distinctive figure emerges from the play of surfaces. He created his early portraits by using optical lanterns to project superimposed images and then photographing the screen on which the composite figure appeared. "The blended result," he comments, "will always have a curious air of individuality, and will be unexpectedly well defined; it will exactly resemble none of its components, but will be an ideal family likeness to all of them, and it will be an ideal average portrait." This new device eliminated the need for optical lanterns and thus made it possible to create "portraits" by subjecting photographic plates to multiple exposures of different durations. After a detailed explanation of the advantages of the new apparatus and showing the audience some of the images he had produced, Galton explains the purpose of his work: "The first consists of 57 hospital

story of the Tower of Babel as a commentary on the Genesis account of the fall.

This is where Stillman's argument would have ended had it not been for an accidental discovery. While rummaging through some papers in the attic of his family's house in Cambridge, Massachusetts, he uncovers the only surviving copy of a sixty-four page pamphlet by a certain Henry Dark. Published in 1690, *The New Babel* presents the case for rebuilding paradise in America. A Boston clergyman born in London in 1645, Dark came to America in 1675 and died in a fire in Cambridge in

Pl. X.

1691. Upon investigation, Stillman discovers that Dark had been Milton's private secretary from 1669 until the poet's death in 1674. The unexpected discovery of Dark's pamphlet enables Stillman to bring his argument full circle by joining his account of precolonial America and Milton's theology of language. A committed Puritan and devoted follower of Milton, Dark concludes that if the fall had come about through the defilement of the Word, redemption would arrive when language was restored to its original purity. "If the fall of man also entailed a fall of language, was it not logical to assume that it would be possible to undo the fall, to

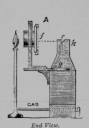

End View.

patients suffering under one or the other of the many forms of consumption. I may say that, with the aid of Dr. Mahomed, I am endeavoring to utilize this process to elicit the physiognomy of disease. The composite I now show is what I call a hotch-potch composite; its use is to form a standard whence deviations toward any particular subtype may be conveniently gauged." It is not only the physiognomy of disease that preoccupies Galton. While pointing out the artistic potential of the technique, Galton is primarily interested in using composite portraiture for diagnostic purposes. Convinced that the inner can be read on the outer, he develops visual norms for detecting physical, mental, and social deviance. These images are the visual equivalents of statistical norms. When used "properly" by skilled detectives, composite portraits make it possible to identify individuals who are predisposed to disease and crime. For Galton, fabricated images play an essential role in police and medical surveillance.

On December 29, 1991, the New York Times published a piece on the op-ed page, "The Last Leninist" by Robert C. Tucker. The essay was

reverse its effects by undoing the fall of language, by striving to recreate the language that was spoken in Eden? If man could learn to speak this original language of innocence, did it not follow that he would thereby recover a state of innocence within himself?" In his visionary reading of the Tower of Babel story, Dark contends that the movement of redemption is from east to west. The fall, which occurred in the far east of Mesopotamia, will be overcome in the far west of America. A series of intricate numerical calculations leads Dark to infer that the construction of the new Tower of Babel will begin in 1960 — the very year Stillman published his book.

Anticipating that distant time, Dark writes: "Once completed, the Tower would be large enough to hold every inhabitant of the New World. There would be a room for each person, and once he entered that room, he would forget everything he knew. After forty days and forty nights, he would emerge a new man, speaking God's language, prepared to inhabit the second, everlasting paradise."

SALVATORE A. brigand de la Calabre

In an extraordinary turn of events, Stillman, not content to let his conclusions linger as words on the page, decides to test Dark's hypothesis by conducting an experiment. His wife having recently died, he resigns from Columbia to devote full time to his research. In an effort to discover whether "God had a language," Stillman isolates his infant son, Peter Jr., by locking him in a small dark room for nine years. When someone finally discovers his demonic experiment, Stillman is declared mad and confined to a mental institution; his son is hospitalized and, after years of physical and psychological therapy, eventually recovers enough to lead the semblance of a "normal" life.

CAVAGLIÁ dit FUSIL assassin

The story "begins" with a phone call – apparently a wrong number – in the middle of the night. Daniel Quinn is lying in bed reading the first page of Marco Polo's Travels: "We will set down things seen as seen, things heard as heard, so that our book may be an accurate record, free of any sort of fabrication. And all who read this book or hear it may do so with full confidence, because it contains nothing but truth."

O.... Voleur napolitain

"Is this Paul Auster" asked the voice. "I would like to speak to Mr. Paul Auster.

"There's no one here by that name."

"Paul Auster. Of the Auster Detective Agency."

"I'm sorry," said Quinn. "You must have the wrong number."

G. SANA de Galiuccio brigand

Quinn is intrigued by the call and as soon as he hangs up regrets not having played along by pretending to be Paul Auster. A writer of detective stories, Quinn is fascinated by disguises and drawn to duplicity. He never writes in his own name but always in disguise. Quinn publishes his works under the pseudonym William Wilson, which he borrows from the inventor of the modern detective story – Edgar Allan Poe. As he lies on his bed unable to sleep, Quinn realizes that the strange phone call represented a missed opportunity to play out a "real"-life version of the stories he writes. Initially frustrated, he does not make the same mistake twice. When there is a second call a few days later, he assumes the persona of Paul Auster and becomes entangled in a world of intrigue where the absence of a solution renders escape impossible.

G. B. VENAFRO de Caspoli brigand

CARBONE chef- brigand

Paul Auster is one of the most inventive authors currently writing. Best known for works that are commonly regarded as detective novels, Auster uses this popular genre as a disguise for provocative reflections on the nature and limits of language. A long-time student, translator, and critic of major modern writers like Kafka, Beckett, Mallarmé, Celan, and, above all others, Jabès, Auster's subtle fiction can be read as an extended gloss on an observation made by Maurice Blanchot in a work that Auster translated:

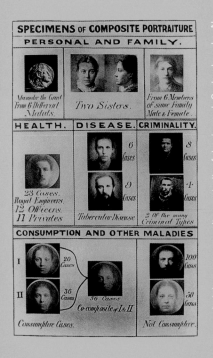

accompanied by a composite portrait of Lenin and Gorbachev by Nancy Burson. Though Burson's photograph recalls Galton's early efforts, advances in technology render her image considerably more refined. Lenin and Gorbachev blend to create a figure that represents neither of them, but in which traces of both can be detected. The *Times's* use of this image is itself newsworthy. As image-processing techniques become more sophisticated, the representational status of photographs (and videos) becomes more questionable. In the past, photographs that had been doctored were always recognizable; digital technology now makes it impossible to detect image manipulation. These developments create enormous problems not only for news organizations but also for law enforcement authorities and the legal system. Photographs and video, which have never been completely reliable, now carry virtually no evidentiary value. The decision to restrict use of the processed image to the op-ed page cannot hide the questions raised by the Lenachev photograph.

Burson's images, like Galton's "portraits," are politically motivated.

History does not withhold meaning, no more than meaning, which is always ambiguous – plural – can be reduced to its historical realization, even the most tragic and the most enormous. That is because the story does not explain itself. If it is the tension of a secret around which it seems to elaborate itself and which immediately declares itself without being elucidated, it only announces its own movement, which can lay the groundwork for the game of deciphering and interpretation, but it remains a stranger to itself. From this, it seems to me, and even though it seems to open up the unhappy possibilities of a life without hope, the story as such remains

> light, untroubled, and of a clarity that neither weighs down nor obscures the preten-
> sion of a hidden or serious meaning....There are appearances, there are only appear-
> ances, and how to believe in them, how to call them anything but what they are?

"The story... remains light, untroubled, and of a clarity that neither weighs down nor obscures the pretension of a hidden or serious meaning.... There are appearances... there are only appearances."

City of Glass is the first part of Auster's critically acclaimed New York Trilogy. Never simply a story, City of Glass is a work in which writers and stories fold into each other endlessly to create a text in which, to borrow a phrase from Baudrillard, "the map engenders the territory." Following the lead established by Poe and embodied in the very name William Wilson, Auster uses the strategy of doubling to generate his narrative. In the stories he tells, every body is always already doubled. As Stillman observes: "Quinn. A most resonant word. Rhymes with twin, does it not?" Daniel Quinn is William Wilson is Mookie Wilson is Max Work is Peter Stillman Sr. is Peter Stillman Jr. is Paul Auster. As Daniel Quinn says upon meeting Daniel Auster, who is the son of Paul — the "fictive" not the "real" Paul —

> "I'm you, and you're me."
> "And round and round it goes," shouted the boy, suddenly spreading his arms and spinning around the room like a gyroscope.

With words whirling and the text threatening to spin out of control, it becomes apparent that the twinning of the characters reflects the duplicity of language. In the society of spectacle, the world becomes a house of mirrors in which we see ourselves nowhere because we see ourselves everywhere.

The action in City of Glass is initiated by the telephonic presence of Peter Stillman Jr., whose call is prompted by the notification that his father has been released after thirteen years of institutionalization. Peter and his wife, Virginia, are convinced that his father will return to murder his son. In order to prevent this crime, Stillman Jr. enlists the services of Auster, who, of course, is Quinn, to shadow his father and to phone daily reports on his activities. In accepting a role usually reserved for characters in his fiction, Auster/Quinn discloses the operating assumptions of every detective. "The detective," he explains, "is the one who looks, listens, who moves through this morass of objects and events in search of the thought, the idea that will pull all these things together and make sense of them. In effect, the writer and the detective are interchangeable."

But the longer Quinn tails Stillman, the less sense things seem to make.

Staking out the flophouse where Stillman takes up temporary residence, Quinn records in his red notebook the suspect's aimless wandering through the city streets. When he attempts to make sense of what he records, however, he can discern neither meaning nor purpose. Instead of successfully discovering the underlying idea, Quinn "hover[s] stupidly on the surface of things." "Quinn was deeply disillusioned. He had always imagined that the key to good detective work was a close observation of details. The more accurate the scrutiny, the more successful the results. The implication was that human behavior could be understood, that

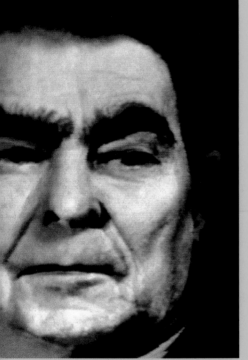

While Galton's photographs are directed to the end of biological purification and social control, Burson's work promotes a social agenda that involves the limitation of nuclear weapons and extension of social welfare programs. The aim of both photographers is to transform rather than to record. Burson's most provocative work, a series entitled *Warhead*, consists of portraits created by blending the faces of world leaders in direct proportion to the percentage of the world's nuclear weapons over which they preside. Using the most advanced digital processing software, Burson is able to average pixel values in a way that generates an image that is virtually seamless. *Warhead I*, for example, is a composite made up of 55% Reagan, 45% Brezhnev, and less than 1% of Thatcher, Mitterrand, and Deng. In another image, Burson overlays images of Stalin, Mussolini, Mao, Hitler, and Khomeini to create *Big Brother*. Burson's technical wizardry tends to obscure some of the most important assumptions informing her work. Like the committed phrenologist, Burson is convinced that since the inner is the outer and the outer is the inner, depth can be read on surface. More precisely, there is no depth because everything is surface. Peel

beneath the infinite facade of gestures, tics, and silences, there was finally a coherence, an order, a source of motivation. But after struggling to take in all these surface effects, Quinn felt no closer to Stillman than when he first started following him." In this moment of discouragement, Quinn's mind wanders to Poe's remarkable work *The Narrative of Arthur Gordon Pym* in which, he recalls, hieroglyphs figure at a crucial point in the plot. Stranded and under attack on an island near the South Pole, Pym and his partner, Peters (n.b.), seek refuge in a chasm where they discover "a range of singular-looking indentures in the surface of the marl forming the termination of the cul-de-sac." "With a very slight exertion of the imagination, the left, or most northerly of these indentures might have been taken for the intentional, although rude, representation of a human figure standing erect, with outstretched arms." While Peters is inclined to read these superficial inscriptions as alphabetic characters, Pym convinces him that they are arbitrary signs bearing no meaning. What neither Pym nor Peters realizes and Quinn fails to detect is that with an additional slight exertion of the imagination the graphs of the underground crypts become hieroglyphs that encode the name of Poe.

Following Poe's suggestions, Quinn plots the course of Stillman's wanderings on a map of New York City. As he gazes at his tracings, a pattern begins to emerge. "After fiddling with them for a quarter of an hour, switching them around, pulling them apart, rearranging the sequence, he returned to the original order and wrote them out in the following manner: OWER OF BAB The solution seemed so grotesque that his nerve almost failed him. Making all due allowances for the fact that he had missed the first four days and that Stillman had not yet finished, the answer seemed inescapable: THE TOWER OF BABEL "The solution is grotesque because it is really no solution at all. While Poe, or more precisely, Pym/Poe, left the readability of hieroglyphic signs undecidable, Quinn, or more precisely, Quinn/Auster, discovers hieroglyphic signs that are signs of the unreadability – or the infinite readability – of signs. If language is not one, meaning, like Humpty-Dumpty, cannot be fixed.

Having hit yet another dead end, Quinn decides to proceed more straightforwardly by approaching Stillman directly. In order not to blow his cover, Quinn "lies" to Stillman by telling him the "truth": "My name is Quinn." On other occasions, Quinn assumes the identities of Peter Stillman Jr. and Henry Dark. In a series of surreal exchanges resembling a dialogue straight out of Beckett, Stillman does not seem surprised by Quinn's claims and never appears to doubt his different identities. Showing no hostility toward his supposed son, Stillman remarks that the imposter looks like Peter Jr., even though his son is blond and Quinn is "dark. Not Henry Dark, but dark of hair." As for Henry Dark himself,

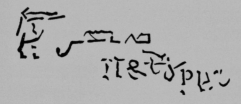

Stillman explains, he never existed but was a character Stillman had invented to advance certain ideas that were too dangerous and controversial to publish in his own name. Though at first reluctant to

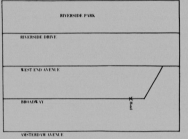

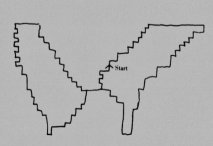

away one layer of skin and you discover nothing but another layer of skin. It is all a matter of facing.

The longer one ponders these "portraits," the more uncanny they become. Consider, for example, *Warhead I*. It is the left eye that captures attention. There is something strangely familiar about that eye; we know we have seen it before. Yet, as we trace the lines of the image, we realize that we have never actually seen this face. This face does not exist; nonetheless we are viewing its image. Burson seems to have done the impossible: she has photographed the missing body.

But Burson is not content to re-present the absence of the body. She has also constructed an interactive environment in which one can watch his or her "own" body disappear. As early as 1968, Burson conceived of building a machine that would make it possible to watch yourself age. It took almost a decade to develop the necessary hardware and software. With an analog-to-digital converter capable of translating video to computer signals that are machine storable, readable, and manipulable, Burson and her collaborator, enter into conversation, Stillman's reservations fade and he quickly proceeds to tell Quinn his entire philosophy of life, which turns out to be a philosophy of language. Remaining thoroughly committed to the ideas that led to the abuse of his son and his own incarceration, Stillman proclaims to Quinn: "The world is in fragments, sir. And it's my job to put it back together again."

> "You see, I am in the process of inventing a new language..."
>
> "A new language?"
>
> "Yes. A language that will at least say what we have to say. For our words no longer correspond to the world. When things were whole, we felt confident that our words could express them. But little by little these things have broken apart, shattered, collapsed into chaos. And yet, our words have remained the same. They have not adapted themselves to the new reality. Hence, every time we try to speak of what we see, we speak falsely, distorting the very thing we are trying to represent...."
>
> "My work is very simple. I have come to New York because it is the most forlorn of places, the most abject. The brokenness is everywhere, the disarray is universal. You have only to open your eyes to see it. The broken people, the broken things, the broken thought. The whole city is a junk heap. It suits my purposes admirably. I find the streets an endless source of material, an inexhaustible storehouse of shattered things. Each day I go out with my bag and collect objects that seem worthy of investigation...."
>
> "What do you do with these things?"
>
> "I give them names."
>
> "Names?"
>
> "I invent new words that will correspond to the things."

The name – especially the proper name – would seem to be the simplest point at which to begin the process of reestablishing the relation between words and things, which promises to restore the original transparency of the world. And yet, as we have seen, from the beginning of *City of Glass*, the propriety of the name is cast into doubt. "Proper" names slip and slide until it is not clear who is who and what is what. Like Potter's players floating across the televisual terminal, Auster's characters fade into and out of each other in such a way that their identities become completely obscure. When he first introduces himself to Quinn, "Peter Stillman Jr." declares:

> "My name is Peter Stillman. Perhaps you have heard of me, but more likely not. No matter. That is not my real name. My real name I cannot remember. Excuse me. Not

that it makes a difference. That is to say, anymore."

"This is what is called speaking. I believe that is the term. When words come out, fly into the air, live for a moment, and die."

No matter...never any matter... nothing ever matters... not even matter. It is not until much later in the story that Peter Stillman Sr. underscores the significance of seemingly frivolous wordplay. Quinn, who is playing the role of Auster, introduces himself as Quinn. Stillman, ever sensitive to puns and tropes, responds that he likes

David Kramlich, developed *The Age Machine*. Once the visitor is seated in the machine, a video camera scans his or her face and feeds the data into a computer. The viewer then registers his or her age and sex and indicates the age at which he or she wishes to see himself or herself depicted. Databases storing information about predictable changes in skin texture, muscle tone, and facial contours make it possible to create a portrait of an aged face in approximately thirty seconds. As the viewer watches the image emerge on the screen, the "real" body virtually disappears. It is as if the thing itself becomes an image before one's very eyes. In this way, Burson's screenplay effectively stages the transformation of "reality" into virtual reality.

In a subsequent development of her digital image-processing technique, entitled *The Composite Machine*, Burson suggests the broader cultural implications of her work. This device invites participants to create "portraits" by blending their own image with images of stars like Cher, Jane Fonda, Marilyn Monroe, Barbara Bush, Marcel Duchamp, Mikhail Gorbachev, Paul McCartney, Nam June Paik, Elvis Presley, Andy Warhol, and Oprah Winfrey.

Quinn's name because it rhymes with twin and then unleashes a series of free associations that seem to have no more diagnostic value than Marlow's game with Gibbon. "I see many possibilities for this word, this Quinn, this...quintessence...of quidity. Quick, for example. And quill. And quack. And quirk. Hmmm. Rhymes with grin. Not to speak of kin. Hmmm. Very interesting. And win. And fin. And din. And gin. And pin. And bin. Hmmm. Even rhymes with djinn. Hmmm. And if you say it right, with been. Hmmmm. Yes, very interesting. I like your name enormously, Mr. Quinn. It flies off in so many little directions at once."

Stillman's remark erases itself in its very expression; moreover, this insight undercuts the project to which he has devoted his entire life. If the name – even the proper name – "flies off in so many little directions at once," then it is impossible to restore the original purity of language by reestablishing a one-to-one relation between word and thing. Rather, it gradually becomes obvious that language is never pure, clear, or unambiguously transparent but is always already duplicitous. As Stillman suggests, without realizing the implications of what he is saying, the duplicity of language is at least double. If language is invented and not discovered, then the sign is arbitrary. Stillman underscores the arbitrariness of the sign by reading the story of Humpty-Dumpty as a theory of language: "Humpty Dumpty: the purest embodiment of the human condition. Listen carefully, sir. What is an egg? It is that which has not yet been born. A paradox, is it not? For how can Humpty Dumpty be alive if he has not been born? And yet, he is alive – make no mistake. We know that because he can speak. More than that, he is a philosopher of language. 'When I use a word, Humpty Dumpty said, in a rather scornful tone, it means just what I choose it to mean – neither more nor less. The question is, said Alice, whether you *can* make words mean so many different things.'" The arbitrary sign is intended to make the thing appear by doubling it. In this way, the word is supposed to re-present the presence of the thing. But contrary to expectation, representation turns out to be depresentation, or, in Jacques Lacan's provocative phrase, "the word is the death of the thing." In the words of another story, which I have, of course, been retelling all along, Sentence... Prison... Sentence; in the words of another story, which I might yet tell in order to retell Auster's story, every sentence is, in effect, a "death sentence." Language, it seems, is the appearance of the disappearance of the body. If the word is the death of the thing, the mystery of language *always* involves a missing body. The search for the body (and the effort to establish its identity) is the search for a signified – transcendental or otherwise – that lends signifiers their thickness, weight, depth, and substance. If the body cannot be found, the mystery cannot be solved.

The duplicity of language does not, however, rest solely on the arbitrariness of the sign. Any signifier taken by itself is completely unintelligible. The identity of the sign – and of everything else – is a function of its relations to, and associations with, other signs. As Auster maintains elsewhere, "nothing is ever named, everything becomes a reference to something else." Since everything is a reference to something else, identity is differential. This is the reason the name "flies off in so many little directions at once." The different directions are the various relations and associations that the articulation of the name presupposes.

If the meaning of signs is a function of their relation to other signs, then linguistic meaning is not secured by binding words to things. Things, which seem to lend words their thickness, weight, depth, and substance, are not an extralinguistic foundation but are always already encoded in an endless (and beginningless) play of signs. Signs cannot be interpreted in terms of things but can only be read in and through other signs. Since language is invented, facts are constructed,

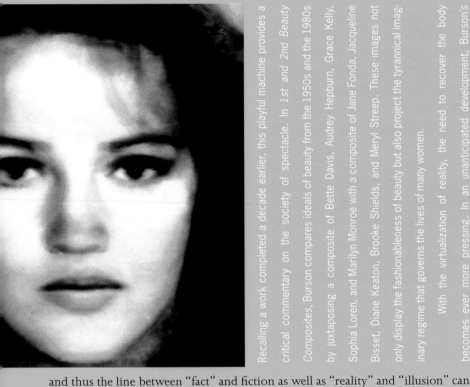

Recalling a work completed a decade earlier, this playful machine provides a critical commentary on the society of spectacle. In *1st and 2nd Beauty Composites*, Burson compares ideals of beauty from the 1950s and the 1980s by juxtaposing a composite of Bette Davis, Audrey Hepburn, Grace Kelly, Sophia Loren, and Marilyn Monroe with a composite of Jane Fonda, Jacqueline Bisset, Diane Keaton, Brooke Shields, and Meryl Streep. These images not only display the fashionableness of beauty but also project the tyrannical imaginary regime that governs the lives of many women.

With the virtualization of reality, the need to recover the body becomes ever more pressing. In an unanticipated development, Burson's strategies for composing images have been appropriated by law enforcement authorities to aid in their detective work. "Beginning in 1982," Lynn Herbert explains, "parents of missing children began to contact Burson. They had seen her 'aged' portraits exhibited, published and on television. Could she provide an updated composite for their missing child? It was not a project Burson had foreseen, but she set about to help these parents....Since 1987, Burson and

and thus the line between "fact" and fiction as well as "reality" and "illusion" can never be drawn clearly. Auster plants a clue leading to this insight early in the story when he describes Quinn: "What interested him about the stories he wrote was not their relation to the world but their relation to other stories." And then, as if to underscore the point, Auster adds a hint about his own rewriting of Poe's "William Wilson": "Even before he became William Wilson, Quinn had been a devoted reader of mystery novels." Since Quinn is both Paul Auster and William Wilson, Auster is also William Wilson, who, in one of his guises, is the invention of Poe.

When the differential character of signs is translated into narratives, every text becomes an intertext that approaches hypertextuality.

Hypertexts subvert traditional strategies of detection. The detective, we have discovered, assumes that "surface effects" disclose deep structures that lend the skin of things its intelligibility. Commenting on the poetry of Laura Riding, Auster suggests that the task of the detective is "to peel back the skin of the world in order to find some absolute and unassailable place of permanence." But rather than the thing-in-itself, this unassailable place of permanence turns out to be nothing but another layer of skin. For Auster, as for Potter, the problem is not the lack of meaning but its excess: "The world of the book comes to life, seething with possibilities, with secrets and contradictions. Since everything seen or said, even the slightest, most trivial thing, can bear a connection to the outcome of the story, nothing must be overlooked. Everything becomes essence; the center, then, is everywhere, and no circumference can be drawn until the book has come to its end." When everything is essence, nothing is essential, and when nothing is essential, the center can never be located and the circumference never drawn. The book does not end, for analysis is interminable. This nonending marks closure of the book, which dispels the spell it has cast for so long.

As *City of Glass* nears closure, Quinn begins to feel "as though the whole thing added up to nothing at all." Gradually, every thing and every body disappear. Shortly after Quinn's and Stillman's bizarre conversations, Stillman vanishes without leaving a trace. Quinn's repeated efforts to contact Peter Jr. and Virginia prove futile; no one answers the telephone. In the wake of this telephonic absence, a previously trivial detail assumes possible significance. As the play of black and white on Poe's southernmost island figures the problem of writing, so the black of Virginia ("dark hair, dark eyes,... a black dress") and the white of Peter ("dressed entirely in white, with the white-blond hair of a child") pose the question of textuality or, more precisely, intertextuality. To the query implied by the "proper" name – Is Stillman still man? – the only possible answer appears to be "No!" Even before the beginning of the story, Quinn had "long ago stopped thinking of himself as real." By the end of the story, Quinn's thought of his own unreality becomes a reality. Having lost the trail of Stillman and unable to contact his son, Quinn stakes out Peter and Virginia's apartment to watch for the return of the father. As days turn into weeks and weeks into months, Quinn drifts into a state of vagrancy. After exhausting all his resources, he turns to Auster, whom he had earlier tracked down and entrusted with the retainer check made out to Quinn in the name of

Paul Auster. Shocked by Quinn's appearance, Auster says that he has been trying to contact him for several months to tell him about newspaper articles reporting that Stillman Sr. committed suicide by jumping off the Brooklyn Bridge. Furthermore, when the "real" Paul Auster tried to cash the check made out to the "fictive" Paul Auster, it bounced. It seems as if Peter Stillman had never really existed.

    After hearing this news, Quinn is hardly surprised when he returns to the apartment of Peter Jr. and finds it empty. "So many things were disappearing now, it was difficult to keep track of them." Quinn realizes that he too is "coming

Kramlich's program has been successfully used by the F.B.I. and the National Center for Missing and Exploited Children to find missing children and adults." It is not difficult to see how this unexpected twist returns the art of composite portraiture to the purposes for which Galton originally designed it. Armed with images, investigators track down criminals and detect deviants. In the age of electronic reproduction, we must learn to reread even faces that have long seemed familiar. For those with eyes to see, everything lies on the surface.

to an end." With only a few pages remaining in the red notebook where his life is now inscribed, Quinn ponders what he has written. The words describing his own life are no more legible than the words recording Stillman's life. The echo of the voice of Auster's son, Daniel, ripples across the page: "I'm you, and you're me... And round and round it goes." Lying on the floor of the empty apartment, Quinn has more than enough time to reflect. "He wondered if Virginia Stillman had hired another detective after he failed to get in touch with her. He asked himself why he had taken Auster's word for it that the check had bounced. He thought about Peter Stillman and wondered if he had ever slept in the room he was in now. He wondered if the case was really over or if he was not somehow still working on it. He wondered what the map would look like of all the steps he had taken in his life and what word it would spell." Though tempted to retrace his life, Quinn does not repeat his hieroglyphic gesture. If he has learned anything, he has learned that, when the map engenders the territory, nothing stands under the play of surfaces and hence understanding is impossible not because there is no meaning but because meanings endlessly multiply. "Quinn was nowhere now. He had nothing, he knew nothing, he knew that he knew nothing. Not only had he been sent back to the beginning, he was now before the beginning, and so far before the beginning that it was worse than any end he could imagine."

But where is this nowhere that is before the beginning? "What I am after, I suppose," Auster admits in a 1989 interview, "is to write fiction as strange as the world I live in." In his strange hypertextual world, it's skin all the way down. Skin rubbing at skin, skin, skin, skin, skin…" 'Somebody's missing.' So the detective really is a very compelling figure, a figure we all understand. He's a seeker after truth, the problem-solver, the one who tries to figure things out. But what if, in the course of trying to figure it out, you just unveil more mysteries?" When unveiling reveals nothing… nothing but further veils, "I'll figure things out. I'll figure it out. I'll figure out who did it" must be translated: "I can't figure things out. I can't figure it out. I can't figure out who did it." Far from writing traditional detective stories that start with the mystery of the missing body and end with its recovery and identification, Auster's fiction begins with bodies that seem present and identifiable and ends with their mysterious disappearance. The mystery of Auster's (dis)solution is the mystery of a world in which bodies vanish as reality becomes virtual. Auster does not refuse "to write about real things in a realistic way" but struggles to write "realistically" in an age in which reality is no longer realistic.

There are appearances

Only appearances

How to believe

How to call

Them

Anything?

TIME

An American Tragedy

BK 4013970 06-17-94

LOS ANGELES POLICE

"All clues. No solutions. That's the way

things are. Plenty of clues. No solutions."

It always begins or seems to begin by chance. "It was a wrong number that started it, the telephone ringing three times in the dead of night, and the voice on the other end asking for someone he was not. Much later, when he was able to think about the things that had happened to him, he would conclude that nothing was real except chance. But that was much later." Begins by chance and ends or appears to end with the disappearance of a body. A disappearance that always seems to be a matter of chance even if it is expected. When the body disappears – especially the body of the mother or the father – our calls go unanswered, for there is no one on the other end of the line. The ringing of the phone becomes a tolling that transforms the *City of Glass* into the city of *Glas*.

This all seems to have begun by chance. A chance gift, which, I now realize, was the gift of chance. What I did not know at the time but have learned since is that gift of chance is a matter of life and death. A matter of life and death whose mystery can never be solved.

As was our custom during professional meetings, Alan and I had met for dinner the night before. In addition to catching up on personal news, we discussed the various projects on which we were working. Always concerned about what is coming next, Alan pressed me for details about plans for my new book. After describing at some length the book I had already started to write, I briefly mentioned a different kind of work that had begun to take shape in my mind. I had little more than a title: Betrayal. I explained to Alan that I envisioned a text that would weave together theological and philosophical discussions with quasi-autobiographical reflections. This kind of work, I stressed, cannot be hurried, for its research involves nothing less than life itself. Alan's interest was obviously aroused, and the more we talked, the more intrigued he became. The next morning when I checked for messages at the hotel desk, there was a package from Alan waiting for me. I opened it and found an inscribed copy of Paul Auster's *Invention of Solitude*.

> For Mark,
>> In the hope that
>>> This will forward
>>>> Betrayal
>>>>> Alan
>>>> 11/21/88

At the time, I had not heard of Auster. I stuck the book in my bag to look at later.

The meetings of the American Academy of Religion always fall on the weekend before Thanksgiving. Weather and the holiday season make travel at this time of year chancy. When I reached the airport, I discovered that a bad ice storm had led to the cancellation of all flights to Albany. Since we were planning to drive to my parents' home in New Jersey for Thanksgiving, I called my wife to tell her that I was taking a flight to Newark and that we could meet in Westfield the next day. On the plane to Newark, I began reading *The Invention of Solitude*: "One day there is life. A man, for example, in the best of health, not even old, with no history of illness. Everything as it was, as it will always be. He goes from one day to the next, minding his own business, dreaming only of life that lies before him. And then, suddenly, it happens there is death." I knew immediately why Alan had given me the book. In this fleeting moment of recognition, my appreciation for his understanding of what I try to do in my writing deepened considerably. I saw my own thoughts reflected in Auster's words. It was not only the evident similarities: same age, growing up only a few miles apart in New Jersey, many of the same experiences. More important but less obvious, it was clear to me that Auster and I were pursued by similar demons and obsessed with the same uncanny *je ne sais quoi*.

The next day, as I lay on the couch with Auster's book, my mother asked what I was reading. An erstwhile English teacher, she always wanted to know what I was reading and what she should be reading. I responded: "You don't want to know." Nothing more was said until a few days later when she handed me *The Invention of Solitude* and said: "You're right; I don't want to know." Three weeks later she was dead.

My mother died five days before Christmas and a little more than a week before the fiftieth wedding anniversary party my brother and I had planned for her and my father. In the confusion and turmoil of those days, two images stand out. The last time I saw my mother alive was in the intensive care unit. She had suffered a massive cerebral hemorrhage, a stroke; her brain, the doctor explained, had exploded. She was being kept alive by a formidable array of machines. This was not the first time I had seen her like this. Nearly twenty years earlier, I had rushed home from Copenhagen, where I was writing my doctoral dissertation, to find her in the same condition in the same hospital. That time brain surgery brought her through the ordeal; this time the doctor told us there was no hope. The "miracle" two decades before made the decision we faced much more difficult. If she had overcome the odds then, why not now? But the doctor insisted that this time the situation was different. With extraordinary hesitation and lingering misgivings, my father decided to stop life support; my brother and I agreed. As I said good-bye, I leaned over to give her warm body and sweaty skin a kiss. Four hours later the silence of that sleepless night was shattered by the ringing of the telephone with the call that my mother had died. The next – and last – time I saw her she was in a casket about to be buried. Saying my "final" good-bye, I leaned over to give her a parting kiss. This time her body was stiff and her skin cold. As I watched, the casket closed and the body disappeared. Forever. "One day there is life.... And then, suddenly, it happens, there is death... the invisible boundary between life and death." What happens in that moment? What disappears?

When I returned to Williamstown, I found a letter from Bob in the pile of mail that had accumulated. Several of us were completing a book, *Theology at the End of the Century: A Dialogue on the Postmodern*, in which we experimented with a new for-mat. Tom, Charlie, and I wrote essays and Bob responded by posing questions to which we, in turn, replied. I entitled my essay "Nothing Ending Nothing." Though touching on a broad range of theological topics, Bob's questions focused on the problem of death. Still suffering from the experiences of the preceding weeks, I neither wanted nor knew how to reply. After considerable deliberation, I decided to organize my response around Auster's meditation on the death of his father. Notes I discovered after my mother's death indicated that *The Invention of Solitude* was not the last book she had read, but it was the last book we shared. In a brief essay, "Unending Strokes," I, in effect, rewrote the death of Auster's father as the death of my mother.

I have nothing left to say. Always nothing left to say. But how to say it? To say it again? And again, and again?...There is no core of the mat(t)er to reach...only surfaces. Surfaces that are not always superficial.... I cast over the written work, over the past body and the past corpus...

One day there is life. A man, for example, in the best of health, not even old, with no history of illness. Everything as it was, as it will always be. He goes from one day to the next, minding his own business, dreaming only of the life that lies before him. And then, suddenly, it happens, there is death. A man lets out a little sigh, he slumps down in his chair, and it is death. The suddenness of it leaves no room for thought, gives the mind no chance to seek out a word that might comfort it. We are left with nothing but death, the irreducible fact of our own mortality. Death after a long illness we can accept with resignation.

Even accidental death we can ascribe to fate. But for a man to die of no apparent cause, for a man to die simply because he is a man, brings us so close to the invisible boundary between life and death that we no longer know which side we are on. Life becomes death, and it is as if this death has owned this life all along. Death without warning. Which is to say: life stops.

The Gift of chance... a mat(t)er of life and death.

As days, months, even years passed, my father showed few signs of overcoming his depression. You don't start over when you are eighty. In the spring of 1990, I had to give lectures in Munich and Helsinki. Between Germany and Finland, I planned to spend a few days in Paris. Hoping to lift my father's spirits, I asked him to go along with me. After much coaxing, he finally agreed. Though he had traveled to Europe several times, he continued to be struck by the little differences he observed: German cleanliness, Munich beer steins, the speed of cars on the autobahn, the early chestnut blossoms in the Luxembourg Gardens, rabbits hanging, hide and all, in open-air markets. I had been looking forward to showing him some of

my favorite Parisian haunts, but chance again intervened. In a state of panic, my father woke me in the middle of the night to tell me he thought he was having a heart attack. Though he was old, he was in the best of health and had no history of illness. As I frantically searched the Paris telephone book for the names and phone numbers of hospitals and cardiologists, he decided the palpitations were subsiding and wanted to wait until morning before doing anything. When dawn arrived, he insisted he did not need to see a doctor. The condition never again returned, and I still have no idea what happened that night.

The next day was our last in Paris, and I had arranged to visit Edmond and Arlette Jabès before leaving. Since I suspected my father would enjoy meeting them, I was delighted when he said he felt up to accompanying me. Though their experiences were worlds apart, age and its challenges brought Edmond, Arlette, and my father together in surprising ways. It seemed as if they had known each other for many years.

In the course of the conversation, the name of Paul Auster came up. Having made plans to include translations of several of Edmond's books in a series I was editing, I commented on the growing recognition of the importance of his work in the States. As evidence, I cited Auster's long appreciative essay in the *New York Review of Books*. Edmond explained that he and Arlette had known Paul for a long time. They had become close during his Paris sojourn and had stayed in touch over the years. Before leaving, my father insisted on taking a picture of me with Edmond and Arlette. That was the last time I saw Edmond alive. In mid-January 1991, Richard called to tell me that Edmond had  died on January 2. He had been ill for several weeks and had been forced to cut short a trip to Spain. But in the days immediately prior to his death, he had seemed to be improving. The night before he died, he and Arlette had welcomed the new year by dancing alone in their living room.

When I returned to Paris briefly in October 1992, I knew I had to squeeze in a visit with Arlette. The death of Edmond was as difficult for her as the death of my mother had been for my father. When she opened the apartment door to greet me, I saw sadness written in the deep lines of her face. Though Arlette obviously had recounted the details of Edmond's death many times, it was important for her to retell the story to me. In the midst of her recollection, she paused to recall my previous visit with my father and to ask how he was doing. I reported that he was still having a hard time; she responded: "C'est difficile, trés difficile." As her account drew to a close, I was particularly touched to learn that Arlette had told Richard to contact three people when he returned to the States after the funeral: Mary Ann Caws, Paul Auster, and me. She asked me if I knew Paul, and when I said no, she encouraged me to get in touch with him because, she thought, we had much in common.

Before taking Arlette's advice, I read more of Auster's work and was persuaded that she was right. In February 1992, I wrote him a letter of introduction in which I expressed my appreciation for his work – especially *The Invention of Solitude*; I included a copy of "Nothing Ending Nothing" along with its postscript, "Unending Strokes." While I did not consider it particularly unusual when I received no response, I was surprised when an answer arrived four months later.

June 21, 1992

Dear Mark Taylor:
Thank you for your extraordinarily kind letter – which has only just reached me. Arlette told you Third Avenue, but the fact is that I live on Third Street – which is a world of difference – and given the intelligence level of Brooklyn postal workers,

a hopeless problem. And since Viking has sometimes held letters of mine for as long as a year, it's finally a miracle that I received your package (dated February 6) as early as I did...

Yes, Edmond and Arlette have been friends of mine for over 20 years – almost like spiritual grandparents – and even though Edmond is now dead, he is still with me. He taught me lessons I will keep for the rest of my life. I'm sure that you and I will meet at some point. It's bound to happen.

With thanks – and all good Thoughts – Paul Auster

A few weeks later, I was leaving for Paris to attend the Cerisy colloquium on Derrida. The timing of Auster's letter seemed odd.

While it is not my custom to keep a journal, I often record my reflections when I travel, for I have found over the years that some thoughts only occur when you are away from home and cannot be recaptured when you return. The day I left for Paris in the summer of 1992, I registered the following observations in a black notebook I keep for such occasions.

July 10, 1992

A certain melancholy accompanies departures – especially when leaving alone for a foreign country. Often the sense of loss that is stronger than the anticipation of gain. I suppose part of it is the solitude and the recognition of the isolation that lies ahead.

But there is something else at work, for such departures often have as their last stop a visit with my father. I know he enjoys the visits; and yet, I also realize that he dreads the partings. When you are 84, you have suffered too many losses for leavetaking to be casual. I know how much my visits mean to him and yet they are difficult for me. It is depressing – terribly depressing – to watch him struggle with age. He has little to look forward to and there is nothing I can say to comfort him. He gets frustrated by the betrayal of his body. As I look at him, he is growing smaller; not just thinner but smaller – as if his body were slowly disappearing. His shoulders are becoming rounded and his gait is steady but not as quick as it once was.

Even more depressing than watching my father struggle with age is anticipating myself in his place. His days are long and his nights longer still. There is not enough conversation to fill the emptiness. In the midst of this silence, I feel a sense of guilt for not spending more time with him. But time seems too precious to spend sitting in New Jersey doing nothing. And yet, when I reverse the situation and think of what Aaron's and Kirsten's visits mean to me, I have a sense of what my trips mean to him. Then, idleness and silent conversations hardly seem a waste of time. But these rare moments always pass quickly.

Confronting – or at least acknowledging – such thoughts as I depart deepens the sense of loss and dislocation. I realize more and more that all departures are glimpses of the unavoidable departure toward which we are inexorably moving.

The ten days at Cerisy were intense and unusually productive. After the colloquium, I had only one afternoon in Paris before returning to the States. I decided to spend it with Arlette. My time with her that afternoon was strangely reminiscent of my visits with my father. Our conversation circled around death and the impossibility of going on. Much of the time we did not speak but simply sat in silence. As I bid her farewell, her melancholy overwhelmed me. The next night I was in New Jersey. My father was eager to hear about my trip and was especially interested to know how Arlette was doing. During the year since his visit with Edmond and Arlette, he frequently asked about them. When I reported then that she was still struggling with her loss, he responded: "She will not get over it; some wounds never heal." Early the next morning, I left for Williamstown. That was the last time I saw my father alive.

Shortly after I returned from Paris, Richard called again. This time he bore the news that Arlette had died on August 12 – less than three weeks after I had seen her. I was speechless; it seemed there was nothing to say... nothing. "So many things were disappearing now, it was difficult to keep track of them." I told Richard that I would write to Auster to give him the news. Paul's response was as prompt as it was poignant.

8/29/92

Dear Mark:

A bad blow. I feel too stunned to say much of anything now – not quite ready or able to absorb the news. But thank you for telling me. I do appreciate it.

All the best – Paul

As I was reading Paul's note responding to Arlette's death, the telephone rang. This time it was not the wrong number – the call was for me. On the other end of the line, the familiar voice of a family friend from the distant past uttered four brief words: "Your father just died."

It always ends or seems to end by chance.... The gift of chance... a matter of life and death. Chance... so many chances... so many missed chances. For what? For whom? Where is the music in these chances? I did not write to Auster for almost a year. I finally got around to sending him another letter but do not remember what I said. I did, however, keep his reply.

July 27, '93

Dear Mark:
We were late in getting to Vermont this year – and I didn't stop at the post office until yesterday, where I found your three-week-old letter waiting for me. I'm so sorry about your father's death.... Never an easy business to face, no matter what the circumstances.
I also should have thanked you for "The Book of Margins," which arrived safely many months ago. I feel guilty about my silence....
I finished a novel about six weeks ago and have been in the doldrums ever since. Burnt out, listless, walking into walls, dropping everything I touch. Most mornings, I have to remind myself to tie my shoes.
I'm very happy you'll be teaching some of my work next year. My sense is that the spring is going to be a hectic time for me – so I don't think it would be right for me to accept the invitation to Williams, since I'd probably have to cancel. But why don't you visit me in New York some time? Surely, you must go down to the City every now and then. It would be a great pleasure to meet at last....

With all good thoughts –
Paul A.

A detail... perhaps a final detail that I neglected to mention when trying to decipher Auster's unreadable hieroglyphs. Shaken by the pattern Quinn thinks he discerns in Stillman's life, Auster writes:

But the letters continued to horrify Quinn. The whole thing was so oblique, so fiendish in its circumlocutions, that he did not want to accept it. Then doubts came, as if on command, filling his head with mocking, sing-song voices. He had imagined the whole thing. The letters were not letters at all. He had seen them only because he had wanted to see them. And even if the diagrams did form letters, it was only a fluke. It was all an accident, a hoax he had perpetrated on himself.

He decided to go to bed, slept fitfully, woke up, wrote in the red notebook for half an hour, went back to bed. His last thought before he went to sleep was that he probably had two more days, since Stillman had not yet completed his message. The last two letters remained the "E" and the "L." Quinn's mind dispersed. He arrived in a neverland of fragments, a place of wordless things and thingless words. Then, struggling through his stupor one last time, he told himself that El was the ancient Hebrew name for God.

Clues... so many clues... Solutions... no solutions. El is not properly a name, for it is the name of the unnameable. The title of the final volume of Jabès's remarkable work, The Book of Questions, is El, or The Last Book. Questions... books of questions that know no end and resist every answer. Letters... horrifying, fiendish letters... letters that might not be letters at all. Had he imagined the whole thing? Was it a fluke, a hoax, an accident? Did it really all come down to chance?

DERMA

I think you can tell a lot about a person just by reading their skin.

Charlie Cartwright

The tattoo becomes more than the image. And in today's context – well, we live in the age of image
overload where we process thousands of photos a month, not to mention TV images.
Because of video and film which simulate more of the dream state, our language is being reshaped;
it's hard to figure out exactly how, but it's happening, and it may well mean a drastic
deterioration of written language and vocabulary, so that the nuances of meaning
disappear along with fine analysis. Thirty years ago you had Walter Benjamin writing about
a whole new way of conceptualizing art in the age of mass reproduction brought about by photographic replication.
And when a painting is reproduced as a tattoo, it becomes really different.

Andrea Juno

If someone asked me, "What's your problem?" I'd have to say, "Skin."

Andy Warhol

GRAPHICS

Hides no longer hiding but on display as precious canvases in a museum devoted to skin...nothing but skin. The body has disappeared and only skin remains...remains as the inscribed surface where image is incarnate and carnality is phantasmic. The skin becomes the site of research whose superficiality is its strength rather than its weakness.

Dr. Masaichi Fukushi, a pathologist and professor at Nippon Medical University, conducted extensive research in dermatology. He was especially interested in moles, which are caused by the excessive production of pigment in the skin. In an effort to understand the biochemical processes that create these disfigurations, Fukushi undertook studies comparing the interior movement of pigment in moles with the effects of exterior pigment introduced into the skin by tattooing. Japan's long tradition of colorful full-body tattooing made Tokyo an ideal place for this research.

As awareness of the extraordinary Japanese art of tattooing has grown, the influence of artists working in this tradition has spread throughout the world. Present-day Japanese tattooing can be traced to the Edo period (1603 – 1867). Prior to this time, the Japanese, under the influence of the Chinese, for whom bodily disfiguration was a crime, used tattooing primarily as a punishment. While the reasons for the change in the status of the tattoo remain obscure, two factors contributed to creating new attitudes. First, ruling classes attempted to maintain social control by imposing strict sartorial regulations prohibiting the wearing of certain garments and fabrics by some members of society. Denied access to high fashion for political and economic reasons, lower social classes made tattooing fashionable. This is not to imply that the practice of tattooing was sanctioned by the authorities; to the contrary, the conservative Tokugawa military government, founded on Chinese Confucian philosophy, did not approve of nonpunitive tattooing. The tattoo, therefore, became a mark of social protest, which, from the point of view of the ruling powers, branded its bearer an outsider. The second factor contributing to changing attitudes about tattooing was the appearance of a twenty-volume Chinese work entitled *Shui-hu Chuan* in which a pseudonymous author, Shih Nai-an, recounts the exploits of a band of rebels who resisted a corrupt government and helped the poor during the last years of the northern Sung dynasty (1117–21). Many of the leading characters in this epic were tattooed. The Chinese edition of *Shui-hu Chuan* appeared in Japan between 1727 and 1759, but the Japanese translation was not completed until 1839. In 1827, a Ukiyo-e named Utagawa Kuniyoshi published an extraordinarily popular series of wood block prints of the tattooed outlaws. These prints, which were widely

available to all classes, exercised an enormous influence on the art of tattooing during the first half of the nineteenth century. Intricate designs weaving together dragons, warriors, vines, and flowers became, in effect, flash (standardized drawings) for Japanese tattooists.

When the modern period in Japan began with the Meiji restoration in 1868, the official attitude toward tattooing did not change. No longer appealing to ancient Chinese codes, the new rulers sought to outlaw tattooing because they feared it would reinforce Western perceptions of Japan as a primitive country. Contrary to expectation, many westerners were intrigued by the Japanese form of this art. From countless sailors and travelers to royalty like Britain's George V and Russia's Nicholas II, a surprising number of foreigners had themselves tattooed. As a result of its popularity among westerners, tattooing, though forbidden for Japanese, was permitted for foreigners between 1868 and 1945. Not until the American occupation after World War II was tattooing legalized in Japan.

The more Fukushi studied the intricate tattoo designs of his patients, the more he became convinced of the value of this underappreciated art form. To preserve these works of art for future generations, he began to photograph and catalogue different tattoo motifs. As his collection grew to over three thousand images, Fukushi began to regret that these remarkable artworks were disappearing with their owners. Using his research skills in pathology and dermatology, Fukushi developed a technique that enabled him to preserve the dermal layer bearing the tattoo. After perfecting this procedure, he approached tattooers and tattooed individuals with a stunning proposal: Fukushi planned to establish a museum dedicated to the preservation and display of tattooed skins. The response to this seemingly bizarre project was remarkably positive. While tattoo artists saw in Fukushi's plan an opportunity to promote their craft, those who were tattooed viewed it as a chance for financial assistance to help defray the high cost of tattooing while securing the notoriety they had always hoped their skins would bring. With the consent and cooperation of the Tokyo medical establishment as well as people throughout the world of Japanese tattooing, Fukushi opened the Medical Pathology Museum of Tokyo University.

After Fukushi's death, his son, Katsunari, who is also a pathologist, took over the museum and continued his father's research into tattooing. The collection of tattooed skins at University Medical Museum currently numbers 105. Writing with all the sensitivity and insight of a trained connoisseur, Katsunari Fukushi explains:

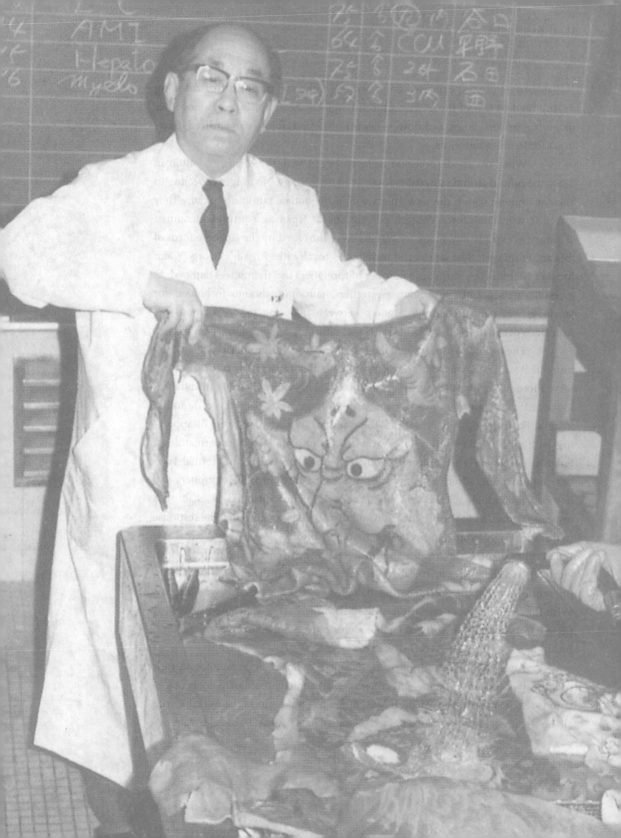

Numbers are not important; I have limited this collection only to tattoo masterpieces which cover the entire body, to hand them down to posterity.... Tattoos are achieved as a result of long-term dedication between tattooer and tattooee, triumphing over the pain and perseverance of the instruments. The passions kindled by both parties in the creation of an unparalleled work fuse their souls together. This is nothing less than a peerless living art.... I would like to devote myself to finishing the fine specimens of tattooed skin I have preserved and to the medical study of them. I feel this would be an appropriate memorial to all those souls who volunteered their skins to me and a duty on my part for their bereaved families and all who are concerned with the subject of tattoos.

Not everyone is so appreciative of the art of tattooing. Throughout much of the world, tattooing has long been associated with criminality and sociopolitical deviance. Not merely a sign marking the criminal, tattooing is actually a crime in seven states in this country. In seven other states, local ordinances outlaw or severely restrict the practice of tattooing. Tattoos are commonly regarded as both symptoms and causes of a variety of diseases. As the trained pathologist can detect traces of disease in bodily tissue, so the educated detective can read the story of crime in lines of tattoos.

On November 6, 1993, three remarkable photographs of tattooed men and an article entitled "Body Language" by Arkady G. Bronnikov appeared on the op-ed page of the New York Times. This piece is an excerpt from a longer essay, "Telltale Tattoos in Russian Prisons," which appeared with additional tattoo photographs in *Natural History*. In these articles, Bronnikov, who had taught criminology at the Institute of the Soviet Interior Ministry in Perm, reports on his thirty-year investigation of tattooing practices among criminals in the former Soviet Union. Having accumulated an archive of over twenty thousand photographs taken in correctional facilities and labor camps in several Soviet republics, Bronnikov summarizes his research. Tattoos, he concludes, are not arbitrary signifiers, but match the crimes committed by the individuals who wear them. Furthermore, tattoos play a crucial role in establishing and maintaining the social relations that structure prison life.

The sheer numbers involved in Bronnikov's analysis are staggering. From the mid-1960s to the 1980s, approximately thirty-five million people were imprisoned in the Soviet Union. If, as Bronnikov calculates, anywhere from 70% to 98% of the prison population is tattooed, then between twenty-eight to thirty million people were tattooed during this period. Tattoos are not, however, evenly

distributed among inmates. The worse the crime, the more likely the criminal is to be tattooed. Bronnikov's data indicate that in minimum-security prisons 65–70% of the convicts are tattooed, in medium-security prisons 80%, and in maximum-security prisons 95–98%. "A prisoner's place in the hierarchy of the criminal world," Bronnikov explains, "depends on his experience as a criminal, his professionalism, his knowledge of the customs, traditions, and unwritten laws of the criminal world. He must be adept at communicating in code, at using cryptography, tapping, gestures, signs, and other secret methods of communication. Tattoos are another kind of secret language, understandable only to the initiated." The skin, in other words, is a text that can be read if one knows the subtext or decoded if one knows the code. The cryptography of tattoos can be quite subtle. For example, an eight-pointed star tattooed on the chest is the sign of a professional criminal, and a cross is the mark of a common thief. Digital cryptograms are especially revealing; indeed, the entire story of a person's life can often be read on his or her fingers. "A black-and-white diamond means the convict pleaded not guilty and is a bitter prisoner and a dangerous neighbor. A domino with six dots indicates a *shestyorka*, a broken man who need not be feared. A gambler wears the symbol of a suit of cards (a spade, a diamond, a club, or heart). A skull or a pirate between the fingers means a murderer, sadist, or robber. The dollar sign indicates a 'bear hunter,' a thief who can open safes. Three dots on a woman's hand means she is a thief." The codes vary widely, but the narrative remains all too familiar. By reinscribing detective stories on the hides of the criminal, Bronnikov and the *New York Times* conspire to reinforce outdated readings of tattoos and well-worn stereotypes of the tattooed.

The April 20, 1994, issue of the *Princeton Alumni Weekly* carried a story written by a member of the senior class bearing the title "Tattoo Me: A Piercing Look at a Fresh Tradition." Katie Hobson begins her account of getting a tattoo by writing:

> I lay back on the padded vinyl table, trying not to think of the sharp buzz grating its way along my right hip, the humiliation of having my jeans pulled down to midthigh, or my parents' forthcoming horror. There wasn't much else to focus on, so I forced myself to watch the Magnum, P.I. rerun over the shopowner's shoulder.... The noise from the television distracted me from what was going on around my middle: Thomi Hawk, tattoo artist extraordinaire, was practicing his craft. He was engraving a beautifully formed P with black-and-orange detailing, the kind a cheerleader might wear on her sweater. But this P was on my skin.

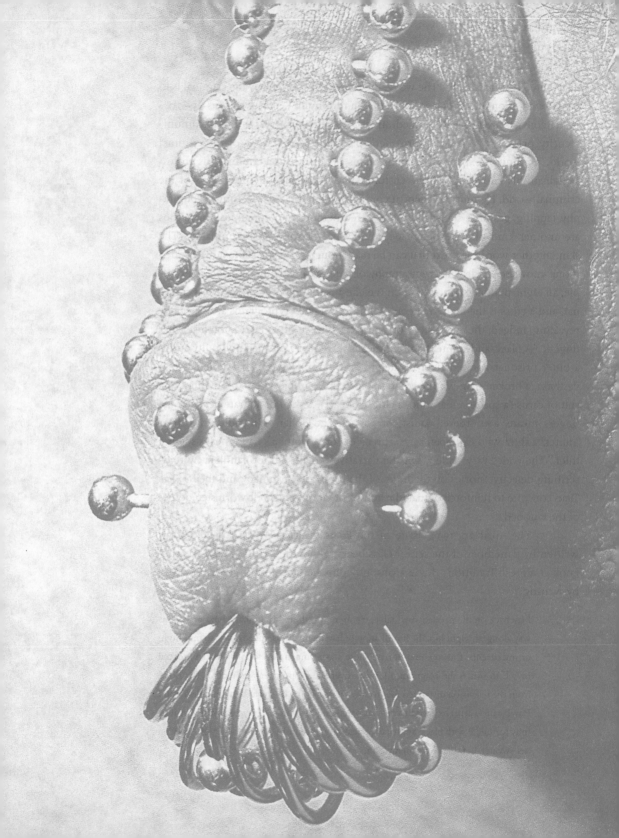

Katie's story is by no means unique. Once limited primarily to criminals, sailors, and bikers, tattooing has, in recent years, gained wide acceptance. Beginning gradually in the late 1960s and early 1970s with the hippie counterculture, rock stars, and the British punk movement, tattooing has expanded steadily and now includes a surprisingly broad cross section of society. In a 1991 *Newsweek* article describing a New York executive who was in the process of getting a full-back tattoo, Michael Mason observes:

> It's the most painful trend since whalebone corsets: tattooing, the art of the primitive and outlaw, has been moving steadily into the fashion mainstream. Haedelt's case, of course, is extreme – most of the rank-and-file "getting inked," as it's called, are following in the more discreet footsteps of celebrities like Cher, Melanie Griffith, Sean Penn, Johnny Depp, Prince and Dolly Parton. Mark Gastineau and Brigitte Nielsen had their names inscribed on each other's epidermis, in much the same way lovers used to carve their initials in trees. Woodstock, the bird from the "Peanuts" comic strip, flutters above Whoopi Goldberg's left breast. At a World Series game, Roseanne Barr and her husband, Tom Arnold, bent over to unveil their own ample art works. From movies like "Cry-Baby" to advertisements for The Gap, tattoos are everywhere.

But the art of disfiguring is not limited to tattooing; as the end of the twentieth century approaches, the practices of piercing and scarification long deemed "primitive" or even "barbaric" are enjoying a surprising revival. The art of body modification is explained, discussed, and promoted in an ever-growing series of videos and glossy publications ranging from predictable tatt mags to extraordinary periodicals like *Piercing Fans International Quarterly*. Other aficionados take advantage of the latest advances in technology like electronic bulletin boards and discussion groups to promote the most recent trends and innovations. From seemingly innocent pierced ears, noses, and navels to not-so innocent nipples, penises, and clitorises, rings, balls, chains, and charms are hanging from places they have not hung for many years. How is all of this to be interpreted? To label such practices a fad does little to explain their current popularity. What social and cultural forces are working to make the body and the marking of its surfaces such an obsession at precisely this moment? How are newly inscribed dermagraphics to be read?

The recent "tattoo renaissance" in America is best approached by placing it within its historical and artistic context. Tattooing is, of course, an ancient art that appears to have been practiced in virtually all cultures since the beginning of human civilization. The earliest known tattoo is on the mummified body of

an Egyptian woman named Amunet, who was a priestess for Hathor at Thebes during the Eleventh Dynasty (c. 2200 B.C.E.). Archeological evidence suggests that in ancient Egypt, tattooing, largely limited to women, played an important role in resurrection rituals associated with the god Osiris. But tattooing did not originate in Egypt; it was imported from Nubia, where there is fragmentary evidence indicating that it occurred as early as the fourth century B.C.E. In most of Africa, however, tattooing was rare. Since tattoos are less effective on dark skin, African cultures tend to prefer body paint and elaborate cicatrization and scarification.

The practice of tattooing disappeared almost completely in the Near East and Europe between the ancient and the modern periods. "Only the nomad peoples of the eastern steppes continued to practice it. Such were the Thracians, of whom Herodotus writes: 'Tattooing they regarded as a token of nobility, and the want of them was taken as a token of the contrary.'" With the beginning of the age of exploration and the era of colonization in the late fifteenth century, tattooing returned to Europe. The art as it is practiced today originated in South Pacific islands where it was rediscovered by European sailors and explorers. The word tattoo derives from the Tahitian word tatu, which means "to strike" and suggests the sound of the mallet hitting the instrument with which the body is cut. The earliest use of tattoo in English occurs in the journals of Captain James Cook. Recording observations during his voyage to Tahiti in July 1769, Cook writes:

> Both sexes paint their bodies, Tattow as it is called in their language, this is done by inlaying the color of black under their skins in such a manner as to be indelible. Some have ill-designed figures of men, birds or dogs, the women generally have this figure Z simply on every joint of their fingers or toes, the men have it likewise and both have other different figures such as circles, crescents, etc., which they have on their arms and legs. In short, they are so various in the application of these figures that both the quantity and situation of them may seem to depend entirely on the humor of each individual, yet all agree in having their buttocks covered with a deep black, over this most have arches drawn one over another as high as their short ribs, which are near a quarter of an inch broad; these arches seem to be their great pride as both men and women show them with great pleasure.

Travelers and adventurers to New Zealand, New Guinea, Indochina, Indonesia, Japan, Micronesia, and Polynesia discovered extraordinarily rich traditions of tattooing. From the intricate full-body tattoos of the Nuku Hiva islanders to the notorious tattooed heads of the Maori, styles varied from area to area and island to island. Visiting Europeans found that the significance of tattoos differed

as widely as their styles. In some contexts, tattoos were primarily marks of achievement or signs of membership in a particular group. As such, tattoos often indicated marital status, social class, or vocation. The use of bodily marks to signal a person's place in the social structure led to the common practice of branding prisoners, slaves, foreigners, and undesirable individuals. In many island cultures, tattooing was a highly ritualized activity. The ceremonies surrounding tattooing were usually rites of passage or status-elevation rituals in which the initiate moves irreversibly from a lower to a higher position in the social hierarchy. The tattoo, in other words, memorializes a significant event in the life of the individual and serves as an indelible mark of his or her new social status.

The ritualized setting for much tattooing suggests that it often carries religious significance. Though the myths informing tattooing practices vary considerably, the religious relevance of the ceremonies tends to remain constant. In addition to establishing membership in a religious group, tattoos are believed to bestow magical powers on those who wear them. In some cases, the tattoo gives a warrior strength or makes him invulnerable to attacks by his enemies, and, in other cases, it bears the gift of wisdom for a leader and fertility for a man or, more often, a woman. In many cultures, tattoos play a crucial role in curative rites. When performed in the proper ritual context, tattooing is supposed to prevent or cure a variety of diseases. Finally, some tattoos serve as lucky charms that are supposed to increase a person's susceptibility to mystical experiences and altered states of consciousness. This use of tattooing is most often found among shamans, medicine men, and spiritual guides who serve as mediators between the visible and invisible spheres.

Though rare, tattooing is not totally absent from the major world religions. The Jewish belief in the transcendence of God leads to the prohibition of idolatry and, correlatively, forbids tattooing. In Leviticus 19:28 it is written: "You shall not gash yourselves in mourning for the dead; you shall not tattoo yourselves. I am the Lord." (Compare Deuteronomy 14:1.) Even though Christianity formally followed the Jewish custom of outlawing tattoos at the second Council of Nicaea in 787, the Christian attitude toward images has always been more complex than Judaism's insistent iconoclasm. Without compromising the transcendence of God, Christians affirm that Jesus is the Word made flesh. The incarnation of the divine in materiality and corporeality confers extraordinary significance on the body. At one point, the New Testament goes so far as to encourage something that seems to approach tattooing. Paul concludes his Letter to the Galatians (6:17) with a plea: "In the future let no one make trouble for me, for I bear the marks of

Jesus branded on my body." Though these words have usually been interpreted figuratively rather than literally, some Christians have sought to imitate the stigmata of Jesus by incising their own skins.

As recently as the late nineteenth century, pilgrims visiting the Italian shrine of Loretto customarily had their wrists tattooed, and even today Bosnian Catholics engage in tattooing for therapeutic and decorative purposes. But the most extensive Christian practice of tattooing is found among members of the widely dispersed Coptic community. After breaking with the Roman Catholic Church in the wake of the Monophysite controversy, which came to a head in the Council of Chalcedon in 451, the Coptic Church spread throughout northern Africa and the Near East. In 1614, only two years after the earliest recorded account of Coptic tattooing, Reverend Edward Terry described a meeting with a Christian pilgrim.

> At Jerusalem this our Traveller had made upon the Wrist of his left Arm the Arms of Jerusalem, a Cross Crossed or Crosslets; and on the Wrist of his right, a single Cross made like that our Blessed Savior suffered on; and on the side of the stem or tree of that Cross these words were written, Via, Veritas, Vita, some of the letters being put on one side of that stem or tree, and some of them on the other; and at the foot of that Cross three Nails, to signify those which fastened our Savior unto it: All these impressions were made by sharp Needles bound together that pierced only the Skin and then a black Powder put into the Places so pierced, which became presently indelible....This poor man would pride himself very much in the beholding of those Characters and seeing them would often speak those words of St. Paul: I bear in my body the marks of Lord Jesus.

In spite of a continuous tradition of Coptic tattooing in the eastern church, this practice received scant attention until the 1956 limited edition of John Carswell's *Coptic Tattoo Designs*. Having stumbled upon a collection of woodblocks used by a Jerusalem tattooist named Jacob Razzouk to stamp outlines of tattoos on the skin, Carswell proceeded to uncover and document a rich array of Coptic designs. Reporting the results of his research in Jerusalem, Carswell writes:

> The craft has been passed down in the Razzouk family for generations; the majority of his customers are Copts from Egypt who want a permanent souvenir of their visit to the Holy Land. Tattooing is a seasonal trade with a peak period of business at Easter.... In an average year, he tattoos at least two hundred Copts. All Coptic pilgrims are virtually obliged to be tattooed as their compatriots would not consider a pilgrimage valid

without this visible sign. As for his other customers, they include pilgrims of most of the Christian denominations. This is confirmed by the presence of Armenian, Syrian, Latin, Abyssinian and Slav designs in the collection.

While the most common Coptic tattoo is a small cross on the inside of the wrist, Razzouk provides an assortment of tattoos for the hands or arms of men, women, and even children. Beyond the Coptic community, Carswell found traces of tattooing in certain sectors of the Muslim population of Jerusalem. Muslims, like Copts, bear tattoos as evidence of their pilgrimages. Unlike Copts, however, some Muslims also engage in tattooing for therapeutic and prophylactic purposes.

As one moves from the Near to the Far East, the popularity of religious tattooing grows. Among Hindus, for example, the image of the god or goddess inscribed on the body is supposed to guarantee divine favor. A present-day devotee of Krishna from the ancient city of Bhaktapur in Nepal explains:

> The image of the god must be placed on the forearm or hand, usually the right forearm because we believe the god must be on our right side. When people tattoo a god on their forearms, it is a special thing. It means that we will always have the god on our forearm and we believe that the god will always do good things for us. If a person chose a more powerful form of a god, such as Hanuman (the monkey-god, trickster), they must be very careful. Why? To wear a tattoo of Hanuman, one must be careful not to offend him, if someone wears a wrong thing against the regulations of the gods, it is believed that that god may trouble that person.

For some sects of Buddhism, rituals associated with tattooing are thought to cast magic spells that predispose the tattooed person to preternatural experiences. It is not uncommon for the tattooist to inscribe magical words, called *gatha*, on the body of the devotee. Only an experienced practitioner can match the power of a particular tattoo with the spiritual condition of the individual. The price of making a mistake, it is believed, can be nothing less than death.

When Europeans rediscovered the art of tattooing between the fifteenth and eighteenth centuries, their experiences were, for the most part, secondhand. Those who were venturesome enough to journey to the South Pacific often brought back with them not only incredible stories about their exploits but also evidence of the strange new worlds they had discovered. In some instances, this cargo was human. In 1691, William Dampier transported a prince named Giolo or Jeoly from his native island of Meangis to England, where he was briefly put on display before eager crowds to raise money for future voyages. Throughout Europe

during the seventeenth and eighteenth centuries, south sea islanders, seamen, and adventurers who were heavily tattooed were regular attractions at carnivals and circuses. By the nineteenth century, this sideshow had spread to America. The Welch Circus, Bartlett's Broadway Circus, the Lion Circus, and P. T. Barnum's American Circus all featured tattooed performers from distant "exotic" lands. The reintroduction of tattooing in the carnival context has had a lasting impact on the way in which it has been understood in Europe and America. In the absence of an adequate appreciation for social and cultural context, tattooing tends to be regarded as aberrant entertainment provided by aliens or freaks.

By the late nineteenth century, however, changing cultural currents provided alternative settings for approaching the practices of non-European peoples. As colonial powers extended their domination, it became necessary to understand more about the beliefs and customs of the people they were trying to rule. One of the results of the response to this political exigency was the emergence of the field of anthropology. Detailed ethnography and extensive fieldwork led to a richer understanding of, if not appreciation for, indigenous cultures. As information and artifacts were accumulated, institutions to store and display them were developed. With the creation of ethnographic museums, distant cultures were put on display in centers of Western civilization. The impact on the European imagination was immediate and lasting. In an effort to come to terms with beliefs and practices never before encountered, Europe constituted an other against which it defined itself. While assuming many guises, one of the most important names of this other was the *primitive*.

European modernism invents itself by inventing primitivism. The modern is what the primitive is not, and the primitive is what the modern is not. Far from preceding the modern temporally and historically, primitivism and modernism are mutually constitutive and, therefore, emerge together. Each defines itself in and through the other. The contrasting evaluations of primitivism reflect alternative assessments of modernity and vice versa. For many people living at the turn of this century, primitivism was regarded as the uncivilized condition that humanity must overcome. From this point of view, the primitive is an immoral savage who is both violent and sexually uninhibited. Modernity represents the culmination of the progressive domination or even elimination of primitive impulses and societies through the cultivation and imposition of rational codes of conduct and systems of control. But the very structures designed to establish order can become repressive and thereby create the conditions for the abrupt return of what seemed to have been eliminated. For growing numbers of urban poor and rural

peasants, modernity appeared to entail the violent enforcement of regulatory structures designed to satisfy the desires of a few through the labor and suffering of the masses. As socioeconomic abuse prepared the way for cultural criticism, it is hardly surprising that many people began to idealize the "primitive" state of humanity as more humane and less corrupt than the so-called civilized life of modernity.

As these remarks suggest, alternative views of primitivism and modernism imply contrasting interpretations of history. For those who believe in the rationality and morality of modernity, history represents a steady march from uncivilized barbarism to cultivated refinement. Progress is marked by distance from the primitive. Borrowing the biological principle according to which ontogeny recapitulates phylogeny, many social critics draw parallels between the development of individuals and of the race as a whole. From this point of view, primitivism represents the infantile state of humanity and modernism epitomizes maturity. Accordingly, the overriding goal is to distance oneself as far as possible from the original condition of the individual and the race. If, however, modernity seems barbaric, then history appears to involve decline and not progress. Instead of an uncensored war of all against all, the original state of humankind is pictured as an ideal world characterized by the absence of conflict as well as by the immediacy and spontaneity of experience. Whether read in terms of the myth of the noble savage or of the biblical story of the garden, the price of historical development is a catastrophic loss of the original condition whose value far exceeds anything that has since been realized. For critics who accept such narratives, the aim of life is to return to this primal state or to find a way to allow the return of the repressed in contemporary life. In this case, primitivism is a reaction to and rebellion against the restrictions and limitations imposed by modern life. When Gauguin fled from the heart of modernist Europe to Tahiti, he literally enacted the journey that many late-nineteenth- and early-twentieth-century writers and artists imaginatively projected. And, as we shall see, when more recent "modern primitives" revive tribal rituals by decorating their bodies, they, in effect, follow Gauguin back to the place where the revival of tattooing originated – Tahiti. By marking their bodies, they silently repeat lines from Gauguin's *Noa Noa*: "I have escaped everything that is artificial and conventional. Here I enter into Truth, become one with nature. After the disease of civilization, life in this new world is a return to health."

But the route from Gauguin's Tahiti to contemporary tattoo parlors and studios is far from direct. As is beginning to become clear, the effort to establish the historical context for the revival of tattooing inevitably leads into the domain

of twentieth-century art. Present-day tattooing cannot be understood solely in terms of the turn-of-the-century idealization of primitivism; it is also closely related to the emergence of body and performance art in the 1960s and 1970s. Body and performance art, in turn, involve critiques of dominant tendencies in art that developed during the first half of this century. Though not widely recognized, what eventually came to be identified as modernism in art is inseparably bound up with an attack on bodily decoration.

In 1908, one year after Picasso completed his revolutionary *Les Demoiselles d'Avignon*, whose irregular shapes and African masks point to a past long forgotten and a future about to erupt, the Austrian architect Adolf Loos published a brief essay that is widely regarded as a classic formulation of the most influential principles of modernism. The essay's title summarizes its argument: "Ornament and Crime." Loos begins his analysis with a remarkable formulation of the interrelation between personal and social development that takes as its point of departure south sea islanders from New Guinea: "The human embryo goes through all the phases of animal life while still inside the womb. When man is born, his instincts are those of a new-born dog. His childhood runs through all the changes corresponding to the history of mankind. At the age of two he looks like a Papuan, at four like one of the ancient Germanic tribe, at six like Socrates, at eight like Voltaire. The child is amoral. So is the Papuan, to us. The Papuan kills his enemies and eats them. He is no criminal. But if a modern man kills him and eats him, he is a criminal or a degenerate." Like his fellow Viennese, Freud, who was at the same time exploring civilization and its discontents, Loos describes the process of maturation as a progression from impulse to control. While it is, by definition, impossible to be immoral in the absence of moral constraints, once moral codes are established and internalized, conduct once deemed guiltless becomes blameworthy. Immediately after establishing the coordinates of his argument, Loos proceeds to insist that tattooing is a prime example of primitive behavior, which, in a modern setting, is a mark of criminality. "The Papuan tattoos his skin, his boat, his rudder, his oars; in short, everything he can get his hands on. He is no criminal. The modern man who tattoos himself is a criminal or a degenerate. There are prisons in which eighty percent of the prisoners are tattooed. Tattooed men who are not behind bars are either latent criminals or degenerate aristocrats. If someone who is tattooed dies in freedom, then he does so a few years before he would have committed murder." The reason Loos places so much emphasis on tattooing is that he sees in this practice the origin of all forms of ornamentation associated with the primitivism that humanity is destined to overcome. The movement from the

primitive to the modern is characterized by the gradual disappearance of decoration.

As if summarizing Marx and anticipating Freud, Loos provides two primary justifications for his position – one economic, the other psychological. Loos's economic argument is as elegantly simple as the aesthetic it promotes.

> Ornament is not only produced by criminals; it itself commits a crime, by damaging men's health, the national economy and cultural development. Where two people live side by side with the same needs, the same demands on life and the same income, and yet belong to different cultures, the following process may be observed from the economic point of view: the man from the twentieth century becomes ever richer, the one from the eighteenth ever poorer....The twentieth century man can pay for his needs with much less capital and can therefore save....Decorated plates are very dear, while the plain white china that the modern man likes is cheap. One man accumulates savings, the other one debts.

Decoration, in other words, involves an excessive expenditure of capital that is unreasonable because it is unnecessary. Such excess impoverishes consumers and enslaves those who produce useless ornaments. The expenditure associated with decoration is not only economic, however, but also psychological. Tattooing and, by extension, all decorative art represent what Loos regards as the lowest human inclinations. With a keen eye to the unexpected implications of graffiti, he observes:

> The urge to decorate one's face and everything in reach is the origin of the graphic arts. It is the babbling of painting. All art is erotic.
>
> The first ornament invented, the cross, was of erotic origin. The first work of art, the first artistic art, which the first artist scrawled on the wall to give his exuberance vent. A horizontal line: the woman. A vertical line: the man penetrating her....
>
> But the man of our own times who covers the walls with erotic images from an inner compulsion is a criminal or a degenerate. Of course, this urge affects people with such symptoms of degeneracy most strongly in the lavatory. It is possible to estimate a country's entire culture by the amount of scrawling on lavatory walls. In children this is a natural phenomenon: their first artistic expression is scribbling erotic symbols on walls. But what is natural for a Papuan and a child, is degenerate for modern man. I have discovered the following truth and present it to the world: *cultural evolution is equivalent to the removal of ornament from articles in daily use.*

As modernism unfolds, ornament is not only removed from articles of daily use but is stripped from most "high" art and architecture. For Loos and his

followers, this development both reflects and promotes cultural progress. With the movement from the primitive to the modern, decoration and color are erased, leaving nothing but pure white skins. "Don't you see," Loos triumphantly exclaims, "that the greatness of our age lies in its inability to produce a new form of decoration? We have conquered ornament, we have won through to lack of ornamentation. Look, the time is nigh, fulfillment awaits us. Soon the streets of the town will glisten like white walls. Like Zion, the holy city, the metropolis of heaven. Then we shall have fulfillment."

But, as always, the restoration of the garden, which is supposed to come with the arrival of the kingdom, is deferred. Though many of the most influential artists and architects of the first half of the twentieth century harbored utopian dreams and millenarian expectations, the removal of decoration that was intended to cleanse the minds of individuals and purify the body politic was gradual and never was completed. To understand what is at stake in this process, it is helpful to turn once again to a thinker who initially might seem to be an unlikely guide: Hegel. In one of his most notorious claims, Hegel once declared art to be a "thing of the past." When this puzzling statement is placed in the context of his overall philosophical system, it is clear that what Hegel intends as a historical summation is actually a surprisingly accurate anticipation of the dominant tendency of the art of this century.

Hegel's analysis of art reenacts the dialectic of surface and depth, which we have already seen at work in his account of phrenology. "Art's vocation," Hegel argues "is to unveil the truth."

> Art shares this vocation with religion and philosophy, but in a special way, namely by displacing even the highest (reality) sensuously, bringing it thereby nearer to the senses, to feeling, and to nature's mode of appearance. What is thus displayed in the depth of a suprasensuous world that thought pierces and sets up at first is a beyond in contrast with immediate consciousness and present feeling; it is the freedom of intellectual reflection that rescues itself from the here and now, called sensuous reality and finitude. But this breach, to which the spirit proceeds, it is also able to heal. It generates out of itself works of fine art as the first reconciling middle term between pure thought and what is merely external, sensuous, and transient, between nature and finite reality and the infinite freedom of conceptual thinking.

To discover the truth of the work of art, one must move from surface to depth by peeling away sensuous appearance like so many layers of superfluous skin that hide immaterial truth. Left to its own devices, art can never completely escape

materiality and thus cannot fully reveal truth. The truth sensuously represented in art is transparently presented in philosophy. When philosophically comprehended, truth is purified of all traces of materiality, which inevitably contaminate its clarity. Though Hegel vehemently denies that truth is inconsequential, he does insist that it is essentially immaterial.

It is not difficult to see that Hegel's argument anticipates Loos's position. Progress, be it artistic, philosophical, or cultural, is marked by the movement from the material to the immaterial or from the sensuous to the conceptual. Within the world of modern art and architecture, development is reflected in transparent glass crystals and pure white walls from which ornamental appearances have been removed. Throughout the first half of this century, there has been a steady movement toward abstraction in art as well as architecture. From Kandinsky, Mondrian, and Malevich to Rothko, Reinhardt, and Ryman, the truth in painting has been consistently abstract. While implicitly agreeing with the principles of speculative idealism, these artists differ from Hegel on one very important point. Whereas Hegel maintains that truth can be realized only by passing beyond art to philosophy, artists insist that truth can be actualized in art and, therefore, philosophy is a supplement, which, though sometimes interesting and informative, carries no special privilege.

For artists, as for Hegel, the distinction between surface and depth or appearance and essence, which their work seems to presuppose, proves difficult to maintain. The insistence on the integrity of the work of art issues in the veneration of its intrinsic value. Consequently, the worth of the art object is not measured in terms of anything other than itself. When immaterial truth materializes in works of art, the object becomes precious. The theorist who most fully articulates this position is, of course, Clement Greenberg. In a highly influential essay published in 1960, Greenberg argues that modernist painting is characterized by the progressive collapse of reference and depth into the surface of the canvas.

> It was the stressing of the ineluctable flatness of the surface that remained, however, more fundamental than anything else to the processes by which pictorial art criticized and defined itself under Modernism. For flatness alone was unique and exclusive to pictorial art. The enclosing shape of the picture was a limiting condition, or norm, that was shared with the art of the theater; color was a norm and a means shared not only with the theater, but also with sculpture. Because flatness was the only condition painting shared with no other art, Modernist painting oriented itself to flatness as it did to nothing else.

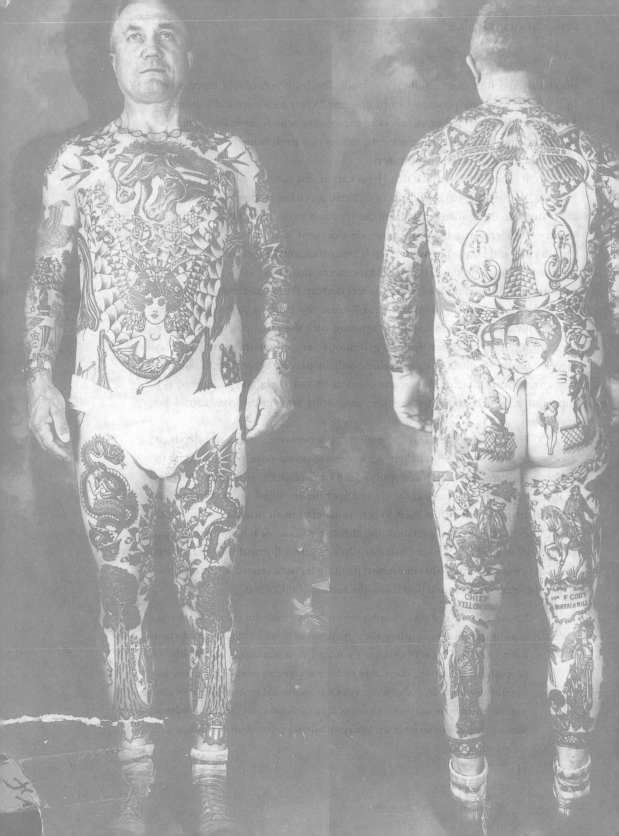

This valorization of flatness, as we shall see, can be understood either as the culmination of the erasure of ornament or as the transformation of l'oeuvre d'art as such into nothing but ornament.

While Greenberg's interest in maintaining the preciousness of the art object is aesthetic and not economic, it quickly became clear that speculation is not merely a matter of thought. The social, political, and economic devastation of two world wars contributed to the migration of "advanced" art from Europe to the United States. Whether the New York gallery system was created to meet or to generate demand, the postwar economy provided ideal conditions for the commodification of the work of art. With these developments, preciousness became less a mark of intrinsic worth than the sign of a currency that seemed as good as gold. This turn of events represents an ironic reversal of the conception art that informed the emergence of modernism. As I have noted, much of the best art produced in this century was motivated by social, political, and even spiritual concerns. But the products of abstraction, which initially were supposed to serve as the intellectual and ethical foundation for social change, become luxurious trophies for the leisure class. When artworks are regarded as precious objects whose value is a matter of speculation, they become little more than superfluous ornaments. Through a "speculative" reversal that is not dialectical, the struggle to avoid ornament ends by making the art object itself ornamental.

In an effort to recover the critical mission of art, artists devised a variety of strategies to resist processes of commodification promoted by galleries and investors. Since the entire market was built around precious objects, one of the most effective tactics was to attack the art object artistically. If the object of exchange were to disappear, it was argued, the market inevitably would collapse and the purity of art's critical vision and social program could be restored. The goal of many midcentury artists became the development of a "postobject art." While dada and Duchamp anticipated many of the innovations of these artists, it was not until the 1960s and 1970s that alternative media and new forms of production gained wide recognition. From the materiality of earthworks to the ephemerality of video and performance art, artists created works that resisted display in galleries and were not readily exchangeable objects. Two of the most important tendencies in postobject art for our purposes are conceptual art and body art.

Conceptual art emerged as an identifiable movement between 1967 and 1972. Developing diverse critiques of the fetishization of l'objet d'art, conceptual artists contend that the "true" work of art is not the material object but the

immaterial idea that lies behind it. When carried to its logical conclusion, this position makes the physical object unnecessary. Conceptual art, in other words, radicalizes abstraction by realizing the complete dematerialization of the art object. In 1969, Sol LeWitt published "Sentences on Conceptual Art" in which he explains: "Ideas alone can be works of art; they are in a chain of development that may eventually find some form. All ideas need not be made physical." In direct opposition to Greenberg's claim that each artistic medium has its unique concern, LeWitt asserts that "since no form is intrinsically superior to another, the artist may use any form, from an expression of words (written or spoken) to physical reality, equally." In semiotic terms previously invoked, the concept is the transcendental signified, which can be expressed through a variety of signifiers. The materiality of the signifier is arbitrary and serves as nothing more than a vehicle for the conception.

Even though conceptual art was devised as a corrective to what many regarded as the degeneration of modern art, it obviously remains committed to some of the most basic principles of modernism. The victory over sensuousness heralded by Hegel and the triumph over ornament declared by Loos are fully realized in conceptualism. Image gives way to concept to create a truth that is insubstantial. At this point, art itself becomes immaterial.

While sharing conceptual art's misgivings about the commercialization of art, body artists are convinced that conceptualism's corrective measures do not go far enough. By extending abstraction to dematerialization, conceptual art reinforces one of the most troubling aspects of modernism. To build upon yet move beyond conceptualism's critical engagement with modernism, some artists turned to a variety of new media. One of the richest resources for these developments is the human body. As a counter to the veneration of abstraction and immateriality, the body artist offers his or her own flesh and blood as artistic media.

To appreciate the significance of body art, it is important to relate this artistic development to broader social and cultural currents unfolding in the late 1960s and 1970s. By the 1960s, unanticipated effects of the postwar economic boom were beginning to be felt throughout society. While almost all aspects of American life were undergoing transformation, many of the most radical changes resulted from what can only be described as an electronic revolution. Even though Edison installed the first central electric-light power plant in New York City in 1881 – 82, electricity was not widely available until President Roosevelt's establishment of the Rural Electrification Administration in 1935. The transformative potential of electricity became evident only after World War II. From refrigerators and washers

to telephones and radios, electronic devices invaded home and workplace to change people's lives. No electronic appliance had a greater social and cultural impact than TV. Introduced to many homes in the 1950s, TV became a standard fixture of American life in the 1960s. With the development of color, TV's quality improved and popularity grew. As demand increased, supporting networks expanded. The general availability of cheap electricity fueled a media explosion of unprecedented proportions. By the mid-1960s, it was beginning to seem that all reality was mediaized.

While these technological developments and social changes might appear to be far removed from the controversies surrounding modern art, many of the issues raised by the emerging electronic culture reinforced misgivings some artists had about modernism. In many ways, the transformation of reality by electronic media is a practical extension of processes of abstraction and dematerialization (pre)figured in high modern art. When the body appears by disappearing on the screen, it becomes effectively immaterial.

Body art represents, among other things, a sustained effort to reverse the dematerialization of art by making the body matter. The lines separating and joining body art to happenings and performance art, which were emerging at the same time, cannot always be drawn clearly. One of the most suggestive antecedents of body art, in which elements of action painting and performance art combine with bodily decoration to create a medium with a different message, is Yves Klein's 1961 *Imprints*, in which he smeared naked women with blue paint and used them as living brushes to decorate a bare canvas spread on the floor. When body art began to distinguish itself as an independent movement, its ways of marking and remarking the body became more and more extreme. In early works, Bruce Nauman thought it was sufficient to perform exercises that were little more than calisthenics, while Terry Fox, Dennis Oppenheim, Dan Graham, and Richard Long were content to photograph or make plaster casts of their footprints after performing a series of choreographed steps. By the late 1960s, such ephemeral traces were regarded as insufficient to overcome the body's artistic erasure and cultural disappearance. In the late 1960s, Vito Acconci, one of the most innovative and outrageous body artists, felt it necessary actually to inscribe his own skin. In a 1969 work entitled *Performance for a Coffee Hour* (*Marking Time*), Acconci repeatedly pressed a bottle cap into his arm. Less than a year later, he performed *Trademarks*, in which he bit as many parts of his body as he could reach.

In spite of the impression they made, Acconci's marks did not last; they were as fleeting as his performance and faded without leaving a trace. It is as if

Acconci feared needles and were satisfied with temporary tattoos that could easily be washed away. If the body matters, it must be marked permanently. On November 19, 1971, Chris Burden pushed body art to its limit: "At 7:45 p.m. I was shot in the left arm by a friend. The bullet was a copper jacket 22 long rifle. My friend was standing about fifteen feet from me." Briefly summarizing his motivation for such an extraordinary performance, Burden describes his art as "acting out the idea, the materialization of the idea." When so understood, body art reverses the movements of abstraction and dematerialization by concretely materializing the idea. The incarnational implications of body art become explicit in Burden's *Trans-fixed*, which was executed in Venice, California, on April 23, 1974. "Inside a small garage on Speedway Avenue, I stood on the rear bumper of a Volkswagen. I lay on my back on the rear section of the car, stretching my arms onto the roof. Nails were driven through my palms into the roof of the car. The garage was opened and the car was pushed half-way out into the Speedway. Screaming for me, the engine was run at full speed for two minutes. After two minutes, the engine was turned off and the car pushed back into the garage. The door was closed." The "original" event is preserved in traces, not all of which can be erased. Photographs record Burden's crucifixion and the two nails that were driven into his hands remain as an independent work entitled *Relic* from *Trans-fixed*, which, perhaps significantly, is in the collection of Jasper Johns. But the most impressive traces of this remarkable work are the scars on the palms of Burden's hands. In these indelible marks, image is embodied as concept becomes flesh.

Burden's staging of *Trans-fixed* in a California garage, as far away as possible from the New York art scene, reflects the anti-institutional and antimarket bias of his work. While persistently critical of modernism, the controversies that led to body art nonetheless perpetuate many of the preoccupations of so-called high culture. Other developments in the art world unfolding concurrently eroded the line between high and low art. In pop art, high becomes low and low becomes high in a reversal that simultaneously subverts and reinforces the codes regulating modernism. For the pop artist, ornament is not a crime but is the very "essence" of art. The signs that intrigue pop artists are drawn from the very commercial culture that conceptualists and body artists criticize. While the appropriative strategies of pop artists prepare the way for a popularized version of body art, pop art is not always popular enough. Painterly signs remain stuck to museum and gallery walls and thus retain vestiges of the elitism they are supposed to reject. Even pop art, therefore, had to be popularized, and for this, media other than galleries, museums, and collections had to be found. The tattoo renaissance represents, among

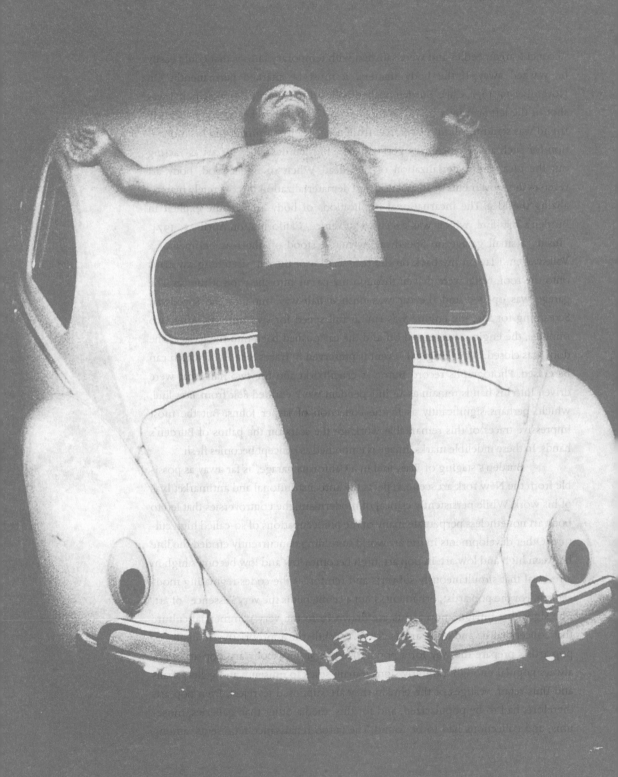

other things, an extension of pop art beyond the white walls of the gallery to the inscribed skin of the body.

Governor Jerry Brown's remarkable letter extolling the artistic virtues of tattooing was written to mark the opening of Tattoo Expo, held in November 1983 aboard the Queen Mary, docked in Long Beach, California. This celebration of tattooing was organized by Ernie Carafa, a New Jersey tattoo supplier; Ed Nolte, a San Francisco printer specializing in T-shirts with tattoo designs; and Don Ed Hardy, the tattooist who has contributed more than anyone else to the revitalization of the art. In many ways, Tattoo Expo represented the culmination of developments that had been unfolding for more than two decades. Prior to the 1960s, tattooing continued to follow patterns that had been established since its rediscovery earlier in the century. Because tattooing was especially popular among sailors from the Pacific fleet, the West Coast became the center of tattooing in the United States. The concentration of naval bases in southern California attracted tattooists from across the country. Most of these tattooists came from blue-collar backgrounds and had no professional training. The designs they offered were not original but were standardized flash that was displayed on parlor walls. Reusable acetate stencils made it possible to trace the drawing directly onto the skin. Coloration was usually limited to black, brown, yellow, blue, green, and red. During this period, almost all the clients were from the military, the working class, and traditionally marginalized groups like bikers, prostitutes, and criminals. Customized work and multiple tattoos by the same tattooist were rare. Since few people stopped with one image, most tattooed bodies became chaotic collages of conventional signs.

This situation changed significantly in the 1960s as the result of the innovations introduced by several important artists. Among the many tattooists who contributed to the revitalization of the art, two in particular stand out: Cliff Raven and Ed Hardy. Unlike their predecessors, Raven and Hardy had formal training in fine arts. Raven received a B.A. in fine arts from Indiana University in 1957, and Hardy studied printmaking at the San Francisco Art Institute in the 1960s. Breaking with traditional tattooing practices, these artists specialize in customized tattoos and are committed to developing original designs consisting of integrated imagery adapted to the interests and bodies of their clients.

Raven was initially drawn into the world of tattooing by Phil Sparrow, an erstwhile professor of English who once had been a member of Gertrude Stein's circle in Paris. Raven spent the early part of his career working with Sparrow in Chicago. Sparrow's chief contribution to the art of tattooing in the United States was the introduction of large-scale oriental designs. Having quickly become bored

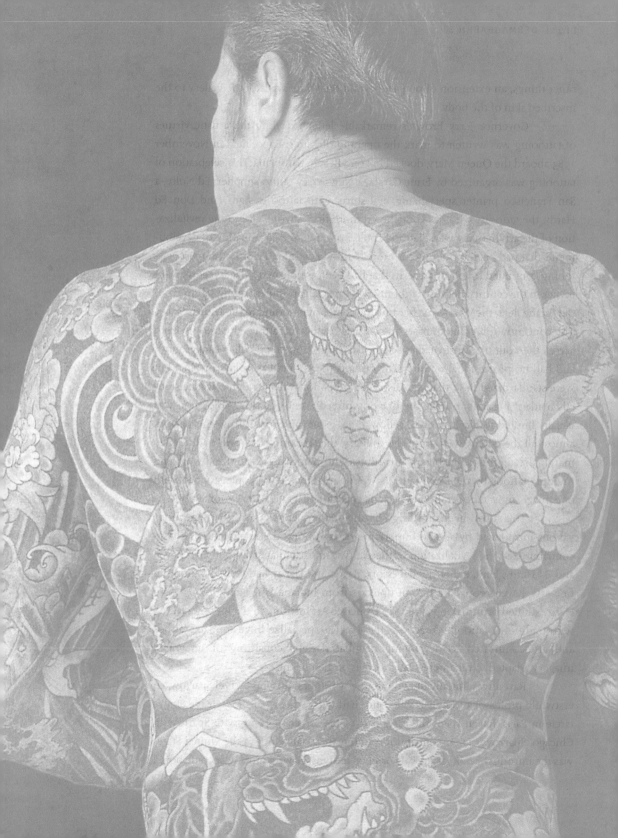

with standardized patterns and repetitious work, Raven was intrigued by Sparrow's innovations. When Sparrow moved to Oakland in 1965, Raven opened Cliff Raven Tattooing, which was later renamed the Chicago Tattooing Company. By the early 1970s, it was clear that the most creative tattooing was being done on the West Coast and in Hawaii, and so, when Lyle Tuttle closed his famous shop on Sunset Boulevard, Raven gave in to the inevitable and moved to California. Tuttle's parlor had been well-known in the late 1960s and early 1970s as the center of counterculture tattooing. For hippies and antiwar activists as well as rock stars like Janis Joplin and movie stars like Peter Fonda, Lyle Tuttle's tattoos became badges of social protest. Raven continued to work in the Sunset Boulevard shop until the early 1980s when, after a brief stint in San Francisco, he set up a studio in Palms, California, where he continues to live and work.

Raven's signature tattoos consist of creative appropriations of Japanese full-back designs. His work is large-scale, freehand, and customized. While borrowing extensively from the Japanese, the colors in most of his early work tend to be somewhat brighter and lighter than traditional oriental tattoos. By the mid-1980s, Raven began to have misgivings about the use of too much color and started experimenting with the large-scale monochromatic black designs from Indonesia that Tuttle had rediscovered. Raven's popularization of tribal designs was a major factor in creating a new movement in tattooing.

On the occasion of Tattoo Expo in 1982, Ed Hardy published the first volume of *Tattootime*, entitled "New Tribalism." Subsequent issues of *Tattootime* and related publications have played a crucial role in the tattoo renaissance. In numerous popular articles, Hardy and his colleagues trace the history of tattooing and keep readers informed about recent innovations. Looking back on developments in tattooing eight years after the appearance of "New Tribalism," Hardy reflects:

> When the first issue of *Tattootime* appeared in 1982 with a cover theme of "New Tribalism," we had no idea of the extent of the impact of this new/old style would have on the tattoo world. This type of design work was a passion of Leo Zulueta, who was just starting to tattoo at the time. Besides Cliff Raven and Thom deVita in America and Roger Ingerton in New Zealand, we knew of no other tattooers working in what Cliff aptly dubbed the pre-technological black graphic style....Within six months we were being deluged at conventions by people showing us the "new tribal" work they were doing and wearing.

Initially involving a straightforward appropriation of traditional designs, the "tribal" revival quickly evolved into innovative reworkings of ancient patterns. As

tattooists become more venturesome, they show a greater willingness to mix and match styles without giving up their commitment to integrated design. Thus, neotribal patterns are rarely used without modification or coordination with other motifs. "Whether adapted from an authentic historic/cultural source or invented by the artist or client, the black graphic look has introduced an important option to modern tattooing – that of clarity, visibility, and an appreciation of abstract form for its own sake. Much of this is achieved through a balanced use of clear skin space, something that was foremost in pictorial tattoo design for the first half of this century but mostly lost since."

Hardy's contribution to the tattoo renaissance is not limited to education and promotion but, more important, extends to the practice of the art. For nearly three decades, he has been one of the most innovative and influential tattooists in the world. Interested in tattoos from the time he was a child, Hardy was by chance encouraged to begin tattooing. In 1966, colleagues at the San Francisco Art Institute asked him to give a talk on the relationship between American tattooing and pop art. Approaching the completion of his B.F.A. in printmaking, Hardy was disillusioned with the dominant forms of contemporary art and had no sense of professional direction. As he prepared his remarks for the Art Institute, he gradually became convinced that tattooing might provide a creative alternative to the sterile art world he had come to loathe.

> When I was at art school, abstract expression had ended and Minimalism, pure form over content, was fashionable – obviously people were starved for ideas. The whole art school environment was so vapid – it was so hideous and still is, with all that ego and self-analysis and everybody caught up in their own petty little problems. The whole concept of art is so important to culture and people's lives, yet so easily diverted and perverted and watered-down. In 1967, I graduated. Then I started tattooing, and it was like getting a giant shock: "Wow, this really has power, and it really has magic; it has real balls to it and a very strong connection to humanity. It's something that people feel really strongly about. Even if it might be corny images, people are very sincere about this; there's a genuine emotional connection.

Tattooing, Hardy concludes, is quintessential pop art, which, unlike its painterly counterpart, is not caught up in the deceitful games of galleries, connoisseurs, and speculators but truly matters in the lives of the people who are devoted to it.

When he began to get serious about tattooing, Hardy, like Raven, turned to Phil Sparrow, whose studio now was located in Oakland. Sparrow introduced Hardy to large-scale Japanese-style tattoos. For the next eight years, Hardy wandered

from southern California, Seattle, and Vancouver to Honolulu and Tokyo, studying oriental design and learning the most advanced tattooing techniques. In 1974, he settled in San Francisco and opened Realistic Tattoo Studio, which was the first by-appointment tattoo parlor in America. While based in the Bay area, Hardy continued to travel throughout the world, studying and tattooing in Japan, Micronesia, England, and on the east coast of the United States. In 1986, he moved from the mainland to Honolulu, where he continues to live today.

The more widely Hardy roamed, the more inclusive and distinctive his style became. Though deeply influenced by Japanese masters, Hardy is never content with simply repeating the lessons he learns from others. His aim is to bring together East and West to create a style that is uniquely suited to a world in which cultural boundaries are hard to define. In addition to Japanese designs, Hardy's repertoire includes monochromatic Indonesian and Micronesian patterns as well as fineline style with imagery drawn from Chicano and Latino prison and gang tattoos, which are particularly popular in the Los Angeles area. Ever sensitive to cultural differences, Hardy nonetheless freely synthesizes images from different traditions. In a 1982 work, for example, he fuses Japanese and Polynesian styles. Committed to erasing the line between elite and popular culture, Hardy also appropriates images from the world of "high" art. In some of his work, he even borrows from artists like the cubists, surrealists, Kandinsky, and Lissitzky.

During the years when Hardy was doing his most creative work, he refused to allow himself be drawn into the controversies and debates preoccupying contemporary artists. Nevertheless, many of his most important contributions to tattooing mirror what was going on in other arts during the 1970s and 1980s. Hardy's use of historical reference and eclecticism extend established postmodern strategies to the art of tattooing. Stressing what he shares with other artists of his generation, Hardy notes:

> I have a client with a lot of tribal work (snakes and grid work on his legs which was Samoan-inspired; a fusion of Samoan and Japanese) who wanted this piece which was like a tribute to Sailor Jerry – a big '40s va-va-voom tits-and-ass nurse. And he wanted it next to a lot of Tibetan Tantric imagery. For years he had been reluctant to ask me, but finally he did: "You don't think it's too dumb?" I said, "It's great!" Because he had grown up in the '40s and had a great affection for this image. I put it on him and thought, "This is real American tattooing" – having all these cultures floating next to each other. I mean, it's all right if some people want to really ape the Japanese, or whatever, but the most exciting possibility for me as an artist is to do this fusion – to be able

to make references to different parts of world culture. There'll probably be more and more of that; I suppose that's kind of post-modernist: making references to references within the business itself.

References to references...signs of signs...skin rubbing at skin, skin, skin, skin, skin. It is, as always, a question of hiding. In Ed Hardy's tattoos, postmodernism becomes incarnate. When the sign becomes embodied, the body becomes a sign.

There can be no doubt that the remarkable changes in styles and practices during the past several decades have contributed significantly to the growth of tattooing's popularity. As designs have evolved from standardized flash to customized work that allows for creative contributions by clients, tattoos have become attractive to people who previously never would have considered marking their skin. Tattooing is not only widely practiced today but in many circles has become quite fashionable. Yet, in spite of growing acceptance, tattooing retains traces of transgression. For many people, tattoos are still badges of protest or rebellion, which are worn with defiant pride. For others, the marked body is unavoidably deviant. The more one studies the contemporary art of tattooing, the more difficult it is to figure. Tattooing inevitably slips between polarities customarily used to organize experience and structure knowledge: nature/culture, savage/civilized, regulation/transgression, simulation/dissimulation, socialization/marginalization, interiority/exteriority, veiling/unveiling, materialization/dematerialization, differentiation/unification, and so forth. By repeatedly alternating between unreconcilable opposites, tattooing marks and remarks a boundary that cannot be fixed. Forever superficial, even when its wounds are deep, the tattooed body is the incarnation of a seam that never mends.

While no tattoo is a sign that can be read with certainty, a consideration of tattooing in terms of its oscillation between processes of differentiation and unification suggests aspects of the art that otherwise tend to be overlooked. We have seen that from its earliest appearance, one of the functions of tattooing is to mark membership in a group that can be as inclusive as the entire society or as exclusive as a small gang or clique. Regardless of the size of the group, identification and differentiation are inseparably bound together. Identity is confirmed by establishing difference and difference is guaranteed by securing identity. Far from a vicious circle, the reciprocal interplay of identity and difference describes concrete social processes. The identity of individuals and groups is a function of their difference from other individuals and groups. To be a member of the bear clan or the Hell's Angels, for example, is to be different from the elk

clan or bourgeois society. Identity, in other words, is difference. But difference alone is not sufficient to constitute identity, because that which is merely different is actually indefinable. If difference is to be articulate, it must involve identification. I am not an elk because I am a bear. Difference, in other words, is identity. The more important the group, the more significant the marks of identification and differentiation. When membership in a group is deemed vital to identity, it is not uncommon for the individual to be permanently marked. Among their many functions, tattoos serve as inscriptions of sociocultural codes and structures on the body of the individual. From this point of view, the tattoo is not the trace of unregulated savage behavior but one of the earliest and most lasting traits of civilization. "Tattooing and scarification," as Michel Thévoz explains, "both being indelible, were intended to stamp the body with the mark of society, of culture, of the institution; they accordingly belong to what might be designated as the secondary process or symbolic order. Practiced as rites, they stand on the same plane of continuity with such rites as circumcision or excision, whose social implications they extend to other parts of the body. Their purpose partly overlaps that of initiation, for they answer to the group need to release the body from the infant fusional relation and set it circulating in the channels of social exchange." In contrast to Loos and his modernist followers for whom tattooing and its extension in decorative art are infantile, uncivilized, and degenerate, the tattoo can be read as a mark of civilization that controls and directs so-called primitive natural impulses.

If understood in this way, inscription within the symbolic order appears to differentiate the individual from the generative matrix that is the site of birth. It is precisely the identification with the social group that precipitates the separation from this all-encompassing milieu. Such differentiation is not a once-and-for-all event but a lifelong process that must repeatedly be marked and remarked. Writing on the body is the trace of codes that simultaneously express and regulate the ebb and flow of desires that are the matter of life and death.

The correlative processes of differentiation-through-identification and identification-through-differentiation are inherently unstable and, when pushed far enough, tend to erase the very distinctions they seek to maintain. While socialization and enculturation wean the individual from the so-called natural milieu, identification with the group can eventually lead to the loss of self. Identities become preprogrammed and pre-scribed like standardized flash that allows no space for individual designs. When this occurs, the badge of group membership becomes the mark of anonymity instead of identity. Flash no longer works; new designs, new patterns, and new styles must be created. Only customized work

satisfies. As an ardent defender of current practices of popular body art explains: "The purpose of the tattoo is to do something for the person, to help them realize the individual magic latent within them. It seems the purpose of the modern world is to wipe out difference. The genotypes of plants, birds, and animals originally generated more difference, more variety. Now we've got this great oppressive force that's trying to homogenize and make everything the same! And that we must resist and fight, because that's anti-life!" But sometimes the very assertion of identity can unexpectedly lead to the loss of identity. If inscription were to break completely with the codes it struggles to resist, it would become illegible even for the person whose body is marked. Resistance, it seems, cannot do without that which it nonetheless cannot bear. For signs to be significant, they might not have to re-present something that is uncoded, but they do have to relate to other already constituted signs. Signifiers comprising the writing of the body are, like all other signifiers, diacritical. If the marked body were to sever relations with all groups and every significant other, the bearer of incarnate signs would become as inarticulate as Peter Stillman Jr., locked alone in his room.

For an increasing number of people, it seems that life is lived in a locked room from which there is no exit. Instead of the glorious kingdom of freedom and fulfillment Loos envisioned, the contemporary world has grown frustrating and repressive. The problem is not merely that the mechanization and routinization of modern life lead to excruciating anonymity and anomie. Even more distressing is the tendency of postindustrial society to create cities of glass in which everything is insubstantial and unbearably lite. As the media invade every aspect of life and electronic networks extend their tentacles to create webs that appear to be virtually seamless, reality itself hides behind screens that are infinite. The postmodern world of images translates the modernist project of dematerialization from the world of art into sociocultural processes. In this way, the culture of simulacra becomes the ironic realization of the avant-garde's dream of bringing art to life.

When reality becomes virtual, the body disappears. This does not mean, of course, that materiality completely vanishes — at least not yet. But as the webs in which we are caught become ether nets, the realities with which we deal become more and more ethereal. For some people, the growing detachment from the body holds the promise of realizing the ancient dream of immortality; for others, the apparent loss of the body and eclipse of materiality are further symptoms of alienation. Having destroyed our souls and ruined our minds, regulatory regimes now conspire to steal our bodies in the name of "progress." Many people who regard

modernization and postmodernization as a fall rather than an advance attempt to resist the march of history by recovering the body. When the body appears to be endangered, it becomes an obsession. This is one of the primary reasons that tattooing (as well as piercing and scarification) has become so widespread during this particular historical and cultural period. *Tattooing represents the effort to mark the body at the very moment it is disappearing.*

It should be clear that in these developments, life is imitating art. We have discovered that one of the most influential strands of modern art defines itself in opposition to the primitive. Within this framework, modernity appears to be the culmination of the progressive control or even elimination of primitive societies and savage impulses through the cultivation and imposition of rational codes of conduct and structures of control. Since bodily ornamentation and figurative decoration are marks of uncivilized desires, they must be wiped away to create the clean white walls, pure white canvases, and neatly pressed white shirts and dresses befitting a civilization that knows no discontents. But, I have also noted, the very structures designed to establish order can become repressive and thereby create the conditions for an unexpected return of the repressed. At this point, history reverses itself; progress becomes decline and what had been labeled degenerate becomes attractive. Instead of attempting to establish distance from the primitive, the challenge is to recover primitive visions and revive primitive practices. From certain turn-of-the-century painters and midcentury body and performance artists, to end-of-the-century tattoo artists, the goal is to reawaken the primitive that forever slumbers in our midst. "Modern primitives" underscore the ambiguity of writing on the body by reading its signs otherwise. What Loos feared can be desired and what Loos desired can be feared. More precisely, Loos's fear is a symptom of desires that can be temporarily repressed but not finally escaped. If ornament embodies desire, then the removal of ornament is the repression of desire, and, conversely, the inscription of ornament is the incarnation of desire. Lines drawn on the body are never univocal but always duplicitous. Not merely the function of a plurality of meanings, this duplicity reflects opposite significations that cannot be reconciled. Drawing opens as much as it closes, to create seams that are as fragile as the bodies they demarcate.

We have already considered the way in which tattooing brands a person as socialized by imprinting the symbolic order in flesh and blood. But the incisive lines of difference separating the individual from the generative matrix also open flows that tend to unite self and other. Scoring the skin transgresses boundaries that are supposed to be closed securely. Tattooing is not only erotic, as Loos insists,

but is also violent. Love and death meet in the ecstatic pleasure of pain. The anguish inflicted by the needle attracts as much as it repulses. What draws in the drawing is loss, radical loss that ends with the loss of self. When loss is counted as gain, the point is not to save or to be saved but to spend and be spent in fluxes and flows that know no bounds. Modern primitives repeatedly testify to the importance of tattooing in creating altered states of consciousness. Like ancient ritual processes, the contemporary practice of tattooing opens the windows of perception. Tattoo Mike (aka Michael Wilson), who has been featured in Dick Zigun's Coney Island *Side Shows by the Seashore* and Bruce Springsteen's "Tunnel of Love" video as well as on the *New York Times* style page, comments on the role tattooing plays in his life: "When I was thirteen I was studying a lot of Surrealist art. I saw photos of a stage production by Jean Cocteau starring a heavily tattooed man and this became a key, signifying a possible way of going through the looking glass for me to achieve a whole other frame of reference, and to elicit experiences beyond the 'normal'...presenting yourself as a signal beacon drawing things to happen to you. In other words: tattoo as a passage to another life." Though details in the accounts of altered states of consciousness brought on by tattooing vary, they commonly include reports of proleptic experiences of death. The association of ecstasy with death is, of course, a familiar theme in Eastern and Western mystical literature. When unity becomes complete, the self disappears in the totality from which it had been separated. At this point eros and thanatos become one. ManWoman, a heavily tattooed Canadian artist who, not insignificantly, has taken for his life's mission the rehabilitation of the swastika, describes the deadly seriousness of his superficial signs.

> The idea of making friends with death, confronting death, transcending death – death as a transformation rather than real death; death in the sense of: die to the ego and transform yourself. The surrender of the ego. There's a point in the mystical experience where the ego peels off and what's left is just an absolute kind of pure essence. Just prior to that there's a moment of fear because the ego is really threatened, and the ego has to drop off. The mystical experience is like a preview of death – you face it, you go through it and you become eternal, you become everything. You really feel all that stuff about becoming one with the universe, one with god or whatever you label it.

"The whole purpose of 'modern primitive' practices," Fakir Musafar explains, "is to get more and more spontaneous in the expression of *pleasure with insight*. Too much structuring somehow destroys any possibility of an ecstatic breakthrough in life experiences." By pushing pop body art beyond the limits of

tattooing, Fakir, who borrows his name from a *Ripley's Believe* It *or Not* account of a nineteenth-century Sufi mystic reported to have "wandered around for eighteen years with daggers and other things stuck in his body," demonstrates the extraordinary potential of body alteration. An unassuming insurance executive by day, Fakir's "other" life was first put on public display in the 1984 film *Dances Sacred and Profane*. Fakir's work testifies to his belief that the microregulation of contemporary life involves precisely the kind of excessive structure that renders "ecstatic breakthrough" both impossible and necessary. Convinced that excess must be met with excess, he attempts to shatter repressive structures by transgressing regulatory codes in practices ranging from self-gilding and penile piercing and elongation to lying on beds of blades and nails, and hanging from flesh hooks.

Evidence to the contrary notwithstanding, Fakir insists that these rituals are not painful and claims that the pleasure they bring is actually transcendent. As one becomes adept in stimulating these experiences, something unforeseen begins to take place: the body becomes the vehicle for passing beyond the body.

> Actually, I wanted an experience that was right on the edge of death. Finally I got my body totally lashed to the wall, my arms in hooks, my head in a restraint, and I had a conscious out-of-the-body experience – and there is nothing else quite like that. You can have a body, but it's fluid; you can walk through walls, earth, iron...you can stay in the present, or walk forward or backward in time, just like walking into another room.... However, this out-of-body experience can be terrifying in that you have to literally go through all the symptoms of real death. And you feel them acutely. Numbness works its way up your legs; your arms go numb; finally it goes up your torso and hits your chest; you go through all the sensations of drowning or suffocating, yet you're not dead. And you wonder, "Why am I not dead?" Then there's a buzzing and a little light and you know your eyes work and you're seeing things with physical sight. At this point I just become a head – all my consciousness, all my attention located in the very center of my head.

A head... just a head... an out-of-body head that roams in a fluid space where walls are not walls and earth is not earth, and a fluid time where past, present, and future flow into each other. The space-time into which Fakir wanders seems strangely similar to the virtuality of cyberspace he is struggling to escape. Just as the search for differentiation-through-identification and identification-through-differentiation collapse into each other, so the effort to mark the body at the moment it withdraws eventually leads to the body's own disappearance. Pondering these endless flip-flops, one begins to feel like a detective who is clueless because

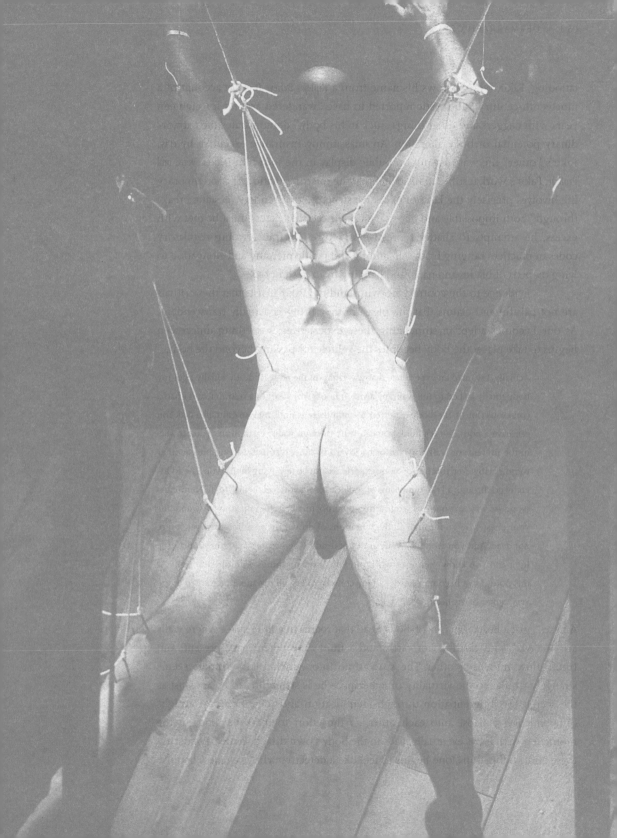

he has nothing but clues and thus cannot recover the body that would solve the mystery that so intrigues him.

EVENT FOR STRETCHED SKIN

WITH THE ASSISTANCE OF TAKAO SAIKI, HIROSHI ITOH
AND THE STUDENTS OF BIGAKKO ART SCHOOL
THIS EVENT WAS REALIZED AT THE

MAKI GALLERY, TOKYO – SUNDAY, 16 MAY 1976

THE BODY WAS SUSPENDED OVER A
1 TON ROCK BY THE INSERTION OF
18 HOOKS INTO THE SKIN
THE INSERTIONS TOOK 1 1/2 HOURS
THE ACTUAL SUSPENSION TIME WAS 15 MINUTES
A LASER BEAM BISECTED THE SPACE
BETWEEN THE BODY AND THE ROCK
ALL ELEMENTS WERE ALIGNED EAST-WEST

While Fakir was hanging from flesh hooks during the late 1970s and early 1980s, Stelarc, a performance artist who was born in Cyprus and works in Japan, was staging a series of events intended to exhibit the "obsolescence of the body." From the beginning of his artistic career, Stelarc has been preoccupied with his body. In early works, he used the latest medical technology to amplify sounds and project images of internal bodily processes like the flow of blood, the beating of the heart, and the contraction of muscles. These practices are a direct response to what he describes as "The Myth of Information." "The information explosion," Stelarc contends,

> is indicative of an evolutionary dead-end. It may be the height of human civilization, but it is also the climax of its evolutionary existence. In our decadent biological phase, we indulge in information as if it compensates for our genetic inadequacies.
>
> Information is the prosthesis that props up the obsolete body. Information gathering has become not only a meaningless ritual, but a deadly destructive paralyzing process, mesmerizing and immobilizing the body, preventing it from taking physical, phylogenetic action....The role of information has changed. Information gathering was once justified because it helped clarify reality. Information overload now creates a new mysticism because of its bewildering array of disconnected data. The body

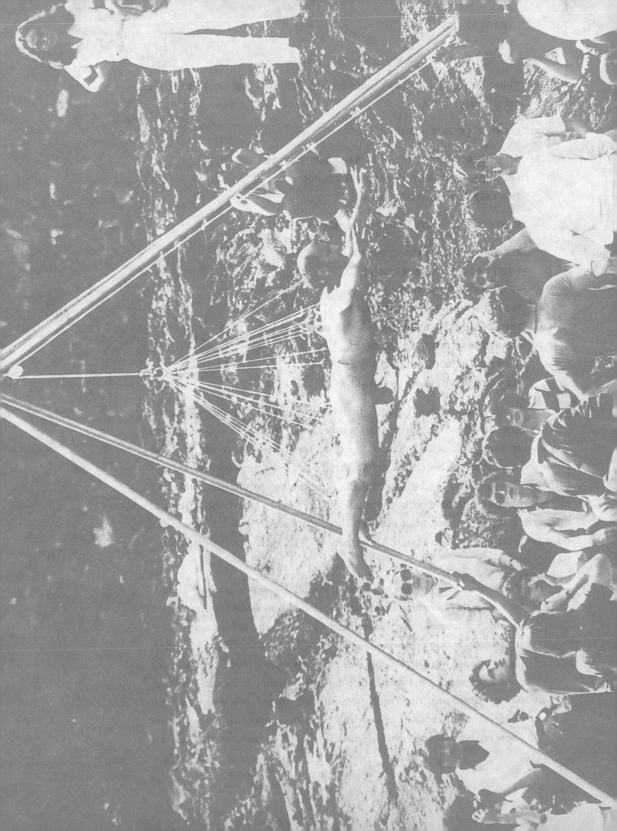

inhabits a hostile landscape of raw bits of undigested data. It is immersed in a deadly
field of fluctuating, fleeting and fragmentary information.

Stelarc's response to this crisis is not to turn away from the information environment in an effort to resurrect the body. Every such gesture, he admits, is futile
because the trajectory of evolution inevitably renders the body obsolete. Faced
with this situation, the challenge is not to return to the body but to leave it
behind. Stelarc's "suspensions" are intended to re-present the disappearance of
the body in the ethereal data clouds that are rapidly spreading across the earth.

Stelarc is not a technophobic fatalist; to the contrary, he remains true to
the modernist tradition of the avant-garde. Never content merely to record what is
taking place, he accepts responsibility for leading the way into the future he
assumes he has glimpsed. According to Stelarc, "the artist can become an evolutionary guide, extrapolating new trajectories; a genetic sculptor, restructuring and
hypersensitizing the human body; an architect of internal body spaces; a primal
surgeon, implanting dreams, transplanting desires; an evolutionary alchemist,
triggering mutations, transforming the human landscape." Unwilling to leave the
reconfiguration of the human body to scientists and engineers, Stelarc develops a
series of prosthetic devices to use in his performances. His best-known apparatus
is a robotic third hand that is controlled by signals emitted by the muscles of the
person wearing it. But in many ways, his most interesting creation dates from the
late 1960s. Between 1968 and 1970, Stelarc developed what can only be described
as a head-mounted display that is a prototype for a virtual reality machine.

> When I was still at art school in Australia, I'd stopped painting and drawing and
> was doing multi-media – like triple screen projections, and a series of helmets and
> goggles which the person put on and it modified their perception. In fact this series of
> helmets destroyed the person's binocular vision – the eyes seeing facets of the same
> image put together to create a three-dimensional impression. The binocular image
> was bisected. What the person saw was unrelated images superimposed. As the per-
> son walked, these images drifted across each other. I was nearly thrown out of school
> because I was supposed to be majoring in painting, and I wasn't painting – I was mak-
> ing helmets and goggles.

In Stelarc's hands, helmets, and goggles, skin graphs are extended to become
body grafts. As technology becomes more sophisticated, dermagraphics become
more subtle and, perhaps, more insidious. While appearing to amplify the body
these supplemental hides might eventually render it obsolete. How are such
grafts to be graphed?

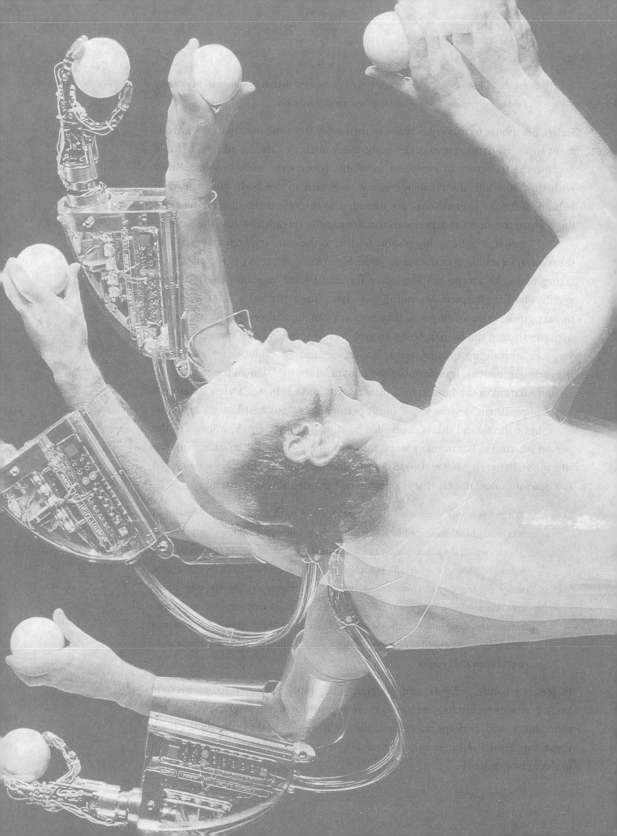

In the end, it all comes down to a question of skin. And bones. When nothing remains... nothing but skin and bones, when bones appear to be nothing... nothing but layers of skin, what once was called "reality" becomes not only unbearably light but impossibly thin. At this point... in this point, the body is deprived of its substance and appears to be on the verge of disappearing.

On November 21, 1993, the *New York Times* published an article by Margalit Fox entitled "A Portrait in Skin and Bones," which reported a performance to be presented that day by the French artist Orlan.

> At noon today, more than 50 invited guests at the Sandra Gering Gallery in SoHo will put down their crudités and fix their eyes on an oversize television screen mounted on one of the gallery's cool white walls. If all goes according to plan, they will witness the live performance of an operation, transmitted via satellite from an Upper East Side plastic surgeon's office. What they will see is no ordinary face lift.
>
> On the operating table, a wide-awake woman in a long black gown will read from a French psychoanalytic text, as the surgeon pauses in the delicate business of rearranging her face. Nearby, a cameraman in sterile surgical garb will record the procedure for network TV as electronic music plays in the background.
>
> The patient is a French multimedia artist who calls herself Orlan. During the last three years, the artist, 46, has undergone a series of plastic surgeries designed to progressively sculpture her face into the quintessential female form, part Venus, part Diana, part Mona Lisa. Today's operation, her first in the United States and first to be transmitted live to a gallery audience, will be her seventh.

Though nowhere acknowledged, the *Times* report on Orlan's performance piece is actually an extension of its publication of Nancy Burson's composite portrait of Lenin and Gorbachev (December 29, 1991) and Arkady Bronnikov's article on tattooing in Russian prisons with the accompanying photograph, which appeared two weeks earlier. Orlan, whose name is a variation of Orlon, a synthetic fiber, appropriates the strategy of composite portraiture invented by Galton and expanded by Burson to create an image that becomes the pattern for her self-transformation. Using sophisticated computer graphics technology, Orlan combines "images of the nose of a famous, unattributed School of Fontainbleau sculpture of Diana, the mouth of Boucher's Europa, the forehead of Leonardo's Mona Lisa, the chin of Botticelli's Venus, and the eyes of Gérôme's Psyche." The images are not only selected for their physical appearance but also for their historical, mythological, and artistic importance. The operations Orlan is undergoing are transforming her face and body into the synthetic image she has fabricated.

The performance reported by the *Times*, entitled *Omnipresence*, is part of a series called *The Reincarnation of Saint Orlan*. In 1971, Orlan gave up her "real" name and assumed a pseudonym. In her earlier incarnation, Orlan staged performances in which she created *tableaux vivants* modeled on classical works in the Western artistic tradition. The most characteristic feature of these pieces is her use of elaborate flowing robes with one breast exposed. In 1990, Orlan decided to make her *tableaux* truly *vivants* by creating *un vêtement incarné*. Acknowledging her debt to body artists of the late 1960s and 1970s like Burden, Acconci, and Schwarzkogler, Orlan labels her work "carnal art." Like her predecessors, Orlan's performances remain as traces in photographs and videos. She does not, however, simply repeat events staged by earlier artists; her carnal art pushes the outer limit of *l'oeuvre d'art* by staging a thoroughgoing translation of art into life in the sustained disfiguring of her own body. This radical gesture is preserved in remainders far more disturbing than photographs and videos. As supplements to her performances, Orlan exhibits and sells framed vials of liquefied flesh and blood removed from her body during the operations.

Orlan's work can be interpreted in many ways. From one point of view, as Barbara Rose points out, her "performances might be read as rituals of female submission, analogous to primitive rites involving the cutting up of women's bodies." If understood in this way, Orlan seems to reinforce practices of female mutilation that have plagued all cultures. But Orlan's performances are too complex to be comprehended by any one-sided reading. Never merely acts of submission, her operations are elaborate performances she carefully choreographs and manages. Doctors, nurses, medical technicians, set designers, photographers, and videographers become actors in a play that Orlan directs while she is undergoing surgery. By putting bloody rituals on display, she raises difficult questions and offers telling criticisms of the ways in which women's bodies have been treated from so-called primitive to so-called modern societies. Orlan's inscribed body becomes a living critique of abusive practices that are as subtle as they are pervasive.

While the context for Orlan's criticism is the world of "high" art, her work can also be read in relation to the practices of pop body art that we have been considering. The importance of the tattoo renaissance is not limited to new forms of old practices. Orlan's carnal art shows that writing on the body need not be inscribed in ornate designs and bright colors that many regard as primitive. Fine shades of white, tan, brown, and black; thin bodies, crafted curves, sculptured muscles, enlarged breasts; to say nothing of layers upon layers of makeup, which

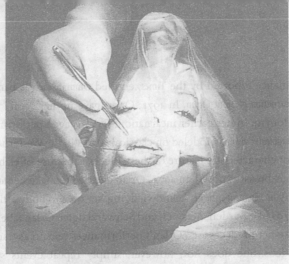

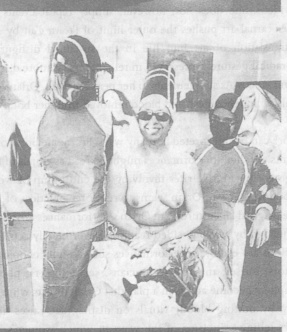

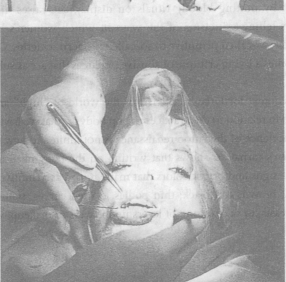

sometimes takes the form of tattoos, are dermagraphics whose implications are rarely figured. In the course of the twentieth century, it has become clear that Loos was wrong; the movement of civilization is not marked by the progressive erasure of ornament. To the contrary, our world is characterized by a proliferation of images in media that multiply at a speed exceeding rational calculation and control. This explosion of images implodes on the surface of civilization and skin of our bodies. We are all tattooed by the media whose creation we have become.

The pamphlet accompanying *Omnipresence* bears a title that echoes Stelarc's suspension of the body: *Le corps est obsolete*. Paradoxically, the more deeply Orlan marks her body, the more steadily it disappears. As media etch themselves into the flesh, circulatory systems become fiber-optic lines and neural networks become worldwide webs. The work of art is not limited to the incarnate image but extends endlessly in cyberspace. Using a satellite as well as visiophone Picture Tel, Orlan transmitted her operation to New York, Paris, Dijon, Nice, Quebec, Antwerp, Cologne, Riga, Milan, Zurich, Geneva, Tokyo, Banff, and Toronto. Stitched to this telecommunications network, she was able to communicate by voice with people in France, Banff, and Toronto and by fax and modem with people at the other venues. Rather than a superfluous demonstration of technological gadgetry, this extension of the performance is a critical component in Orlan's art. Media networks are, in effect, electronic prostheses that supplement the work of art. Though such supplements sometimes seem excessive, they inevitably alter the body "proper" by disrupting its apparent stability. The amplification of Orlan's performance further transforms her work by rendering her body immaterial. With this twist, the lines of communication bend back on themselves to create oscillating loops that cannot be short-circuited: image is transformed into body, which is transformed into image, which is transformed into body, which is transformed into image...

These reversals and counterreversals make it possible to reread the body/prosthesis relation. Perhaps not only electronic webs are prostheses that supplement the human mind and body, but also the human mind and body are prostheses that extend the net. If the body is an extension of the electronic networks that increasingly constitute our world rather than the reverse, then the body's reality becomes virtual. In one of her many interviews, Orlan reflects on a strange experience she had during one of her performances: "I recall when I was doing a very big and long performance: I was present physically but had the impression of being absent: something was able to absent itself, the body was able to be the support where things were able to inscribe themselves without having to be present.

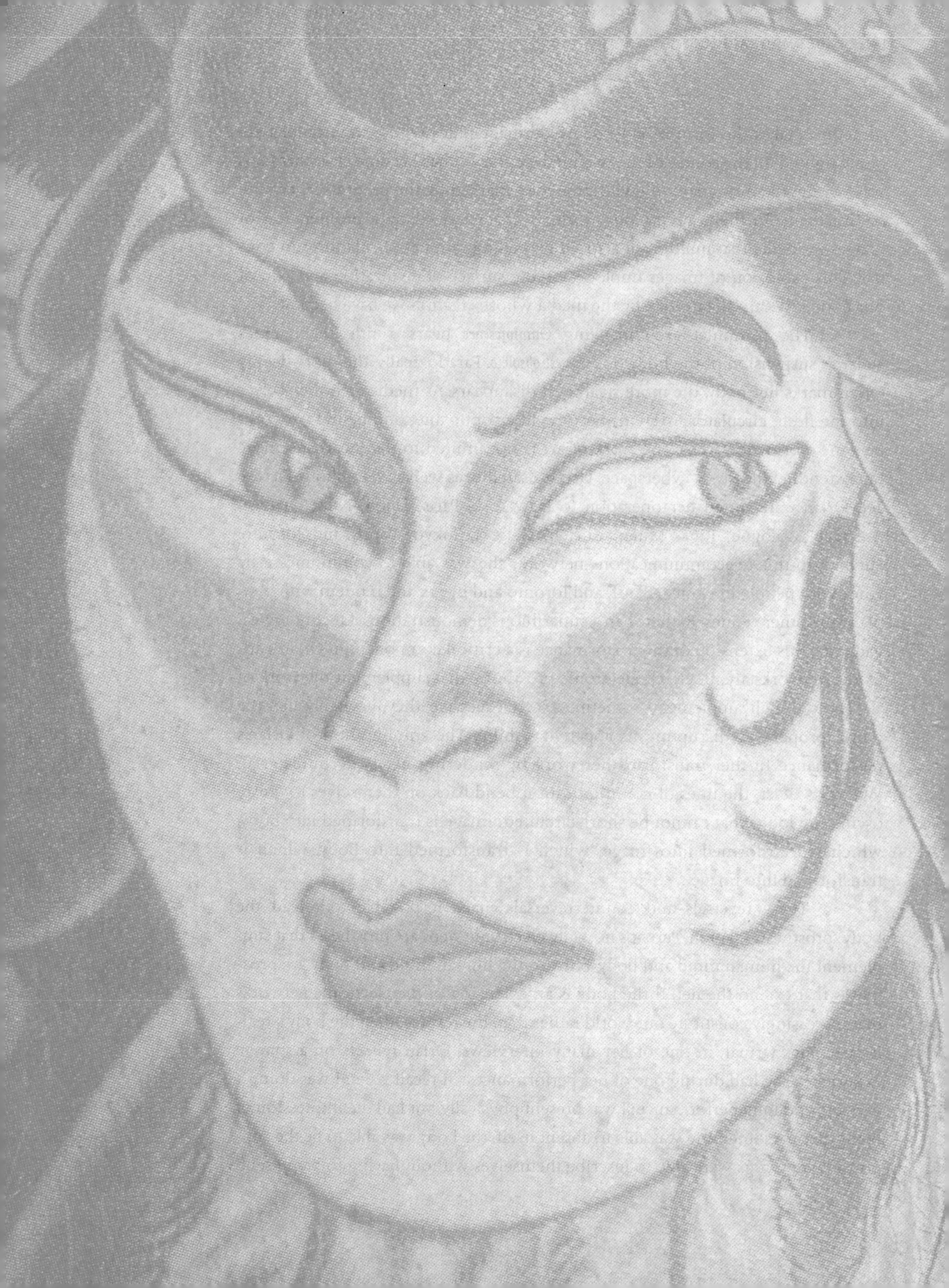

An impression, then, of strangeness where one no longe[r] is real on the exterior and what is not real." *Une impression... d'ét[range] plus exactement ce qui est réellement... et ce qui ne l'est pas... Étrange...très étrange. As* hides that hide nothing...nothing but other hides. As strange as signs that [ ] nothing...nothing but other signs. As strange as surfaces know no depth yet are not simply superficial. In the midst of these endless surfaces, we all become fashion-able signing detectives.

Go Figure

Falling Apart at the Seems

Fashionable Religion

Ralph Lauren

Helmut Lang

Yohji Yaman

As fashion takes a turn toward the sober, the somber, and the monastically austere, **Henry Alford** wonders what this new ascetic aesthetic is all about

S ink to your knees and start atoning for the acquisitive 1980s; designers are increasingly finding inspiration in the vestments of priests, nuns, rabbis, and monks. A veritable interfaith symposium on fashion is currently being held at your better temples of commerce; spiritual equanimity, it seems, is only a credit-card receipt away. The look is one of penitence and personal conviction; if the traditional nun's cape has nine buttons (one for each letter in *obedience*), then this season's clothes should have nineteen (one for each letter in *meditation and denial*). Awning-size sheaths whose only embellishment is a trumpet flare at the cuff, voluminous black robes reminiscent of body bags without zippers—these are not clothes in which to quaff champagne while discussing leveraged buyouts and the Michael Milken hairpiece. These are clothes in which to lurk at airports, frantically begging passengers to buy your pamphlets and your incense.

"There's such an elegance about priests. I think it's a wonderful look," says Calvin Klein, whose collection includes long priests' coats, pared-down black suits, and wide-brimmed Shaker hats. "And I've always loved the minimalist, graphic purity of the Amish. I'm mad for the colors." Black, gray, more gray—a browse through Austrian de- ▶136

habit, 1959

Richard Tyler

Jean Paul Gaultier

Wearing Thin

What's in? What's out?

Disdressing

In Vestment

Jeanetic Engineering

Making It Up

Modeling Reality

Net Effects

Cyberchic

CLUBWEAR

This hard-edged futuristic look for girls is influenced by the sinister and gloomy atmosphere of movies like Blade Runner and by dark science fiction comics. The styling is aggressively sexy, including miniskirts, stretch pants, tight tops and cropped tops. Black, metallics and drab military colours predominate. In a mix of fetish and futuristic fashion, reptile skin effects and latex are used with transparent and holographic fabrics.

Trendy Nomads

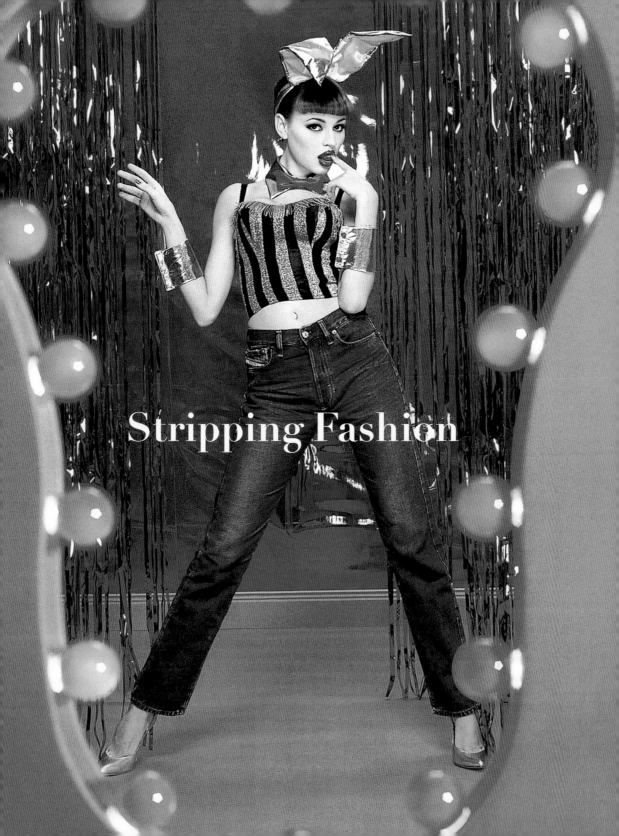

Stripping Fashion

Why must it be that men always seek out the depths, the abyss?
Why must thought, like the plumb line, concern itself exclusively
with vertical descent? Why was it not feasible for thought to change
direction and climb vertically up, ever up, towards the surface?
Why should the area of the skin, which guarantees a human being's
existence in space, be most despised and left to the tender mercies
of the senses? I could not understand the laws governing the motion
of thought – the way it was liable to get stuck in unseen chasms
whenever it set out to go deep....
If the law of thought is that it should search out profundity, whether
it extends upwards or downwards, then it seemed excessively
illogical to me that men should not discover depths of a kind in the
"surface."...Why should they not be attracted to the profundity of
the surface itself?

Yukio Mishima

Fashion is profound in its superficiality.
The profundity of fashion does not involve depth but reflects
the infinite complexity of a play of surfaces that knows no
end. In the absence of a depth that grounds, fashion remains
fraught with ambiguity – irreducible ambiguity. This ambiguity, which borders on the enigmatic, is what renders fashion simultaneously attractive and repulsive. On the one
hand, to label something fashionable is to embrace it as smart,
sophisticated, elegant, current, and timely. On the other hand,

to characterize something as fashionable is to dismiss it as trendy, trivial, inconsequential, insignificant, and fleeting. The positive and the negative intersect only for an instant: timely yet fleeting. The ambiguity of fashion mirrors the enigma of time.

The fabric of fashion is woven from the warp and woof of thanatos and eros. Dedicated to the eternal return of the new, fashion remains irrevocably committed to that which passes

Go Figure

AUSTIN (Nov. 11, 1993) *Jennie casually strolled into Jacques', an up-scale coffee house in downtown Austin, ordered a cappucino, grabbed the Times, and joined her friend at a table near the window. "I did it!" Jennie confessed with obvious satisfaction. "No, you didn't! I don't believe you," Sylvia responded incredulously. Saying nothing, Jennie unbuttoned her blouse just enough to expose a small rose and lone star tattooed on her shoulder. Sylvia giggled with delight. Jennie just smiled.*

From college dorms and uptown health clubs to malls and runways, tattoos and piercings are popping up everywhere. Once a badge of honor sported by sailors and bikers, tatts have gone mainstream. While the art of disfiguring is ancient, times as well as tribes now are different. It began quietly, even discreetly, with small tattoos hidden in private places for "intimate admirer's eyes only. It wasn't until the eighties, when supermodels like Stephanie Seymour and Carré Otis and Hollywood actresses like Julia Roberts and Drew Barrymore began flaunting their very public 'pieces' on their shoulders,

ankles, and lower backs that tattooing took a decidedly glamorous turn." Now "fashion watchers barely flinch when more elaborately tattooed models like one-time car mechanic Jenny Shimizu (who has a bawdy tattoo of a near naked woman riding a wrench on her upper arm) or the buzz-cut model Eve Salvail (who has a large tattoo of a serpent across one side of her head) strut down the Chanel, Versace, and Calvin Klein runways of Paris, Milan, and New York."

So what's the deal? Why this obsession with carnal scripture? Teena Mareer, Los Angeles native and piercer

for the stars, sees the tattooing and piercing craze as a nostalgic search for body and place. "The origins of body piercing," she notes, "are dotted all over the planet. I suspect there is a little bit of tribal identity, with people trying to find roots and connect back. Our society tried to alienate ourselves from our bodies." The lines that mark the body, then, reaffirm the physical and material in a world where everything is uprooted and immaterial. Global nomads plugged into ether(eal) networks seek to reconnect with a tribe they can call their own.

Or so it seems. But in the

away: the transient, the momentary, the ephemeral. To say no to fashion is to flee time in search of eternity. "What we wished to express in art," Amédée Ozenfant confesses, "was the Universal and Permanent and to throw to the dogs the Vacillating and the Fashionable." To say *yes* to fashion is to affirm the inescapable eternity of time.

How should something as elusive as fashion be approached? Is it possible to comprehend fashion fashionably? Or is every understanding of fashion an unfashionable misunderstanding?

The tradition of interpretation suggests that fashion has always been treated unfashionably. But what does it mean to treat fashion unfashionably, and what would it mean to consider fashion fashionably?

Fashion is a recent invention. Indeed, fashion did not exist prior to the advent of modernity. It is, therefore, no more possible to understand modernity and modernism apart from

world of fashion, like everywhere else, what you see is rarely what you get. As the tattoo and piercing fad spreads, the line separating the real from the fake becomes harder and harder to draw. Whether mimicking the custom designs of a Don Ed Hardy or the flash of a local tattoo parlor, temporary tatts have become the rage for wanna-bes who are unwilling to make permanent commitments. Always slightly ahead of the curve, Rei Kawakubo recently hired makeup artist Stáphane Marais to stencil "necklaces, bracelets, and anklets in primitive patterns" on her models. For those who can't afford such customized work, there is always the ready-to-wear. New York City's Temptu, Inc., recently introduced a new line of temporary tattoos, "which are applied to the skin with an alcohol-soaked pad, removed in seconds with baby oil. Temptu's credits run the gamut from film stars (Robert De Niro in Cape Fear, Winona Ryder in Night on Earth) to fashion models (at both the Anna Sui and Comme des Garçons shows), and their handiwork covers everything from hearts and flowers (packet of four designs, from $4) to stencils with special body paints ($20 for a six-color kit)." If decals and paint are too much trouble or you want a recyclable hide, tattoo dresses, blouses, shirts, and pants might be the answer. From Karl Lagerfeld's revealing Skindress to colorful tattoo designs, clothing is being treated like a second skin. Predictably, Jean-Paul Gaultier is leading the way. His tattoo T-shirts and dresses, "which fit like a sheer body stocking, are the fashion prize of the summer." For women with less inhibition and more money, Gaultier offers a pastiche of "global-village chic" that is guaranteed to make even postmodernist heads spin: "A veil-like cropped top – stripped of one sleeve and 'tattooed' with magnified European money – teams up with a pareo emblazoned with all-American motorcycle motifs. Injecting some out-of-India detail: clusters of silver jewels." By craftily mixing painted tattoos with tattooed fabrics, Gaultier makes it virtually impossible to be sure where skin ends and garment begins. Commenting on the collection, Gaultier explains: "I wanted to point out the tribal roots of body art and offer a little history lesson." History lesson or not, the street, which rarely preserves anything, once again is leading

fashion than it is to understand fashion apart from modernity and modernism. The relays joining fashion and modernity intersect in the word *modern*. Modern derives from the Latin *modo*, which means "just now" and, by extension, "of today." Accordingly, the modern is current, up to date, and of the moment; it is, in other words, fashionable. The fashionable, in turn, must always be new and thus modern. The convergence of the fashionable and the modern suggests that the ambiguity of fashion extends to modernity. This ambiguity comprises the enigmatic coincidence of affirmation and negation in the moment of time. The affirmation of the modern is inseparable from the negation of the outmoded, the customary, and the traditional. To be modern is to be of the present rather than of the past. Yet the past, from which the modern seeks to distance itself, does not merely pass away but continues to haunt the present. The specter of the past assumes at least two guises.

the way. As fake tatts and inked garments parade down runways, the force of Maree's explanation of tattooing and piercing fades. What is at stake seems to be not a longing to recover the body but a reveling in the loss of its substance. Guido Palau, one of Calvin Klein's leading hairstylists, comes closer to the point when he observes that "women are trying to look as fake as possible." If faking it is what really matters, everything is even less than skin-deep. As Andre Agassi preaches from his Las Vegas pulpit: "Image is everything."

Back at Jacques', Jennie

patiently answered Sylvia's endless questions. "No, I haven't told my parents or Rob yet; yes, it's legal in Texas. No, it didn't hurt; yes, it's safe. No, I'm not sorry; yes, I'm pleased – very pleased. Actually, I'm thinking of getting another one. But this time I'm not going to use flash; I'm going to create my own design."

Postmodern primitives. Go figure.

First, inasmuch as the affirmation of the modern is a negation of the customary, the past persists in the present as negated. Though not properly present, the past is not simply absent. Second, modernity can remain dedicated to the present only by affirming every present as always already passé. As soon as the modern arrives, it is not only dated but obsolete and thus must be replaced. Far from antimodern, obsolescence is a condition of the possibility of modernity itself. Since the modern can arrive only by disappearing, it is never present or, more precisely, is always present as passing. The inescapable passing of the modern is what makes fashion both so unsettling and so seductive.

Any treatment of fashion that explains the ephemeral in terms of the abiding is unfashionable. Though unfashionable inter-pretations of fashion vary considerably, they all share a common architecture in which a transient suprastructure is grounded in a more-or-less permanent infrastructure. This infrastructure/suprastructure polarity is a reinscription of classical theological and philosophical binaries like

BEING/BECOMING

ESSENCE/APPEARANCE

ETERNITY/TIME

The terms of these interpretive binaries are never equivalent but are hierarchically ordered in such a way that the former is consistently privileged at the expense of the latter. When elaborated and extended, this structural model generates a conceptual grid that can be applied to interpret fashion.

REAL/FAKE

NATURAL/ARTIFICIAL

MASCULINE/FEMININE

SERIOUS/FRIVOLOUS

RELIABLE/FICKLE

REASONABLE/SENSUAL

UNIVERSAL/PARTICULAR

NECESSARY/SUPERFLUOUS

USEFUL/USELESS

AUTHENTIC/INAUTHENTIC

PROFOUND/SUPERFICIAL

Within this taxonomy, fashion is classified as fake, artificial, feminine, frivolous, fickle, sensual, particular, superfluous, useless, inauthentic, and superficial. The truth of fashion is supposed to be disclosed when the transient suprastructure is reduced to an enduring infrastructure. The infrastructure that appears to form the foundation of fashion can be construed in psychological, sociological, economic, and linguistic terms. Interpretation, then, involves a process of translating the manifest (i.e., the superficial) into the latent (i.e., the profound) through an irreversible process of decoding. Since the locus of truth is always the hidden, under-standing requires a grasp of

Falling Apart *at the* Seems

First it was philosophy, then literature, theology, even architecture; now it's fashion.

Everything is falling apart at the seems. Responsibility for this catastrophe, many argue, lies squarely on the Left Bank. For years, distraught critics have been blaming "fashionable" Parisian philosophers for the imminent collapse of Western civilization. No one has been the focus of a more sustained and vitriolic attack than Jacques Derrida. Though bordering on inaccessibility for the uninitiated, Derrida's dense writings have provoked extraordinary reactions in the media and popular press. Labeling Derrida's writings "merely fashionable" does not disguise the panic they provoke. What makes Derrida so threatening and why are people either so anxious to condemn or so eager to embrace his work?

Derrida's philosophy, if it is a philosophy, is commonly

known as deconstruction. For most critics, "deconstruction" is indistinguishable from "destruction." Thus, when Derrida deconstructs the Western philosophical, literary, religious, and artistic traditions, he is charged with effectively destroying the very foundations of society and culture. This criticism, however, misses Derrida's point and distorts the insights he offers. Rather than a destructive attack on valued traditions and institutions, deconstruction is a sympathetic diagnosis of pervasive symptoms of psychological insecurities and social uncertainties we are inclined to overlook or conceal. When subjected to Derrida's careful analyses, the ground that once seemed firm turns out to be suspended over abysses we can never fathom. Deconstruction does not so much shatter foundations as expose fissures that cannot be closed and faults that cannot be mended. Though we struggle to deny it, these faults and fissures rend the very fabric of our lives.

After the confidence and optimism of the eighties and early nineties, the world now seems less certain and secure. Haunted by foreign threats and internal dangers, things seem to be unraveling and spinning out of control. While the old world order has passed away, a new world order has not

that which stands under the insubstantial play of appearances. Once the underlying historical, psychological, social, economic, or linguistic processes have been laid bare, the sub-stance of fashion becomes apparent. While the nature of this substance varies, the architecture of the argument remains constant.

Fashion, however, calls into question the architecture of every version of this style of interpretation. The practices of fashion present an indirect critique of all theories that presuppose a hierarchical distinction between suprastructure and infrastructure. As if echoing the remarkable Japanese writer Yukio Mishima, fashion de-signers implicitly ask why we are not "attracted to the profundity of the surface itself?" To discover the depth of surface and the profundity of superficiality, it is necessary to develop a *fashionable* approach to fashion. Even the most perspicacious readers of fashion overlook the contradiction between their theories and what

yet emerged. Promises of unlimited growth have given way to warnings about impending scarcity and burdensome debt. The Wall might have fallen, but new walls are being built every day. In the midst of all this confusion and turmoil, principles and policies that have long guided the lives of individuals and societies are torn to shreds and shot full of holes.

In the face of such world-transforming events, the distance separating sophisticated Left Bank philosophy from the Parisian runways might seem unbridgeable. But gaps can be as illusory as the stuff that is supposed to fill them. If philosophy can be fashionable, why can't fashion be philosophical?

The stirrings of a philosophical turn in fashion can be traced to Rei Kawakubo's 1992 Comme des Garçons collection. Not only the designs but also the setting in which they were introduced signaled a seismic shift in the foundations of fashion. The stage as well as the clothing displayed seemed to have been deconstructed. "Instead of a sleek runway there were plywood planks in midconstruction hung with bits of canvas. Models emerged in paper dresses, ripped toile suits, and trench coats hacked off above the waist. Kawakubo's idea was to show clothes in stages of their development – from paper patterns

to cloth. But nothing was finished. Linings slipped out from under jackets with missing sleeves and collars; the raw edges and seams on slip dresses were sealed with rough stripes of paint." "I'm not breaking something, I'm rebuilding," Kawakubo insisted. "Too much importance has been placed on slick, polished images. I show clothes that aren't finished and expose their construction to indicate the value of things that are primitive and imperfect."

The imperfect and unfinished have become trademarks of deconstructionist fashion. Blouses are misbuttoned, shirts torn, slacks ripped, sweaters unraveled, skirts frayed. As if this were not enough, something is always either missing or added as a useless supplement: "a shoulder, half a collar, several inches of a skirt's hem, revealing the lining beneath – or four sleeves or two necklines set into the same dress." "Whereas completion can sometimes be static," Kawakubo observed, "here I saw an energy and beauty in the unfinished state."

While Kawakubo and her colleagues Jean-Paul Gaultier and Yohji Yamamoto were introducing the tattered-and-torn look, a new generation of Belgian designers was busily watching and taking notes. Martin Margiela, Ann Demeulemeester, and Dries

they attempt to theorize. Every effort to understand fashion by reducing it to a permanent or quasi-permanent foundation misses fashion's most telling point. While critics have been all too eager to apply theories to fashion, they have been reluctant to read their own theories fashionably. When fashion turns back on the theories designed to capture it, theory itself becomes fashionable.

An examination of the unexpected imbrication of fashion and modern architecture prepares the way for a deconstruction of the architectonics undergirding different theories. In a suggestive article entitled "White Out: Fashioning the Modern," Mark Wigley goes so far as to argue:

> Modern architecture was indeed explicitly launched against fashion, and its white surfaces played a key role in that attack. Its very modernity was repeatedly identified with the rejection of architecture's nineteenth century immersion in the world of fashion. As

van Noten, who eventually came together at the Royal Academy of Fine Arts in Antwerp, reacted even more strongly to the excesses of the eighties. "The power suits. The gold buttons. The designer logos plastered on everything. The whole haute couture opera, with Brünnhilde trussed up in embroidery, clacking beads and drapery velvet. And the international press, running around with thesauruses to find one more word synonymous with gilt.

"A satire would have been redundant. If that were the future of fashion, few of the academy group wanted it. As a backlash against established eighties excesses a new style was born. It was one that offered a sort of asbestos against the bonfire of the vanities."

So-called deconstructivist fashion is far from a unified movement. "Without abandoning any of their rigorous training, the three young designers set about creating clothes that would not overwhelm the wearer. Clothes that didn't seem oblivious to the realities of an often unhappy world. Each of the Belgians pursues that end in a different way: Mr. Margiela with a vengeance, Ms. Demeulemeester with femininity and Mr. van Noten with studied simplicity." What joins these otherwise distinct approaches is not only a shared sense that fashion should reflect the times but the conviction that design is a formative force that bears social

responsibility. If the cuts of the nineties are the price we are paying for the binge of the eighties, then fashion must share part of the blame. Tattered garments expose worn ideas and frayed ideals.

But we need to see only so much seamy fashion to be reminded that everything is falling apart. At a certain point, criticism fades into irony in which rejection and endorsement become indistinguishable. In an unexpected twist, deconstructivist fashion has recently come perilously close to precisely the kind of nihilism often attributed to deconstructive philosophy. As if to parody the repeated charge that deconstruction leads us down the slippery slope of relativism and nihilism, which eventually leads to the death camps, "Kawakubo presented her Comme des Garçons men's collection for fall, titled 'Sleep.' An assortment of striped pajamas worn with sweaters, jackets and bathrobe coats, it was, she said, her attempt to revive lounge wear, which had once been an important category in the gentleman's wardrobe. The date assigned to Kawakubo for her show was, as it happened, the fiftieth anniversary of the liberation of Auschwitz, and two critics saw in the striped pajamas a reminder of the Nazi death camps. The outraged reviews

the movement's most influential manifesto – *Vers une architecture*, published by Le Corbusier in 1925 – puts it, the "styles" of nineteenth century architecture are but "the old clothes of a past age," clothes that "are to architecture what a feather is to a woman's head; it is sometimes pretty, though not always, and never anything more."

Le Corbusier obviously presupposes a hierarchically structured grid in which fashion is directly related to the feminine and indirectly associated with the artificial, frivolous, fickle, sensual, and most important, the useless or nonfunctional.

Consistently committed to reasonableness and functionalism, modern architects claim to be resolutely opposed to fashion. Le Corbusier's resistance to fashion should not be surprising, for, as I have noted, his partner in purism, Amédée
Ozenfant, declares: "What we wished to express in art was
the Universal and Permanent and to throw to the dogs the
Vacillating and the Fashionable." Ozenfant's opposition

in *Le Figaro* and the *International Herald Tribune* prompted a
visit to the Comme des Garçons showroom by members of
the European Jewish Congress and a spate of articles denounc-
ing Kawakubo as, at best, an unwitting anti-Semite. As a gesture of conciliation, she withdrew the pajamas from the line.
Other items in the collection had been stenciled with numerals,
randomly scattered, and with footprints. As the scandal esca-
lated, the pajamas came to be described as stamped with 'identification numbers'; the models as 'emaciated,' with 'shaved
heads'; and the footprints, as made by military boots trampling
the Jews underfoot. (In fact, no numbers appeared on any
of the striped garments; many of the models had long hair;
and the tread had been made by a basketball sneaker.)" In an
attempt to close the file on this whole unfortunate episode,
Kawakubo actually added fuel to the controversy by insisting:
"There is no meaning."

While the charges of the critics are obviously excessive,
Kawakubo's response is inadequate. Deconstruction's effort
to display the inescapable faults in systems and structures
of power is both necessary and important. But criticism alone
is not enough. If we are to fashion a future that is something
more than an endless repetition of the present, we must do
more than preach, "There is no meaning." Can fashion help us
to meet this challenge or is it forever condemned to prove
the pointlessness of Rei Kawakubo's point?

between the universal-permanent and the vacillating-fashion-
able both repeats and inverts the contrast that Baudelaire considers to be definitive of modernism. In his influential essay
"The Painter of Modern Life," Baudelaire writes: "By 'modernity' I mean the ephemeral, the fugitive, the contingent, the
half of art whose other half is the eternal and the immutable."
While Baudelaire correlates the modern with the eclipse of
the eternal and the immutable as well as the proliferation of
the ephemeral, the fugitive, and the contingent, Ozenfant and

Le Corbusier reverse historical and theoretical directions by relating the modern to the universal and permanent, and the primitive to the vacillating and fashionable. In developing their account of modernism, Ozenfant and Le Corbusier follow the lead of Adolf Loos.

For architects preoccupied with form and structure, garments are a second skin that is both endlessly fascinating and profoundly disturbing. As we have discovered in our consideration of tattooing and bodily decoration, Loos associates ornamentation with criminality, femininity, primitiveness, infantilism, and madness. By translating synchronic structure into diachronic process, he effectively historicizes hierarchical binaries in such a way that the superior term is identified as modern and the inferior term as primitive. In a series of remarkable essays devoted to topics ranging from "Men's Hats," "Footwear," and "Shoemakers" to "Underclothes" and "Ladies' Fashion," Loos sets up an evolutionary scheme in which personal growth and sociocultural development reflect a movement from the decorative to the nondecorative or from the ornamental to the formal. This course is, as we have seen, part of a more general progress from sensuality to reason. When situated in this narrative, fashion appears to be a primitive obsession from which civilized people must be liberated.

The clothing of the woman is distinguished externally from that of the man by the preference for ornamental and colorful effects and by the long skirt that covers the legs completely. These two factors demonstrate to us that the woman has fallen behind sharply in her development in recent centuries. No period of culture has known as great a difference as our own between the clothing of the free man and that of the free woman. In earlier eras, men also wore clothing that was colorful and richly adorned and whose hem reached to the floor. Happily, the grandiose development in which our culture has taken part in this century has overcome ornament. Ornament is something that must be overcome. The Papuan and the criminal ornament their skin. The Indian covers his paddle and his boat with layers and layers of ornament. But the bicycle and the steam engine are free of ornament. The march of civilization systematically liberates object after object from ornamentation.

While the terms of Loos's analysis are manifestly racist and chauvinist, his undeniable but not unproblematic sexism deserves further consideration in this context. Loos consistently associates fashion with women and identifies women with sensuality. Sensuality, he insists, is a dreadful disease.

> Ladies fashion! You disgraceful chapter in the history of civilization! You tell of mankind's secret desires. Whenever we peruse your pages, our souls shudder at the frightful aberrations and scandalous depravities.... This unnatural sensuality erupts in different ways in every century, indeed in every decade. It is in the air and it is infectious. Sometimes it spreads through a country like a pestilence that cannot be hidden; sometimes it sneaks through a nation like a secret and contagious disease, and those who are afflicted by it know how to conceal it from others.

The primary agents for the spread of this disease are women whose modus operandi is fashion. Reduced to a position of subservience by men, women regard fashion as an exercise of the will to power that not only reinforces but can also disturb social hierarchy.

> That which is noble in a woman knows only one desire: that she hold on to her place by the side of the big, strong man. This love makes her the man's subordinate. It is an unnatural love. If it were natural, the woman would be able to approach the man naked. But the naked woman is unattractive to the man. She may be able to arouse a man's love, but not to keep it.... Woman covered herself, she became a riddle to man, in order to implant in his heart the desire for the riddle's solution.... Once she is married, the woman acquires her social stamp through her husband, regardless of whether she has been a coquette or aprincess. Her position is relinquished completely. Thus the woman is forced to appeal to the man's sensuality through her clothing, to appeal unconsciously to his sickly sensuality, for which only the culture of the times can be blamed.

Fashion and, by extension, the women who sport it are artificial, deceitful, disingenuous, degenerate, and diseased. Expressed in theological terms, fashion is sinful.

Loos's account of the feminine wiles from which fashion is spun discloses easily overlooked aspects of the implicit theology of history that informs his interpretation of both fashion and architecture. History, I have noted, is marked by the

Fashionable Religion

GOD, RELIGION IS BACK!

Not just in the heartland but in the midst of the "secular city."

NEW YORK (Sept. 5, 1993) – The fall collections surprised just about everybody this year. Three decades after the proclamation of the death of God, religion is back – back with a vengeance. Not just in the heartland and the pious platitudes of politicians but in the midst of the "secular city."

"Everywhere this season designers are giving new meaning to the term 'religious follower of fashion.' Poverty and chastity were the themes at Martin Margiela, with 'poor,' earth-tone fabrics fashioned into long garments that covered the body from neck to ankle. Meanwhile, at Jean-Paul Gaultier, the clothes told a similar story, only with Jewish details: As violinists played traditional klezmer music, models walked the runway in wide-brimmed rabbinical hats, skullcaps, big shawls resembling the tallith (prayer shawl), and superlong black coats, their hair styled in tight ringlets to resemble payess, the side curls worn by Hasidic men. It seems nothing is sacred – or is everything sacred?"

The religious traditions designers find inspiring are those that are most hostile to images, decoration, and, by extension, fashion: Protestantism and Judaism. This should not be surprising because the art world has long been fascinated by the pure simplicity of ascetic aesthetics. If art museums have become our temples and shrines, worshippers have learned how to dress when they enter them. Art openings are more like somber gatherings of morosely clad rabbis and pastors than festive occasions to celebrate the true colors of art. Everything is as hushed and muted as the sounds and tones of a synagogue or church. Always a step behind, while attempting to appear a step ahead, fashion (for the moment) has deserted profane streets and is invading sacred precincts.

Minimalism in fashion is, of course, nothing new. Indeed, the history of modern fashion represents repeated fluctuations between ornament and its removal.

movement from sensuality to reason, which is reflected in a progressive disappearance of decoration. Accordingly, while so-called primitives indulge in excessive ornamentation, so-called modern civilization eschews every temptation to decorate. It now becomes clear that Loos regards sensual desire as "unnatural." Prior to the beginning of history, men and women lived in a natural state in which they lacked nothing and hence were undisturbed by desire. In this prelapsarian garden, innocents were free to run naked without feeling any need for supplemental clothing. But, as the story goes, the feminine temptress disrupted this harmonious condition by engendering desire in man. The symptom of this transgressive desire is the first article of clothing – the fig leaf. Throughout history, clothing – especially feminine fashion – has been a sign of sin. The only way in which sin can be overcome is through the control of desire. For Loos, as for his fellow Viennese Freud,

Periodically, iconoclasm seems to be iconoclastic. What is new about the current return of a minimalist aesthetic is the eagerness with which designers claim religious sources for their work.

"'There's such an elegance about priests. I think it's a wonderful look,' says Calvin Klein, whose collection includes long priests' coats, pared-down black suits, and wide-brimmed Shaker hats. 'And I've always loved the minimalist, graphic purity of the Amish. I'm mad for the colors.' Black, gray, more gray – a browse through Austrian designer Helmut Lang's offerings this season suggests that he, too, is mad for colors not prominent in the films of Disney. 'We're finding a new way of being elegant,' says Lang of the many designers who, like him, are making spare, clean

clothes. 'We had so much of a certain kind of glamour in the past. Now designers are trying to capture a more sensitive feeling.'"

For some, the return to purity and simplicity expresses repentance for the excesses of the eighties. " 'I suppose there is a need for new values,' says Belgian avant-garde designer Ann Demeulemeester about the origins of monastic fashion. 'I think people are fed up with superficial and vulgar codes of sexuality.'" Others insist that fashion's newly found puritanism reflects a response to the growing AIDS crisis and all it represents. "'We are in a period of being more humble, of spending less, of being more frugal,' says Robert Lee Morris, a jewelry designer whose use of the cross helped spark the trend. 'These

crosses just emphasize that sense of self-denial. Also, there's the AIDS crisis. Literally, we're keeping our pants up, and holding back – using our will power to control that hedonism we had in the 80s.'"

It's hardly surprising that not everyone is persuaded by such claims of value, frugality, and self-control. After all, how much self-denial does it take to purchase a fashionable monk's hooded cape and coat by Geoffrey Beene for a cool $3,900?

Many find fashion's exploitation of religious motifs offensive or even sacrilegious. Reacting to Gaultier's appropriation of Hebrew traditions, Rabbi Shmuel Butman, director of the Lubavich Youth Organization and spokesperson for the Crown Heights Jewish community of Brooklyn, explained: "The Jewish garb is

historical progress is marked by increasing repression. When psychoanalytic insight is translated into fashionable architectural terms, "where id was ego shall be" becomes "where ornament was form shall be."

But how can sin be overcome, desire controlled, the body disciplined, transgression punished, the garden restored, and the kingdom realized? The unlikely means to such lofty ends, Loos and some of his fellow modern architects insist, is the reform of fashion. Indeed, not only the progress of civilization but the emergence of modern architecture presupposes controlling the excesses of fashion. Wigley goes so far as to contend that "the whole logic of modern architecture is actually that of dress reform.... The discourse of modern architecture thus literally occurs within that of clothing reform. All the standard arguments on behalf of modern architecture had already been made in the realm of dress design. The reformists

holy; it is part of our tradition. It should not be exploited on the economic level. It is doubly offensive if it violates biblical precepts, which dictate that men should wear men's clothing and women should wear women's clothing." Margaret R. Miles of the Harvard Divinity School insists that the effects of fashion's turn to religion are even more pernicious. "'The way to discount a symbol is not to walk away from it and ignore it,' she explains, 'but place it in a decorative rather than religious context. I regret that the religious symbolism is being trivialized and secularized in this way.'"

While it is easy to be suspicious about religion that is worn on one's sleeve or skirt, things are not as simple as Miles assumes. Even when they appear to be opposite, the secular and the sacred are inseparable; the religious can no more be dissociated from the decorative than

the decorative can be divorced from the religious. These lessons are as old as religion and as new as the ongoing debate between modernists and postmodernists.

From colorful masks and body paint to dark robes and suits, religion has always involved fashion. Throughout the history of religion, some of the most fashionable characters have been the ones who have most devoutly denounced fashion. "When Cromwell reformed the monarchy, the white collars and black coats of austere Protestant costume became all the rage, a reaction to Catholic `popery' and elaborate ecclesiastical vestments." The switch from the iconophilia of Catholicism to the iconophobia of Protestantism was not the shift from fashion to antifashion but was a change of fashions.

Fashion, we are finally coming to

realize, is ubiquitous and, therefore, unavoidable. As ubiquitous and unavoidable as the sacred once seemed. The return of religion as fashionable becomes possible in a time when fashion has become a religion. Perhaps the current religious revival actually completes the death of God by sacralizing the image. Can we any longer claim with confidence that a priest's robe is any less fashionable than Madonna's bra? Or are we any longer sure that the priest's crucifixes are any more religious than Madonna's crosses? Isn't fashion always something of a religion and religion always somehow fashionable?

had long argued for the simple cut, the pure line, and the reduction of ornament as part of the general argument about function (and the related discourse on hygiene and exercise) that formed the basis of their position. The virtues of the clean white surface had, of course, first been elaborated in the realm of dress." As early as the late nineteenth century, followers of William Morris's Arts and Crafts movement organized the Rational Dress Society (1881) and Healthy and Artistic Dress Union (1890). A decade later, at the same time that Freud's

Interpretation of Dreams appeared, Henry van de Velde, as Wigley points out, published *Die künstlerische Hebung der Frauen-tracht* (*The Artistic Improvement of Women's Dress*), in which he maintains that "clothing designers, like all other industrial artists, can successfully resist the degenerate forces of fashion." Convinced that a common principle should underlie clothing and architecture, van de Velde argues

that the rule of logic that preceded the rule of fashion in all the arts, and that should be restored, is "the beauty of the skeleton (*Gerüst*)" that "is these days so hidden, so covered over with wandering, unfitting and fantastic decorations, that it is truly a labor to detect it." This skeleton is always understood as that of a building. Fashion, then, is no more than the complete burial of the underlying skeleton by an irrational façade, "highly illogical constructions that, without a visible skeleton, allow a cloud of bows, puffs, flounces, and pleats to run amuck over all the contours of the body, and reconfigure it to an unformed mass of flesh, which doesn't permit the least inkling of the proportions of limbs and joints, and in which the beauty of the human figure has been completely lost."

Wearing Thin

Fashion once again is wearing thin. It's not about lite clothing but fading bodies. As models have followed designers by emerging from anonymity to celebrity, fashion has become as much a matter of stylish bodies as of styled apparel. For the past several seasons, runways have been dominated by megamodels like Cindy Crawford, Naomi Campbell, and Christy Turlington whose presence is unmistakable. But recently things have been changing. In place of Cindy, Naomi, and Christy, we now have Claudia Mason, Lucie de La Falaise, Amber Valletta, and, above all others, model-of-the-moment Kate Moss, upon whose fragile body Calvin Klein has hung his future.

"The smaller and thinner, the better to heap on more clothes," Klein confidently declares. It seems we have been down this road before. In the 1960s, Twiggy "was a shocking sidetrack from the womanly, fully packed models of the day. Bert Stern, one of *Vogue*'s photographers, was practically a solo voice in a forest of negatives. 'She's perfectly pure and clear, like fresh water,' he gushed. Twiggy's tiny teeth had chomped into the notion of conventional beauty. Her minimal hair and her major makeup were copied; her figureless figure launched a glut of madly dieting wanna-bes."

But like, like fat, is not always the same. There are different kinds of fat and thin and to confuse them is to miss their point. Twiggy's slender figure appears to be virtually sexless. "In the 1960s, it was indeed more comfortable to think of Twiggy as a childlike woman without a sexual history, as if her thinness made her neuter. It was widely and approvingly reported that she slept with teddy bears." Twiggy seemed familiar and reassuring.

The longer you stare at Kate Moss, the less like Twiggy she appears. Gazing back at us from resolutely black-and-white ads, slight Kate does not look familiar and reassuring but hauntingly ghostlike. Her body is unreal, ethereal, even illusory. It is as if "madly dieting wanna-bes" had become gaunt anorexics. Moreover, anorexic bodies seem to reflect an anorexic culture that is obsessed with fat and intent on becoming lean even if not always mean. It is not merely clothing that has become transparent; the body itself is rapidly becoming immaterial. A latter-day ascetic worshipping a God that no longer appears, Kate Moss transforms herself into skin and bones — nothing but skin and bones. Hers is an inner "beauty" that is finally indistinguishable from death.

Never skin-deep, such beauty is a matter of bones. In ways that will become increasingly apparent in what follows, eros and thanatos meet in the "unformed mass of flesh" and "beauty of the skeleton." Paradoxically, the only way to achieve liberation from the woes of the flesh is through greater control of the body and its supplements. To restore psychosocial order, desire must be disciplined by regulating fashion.

Though critical of van de Velde's promotion of art nouveau in architecture, Loos strongly endorses the "structural principle" according to which form is privileged over ornament. While Loos tends to identify fashion with useless ornamentation that must be removed, a careful consideration of his arguments suggests that he actually calls for the reform rather than the elimination of fashion. What is at issue is not the struggle between fashion and antifashion but a contest between alternative fashions. If civilization is to prosper, "ladies' fashion" must be replaced by "men's fashion." This evolution of fashion reflects the sublimation of desire. As feminine fashion gives way to masculine, desire is simultaneously sublimated and repressed. The movement from ornament to form is marked by the "progress" from sensation to reason, materiality to immateriality, and sensual to Platonic love.

> A great and constant tendency has characterized the last hundred years.... The most important, whose end is still by no means in sight, and, because it emanates from England, is thereby the strongest, is the persuasion invented by the refined Greeks: Platonic love. The woman may be no more than a good friend to man. This tendency too has been taken into account; it has led to the creation of the "tailor-made costume," clothes made by the man's tailor. But in that class of society in which the woman's aristocratic blood is also taken into consideration, in the high nobility where the woman's birth is a factor after many generations, one can discern an emancipation from the prevailing ladies' fashions in which homage is also paid to outward elegance. People thus never cease to wonder at the simplicity that prevails among the aristocracy.

Whereas women's fashion is artificial, frivolous, idiosyncratic, sensuous, and useless, men's fashion is natural, serious, universal, reasonable, and functional. Fashion is most civilized, Loos argues, when it is least obvious: "To be dressed correctly! I feel as if I have revealed in these words the secret that has surrounded the fashion of our clothes up to now. We have tried to get at fashion with words like 'beautiful,' 'stylish,' 'elegant,' 'smart,' and 'strong.' But this is not the point. Rather, it is a question of being dressed *in such a way that one stands out the least.*" That which stands out least is either common or universal. Refined fashion is neither idiosyncratic nor ostentatious but standardized or uniform.

This preference for the uniform both presupposes and subverts the architectural structure of every unfashionable treatment of fashion. Loos consistently dismisses the artificial, frivolous, idiosyncratic, sensuous, and useless (i.e., the feminine) and embraces the natural, serious, universal, reasonable, and functional (i.e., the masculine). At first glance, Loos's principle of uniformity seems to anticipate Ozenfant's and Le Corbusier's desire to capture "the Universal and Permanent and to throw to the dogs the Vacillating and the Fashionable." But Loos admits what other modernists refuse to acknowledge: the uniform is undeniably fashionable. Loos, in other words, does not pose an opposition between fashion and antifashion but stages a contest between competing fashions. The removal of ornament is not the negation of fashion but the affirmation of a new fashion. Since everything is always already fashioned, all fashioning is refashioning. One can no more escape fashion than one can flee time, because fashion is the indelible mark of our temporality.

Loos did not fully appreciate the far-reaching implications of his analysis of fashion for the theory and practice of modern architecture. Nor did he realize that his recognition of the inescapability of fashion creates the possibility of formulating

Transparen

a fashionable approach to fashion. To unfold the implications of Loos's arguments, we must turn to the fashionably unfashionable bare façades, white surfaces, and transparent walls of modern architecture.

Le Corbusier is preoccupied with surface – naked, clean, smooth,pure surface. On the face of it, this virtual fixation on surface appears to stand in tension with his critique of fleeting fashions and ceaseless search for universal structures and eternal essences. Summarizing the course of his work up to 1929, he writes: "As I believe profoundly in our age, I continue to analyze the elements that are determining its character and do not confine myself to trying to make its exterior manifestations comprehensible. What I seek to fathom is its deeper, its constructive sense. Is not this the essence, the very purpose of architecture? Differences in styles, trivialities [*frivolités*] of passing fashion, which are only illusions or masquerades, do not concern me." The depth that Le Corbusier seeks to fathom is, however, superficial. His effort to free himself from illusions and masquerades by turning

Just when you thought you had seen it all, you discover that you ain't seen nothin.

But now it seems nothing is on display everywhere. Fashion has become utterly transparent. Unwilling to let his provocative designs speak for themselves, Karl Lagerfeld gleefully declares: "Possy is in!"

away from "the trivialities of passing fashion" does not lead to a rejection of the importance of surface. To the contrary, in Le Corbusier's architecture, *surface is essential.* In a section of his manifesto, which arguably launched modern architecture, entitled "Surface," Le Corbusier declares: "Architecture, being the masterly, correct and magnificent play of masses brought together in light, the task of architecture is to vitalize the surfaces which clothe these masses but in such a way that these surfaces do not become parasitical, eating up the mass and absorbing it to their own advantage: the sad story of our present-day work." This association of surface with clothing borrows a distinction between clothes and fashion that was commonplace among fashion critics of the time. Though clothing is obviously necessary, fashion, many argued, it is not essential and thus is excessive, extravagant, and useless. But Loos's exposure of the fashionableness of antifashion implies

"On both continents, at every show, models walked the runways virtually undressed below the waist. There were transparent pants, skirts with no fronts, G-strings, briefs, nothing at all. Designers have been using sheer fabrics for several seasons, but this time the underlayers were lifted, and the clothes, particularly the once-practical pair of pants, all but disappeared. At Mizrahi the show-finale bride became a divorcée in pants so sheer they looked like Saran Wrap with sparkles, and at Gaultier the pants weren't just sheer, they were shredded. For Fendi, Lagerfeld wove string trousers so loosely you could stick your fist through them, but for his own collection he topped himself with 'pool skirts' of clear plastic inner tubes."

Are these guys kidding? Surely they jest even more than the ever-didactic Robert Altman. Yet the designers are serious – deadly serious. When Saran Wrap becomes a film that overexposes, it is impossible to know whether art is imitating life or life is imitating art. The parading of nude models in the concluding scene of *Prêt-à-Porter* repeats a criticism that is as old as fashion itself: fashion, Altman suggests, is much ado about nothing. This season it has

become all too clear that designers have finally concluded that it is hopeless to resist such charges, and so they are embracing the criticism by taking it literally. "You say fashion doesn't matter – that it's nothin? We'll show you what matters and doesn't matter. In fact, we'll show you nothin. And we'll even make you pay for it!" As fashion becomes transparent, clothes cease to matter. Like so much else that once made up the fabric of our lives, fashion has become immaterial.

Or has it? Perhaps as the scene shifts to the ob-scene, fashion actually becomes more deeply etched into our lives than ever before. Strip away layer after fashionable layer and you discover not an unadorned body but a body that has become fashionable. With virtually everyone strapped to exercise machines that future generations of archeologists will surely see as direct descendants of medieval torture devices, it should be obvious that the body is no more natural than the clothes it wears. But we resist this conclusion because we desperately want to believe that there is something that is not fashion. Cunning designers, however, won't let us off the hook. Their free or not-so-free admission that fashion is immaterial leads to the transparent conclusion that the immaterial is inescapable.

that this opposition finally collapses. In the modern era, clothes are always fashionable, even, perhaps especially, when they are trying not to be so.

The surfaces that absorb Le Corbusier are not merely essential; they are consuming, or more precisely, all-consuming. Surfaces and consumption are inseparable. In an effort to overturn the long-standing hierarchy that subordinates surface to substance, Le Corbusier insists that surface is not "parasitical."

Rather than a parasite that feeds on the body of mass or mass of the body, surface consumes bodily mass, thereby rendering substance superficial. Far from insign-ificant clothing for essential structures, surfaces actually constitute the masses they appear to adorn. *"A mass,"* Le Corbusier maintains, *"is enveloped in its surface, a surface that is divided up according to the directing and generating lines of the mass; and this gives the mass its individuality."*

What's In?

PRADA

We should have seen it coming!

As soon as Madonna and her troupe burst on stage and screen in their undies and Gaultier cone bras, it was inevitable that Victoria's Secret would be told. As if to imitate one of our era's most notorious imitators, the fashion world seems intent on rewinding and replaying the spectacle of *Truth or Dare*.

On the runway this spring, everything has been turned inside out and outside in. "Lingerie," reports Vogue's Paul Rudnick, "has busted out of the boudoir and into the ballroom." "Everyone is experimenting with frothy near nudity: Geoffrey Beene has shown countless gowns with spiraling panels of net, panels that do not allow for any undergarments whatsoever; if Givenchy sketched with Audrey Hepburn in mind, Geoffrey has clearly been fixating on Dolly Parton. Bill Blass has offered hip-baring parfaits of sheerest Chantilly swirled in gauze, as if demonstrating how to gift wrap a centerfold. Azzendine Alaïa, once enslaved to second-skin knits, has just rediscovered the white Swiss eyelet of Victoria's Secret camisoles. Even the ordinarily practical-minded Donna Karan has paraded models with both jacket and blouse unbuttoned and gaping, highlighting a triple strand of pearls and a peeka-boo bra, an ensemble presumably intended to cement respect in the workplace. What's next, Donna – carelessly unzipped flies or charmeuse halters worn nonchalantly tucked into control-top panty hose?"

Why this compulsion for self-exposure? It is easy, all too easy, to see the lingerie craze as yet another example of fashion's insatiable need to push the envelope with designs that are evermore outrageous. But something else is going on (or coming off) here. Stepping Out's Alvin Brass suggests

When surfaces become consuming, the ground of architecture, as well as everything else, not only shifts but, in a certain sense, disappears. It was left for Theo van Doesburg, Mondrian's erstwhile colleague and cofounder of de Stijl, to draw the consequences of the switch from ground to surface: "Man does not live within the construction, within the architectural skeleton, but only touches architecture essentially through its ultimate surface.... The functional element becomes automatic, only the summarizing surface is of importance, for sensory perception as well as for psychological well-being. It has an impact on the morale of the inhabitant.... Houses are like people. Their features, posture, gait, clothing, in short: their surface, is a reflection of their thinking, their inner life." When inner becomes outer in superficial display, surface is rendered transparent.

Transparency is not merely an artistic or architectural effect

that "provocative designs that turn everything inside out and outside in are well-suited to a world in which radio and TV talk shows and tabloid journalism are erasing the boundaries that once separated the public and the private. Everyone's dirty and not-so-dirty laundry now is hung out for all to inspect."

What is remarkable about all of this is the lack of resistance to such overexposure. Instead of evading probing private eyes, people, eager for their fifteen minutes of fame, are willing to bare more than their souls. Nothing, it seems, remains unspoken or unspeakable. It is as if

secrets had become crimes against humanity; everything not only can but must be told. When all is said (and done), Victoria's secret is that she has no secrets. Like the guests of Oprah, Phil, Geraldo, and Sally, she will show and tell all. There is an obscenity in all of this that is more than a matter of sex.

What's next, Mr. Rudnick? The answer is obvious – as obvious as the clothes on your back(side): total exposure, which is, of course, the end of fashion. After *Truth or Dare*...Sex: S/M in a full-metal jacket.

What's out?

but a modernist ideal that assumes the force of a psychological, social, and cultural imperative. Commenting on the modern philosopher par excellence, Kierkegaard writes: "The Hegelian philosophy assumes no justified hiddenness, no justified incommensurability. It is, then, consistent for it to demand disclosure." The demand for disclosure – total disclosure – is the demand to say and show (the) all. Glass façades that reveal everything by showing nothing represent one of the most telling responses to this demand for transparency.

Modern architecture is, of course, unthinkable apart from the curtain wall. When technological developments made it possible to separate skin from skeleton, architecture was freed to become superficial. Reflections on the glass wall disclose a reconfiguration of foundational polarities like exteriority/interiority and surface/depth. As Le Corbusier suggests, once surface is liberated, it quickly becomes all-consuming. If nothing separates inside from outside, skeleton and skin converge; there is no longer anything to hide because nothing remains but hides and skins. Just as the bodily skeleton is actually epidural, so ostensible infrastructure turns out to be involuted suprastructure. The utter transparency of inner and outer betrays the superficiality of depth and the profundity of surface.

When surface consumes depth, everything is turned inside out. Once regarded as essential, structure now appears to be as fashionable as ornamental façades. In what Baudrillard labels "*l'effet beaubourg*," essential structure is transposed into supplemental artifice. This reinscription of form as ornament is not merely the inversion of a classical binary but a subversion of the hierarchical structure that all previous architecture presupposes. In this subversive moment, the modern begins to slip into the postmodern. To trace this slippage, it is necessary to follow other threads that bind fashion, surfaces, and consumption to naked skins and diaphanous walls.

Fashion and modernity, we have discovered, intersect in the moment, which is always "just now." While resisting the timeliness of fashion, modern architects nonetheless remain devoted to erasing the past by constructing bare walls dedicated to the present. If to be modern is to be of the present – always of the present – then modernity must be as committed to planned obsolescence as fashion is. Since the new is old as soon as it appears, it is necessary to renew it constantly through a process in which repetition becomes a virtual compulsion.

Planned obsolescence is, of course, not simply an artistic tactic and fashionable strategy but a sociocultural practice without which the modern economy cannot function. Never simply a question of style, the modernity of fashion is also a matter of economics. The modern economy needs fashion as much as fashion needs the modern economy. Fashion sensu strictissimo does not actually emerge until the middle of the fourteenth century. In earlier societies, costumes were regulated by standards and norms that remained relatively constant over long periods of time. The preservation of a reliably recognizable past took precedence over the invention of a radically new present. For centuries, the commitment to sartorial tradition tended to provide personal and social stability as well as historical continuity. But during the late Middle Ages all of this changed. As a mercantile economy concentrated in towns and cities gradually displaced an agrarian economy centered in feudal estates, the rudiments of a market society began to take shape. Newly developed manufacturing processes and trade practices brought with them a money economy based on surplus production and the free exchange of goods. The circulation of wealth was accompanied by a growing social mobility that threatened the hierarchical structure of feudalism. The distinguishing mark of newly won mobility was fashion. As Stuart Ewen points out:

> Fueled by their desire for franchise and status, the merchant class mimicked and appropriated consumption practices of the nobility. Commercial activity made luxurious items more readily available than before and provided prosperous merchants the wherewithal to acquire them. Although the merchants' fortunes were a product of commercial enterprise, their consumption patterns were designed to obtain the imagistic trappings of landed heritage. The results of this tendency characterized – to a large extent – the genesis of the bourgeois ideal of style on into the nineteenth century. *Conspicuous consumption*, as Thorstein Veblen would name it, was the mark of status. In a world where nobility still ruled, the merchant class seized upon symbols of excess which had customarily been prerogatives of landed elites.

Established powers were quick to realize the explosive social and political implications of changing fashions. To preserve waning power, representatives of the feudal order initiated a series of sumptuary laws. By regulating dress, they hoped to avoid economic, social, and political revolution. As late as 1530 the town of Augsburg adopted a law according to which "only princes, knights and their ladies were permitted to wear brocade" and "velvet garments were for patricians." "Upper bourgeoisie" were permitted "three ellens of velvet to decorate their headdresses." But such regulatory efforts were doomed to fail; the tide of change could not be stemmed. Once released, market forces rapidly became as all-consuming as fashionable images fabricated to promote the modern economy.

Markets, of course, thrive only when they expand. During the early stages of market capitalism, demand within Europe was sufficient to fuel constant growth. But as industrialism steadily extended its reach, new resources and markets had to be found. The transition from market to monopoly capitalism went hand-in-hand with the emergence of colonialism and imperialism. As empires grew, new markets for exported manufactured goods were created, and a steady flow of foreign luxury items returned to Europe. In many circles of high society, the more "exotic" something was, the more fashionable it seemed. But geographic expansion has limits. With the passing of the age of empire, new ways of ensuring economic growth had to be created. By the beginning of the twentieth century, it had become obvious that strategies that had worked in previous stages of capitalism were no longer effective. In their early phases, industrialism and the market were able to thrive by manufacturing and distributing products that met human needs. As more and more people acquired needed commodities, demand inevitably declined and markets weakened. With little or no outward expansion, inward growth became the only viable alternative. If people bought no more than they needed, the economy inevitably would falter. The challenge industry faced was to create desire where there was no need. Masses of people had to be made to want what was unnecessary, excessive, extravagant, frivolous, and impractical. It became an economic necessity to make fashion desirable. In a circle that borders on the vicious, the market creates fashion, which, in turn, creates the market.

In fulfilling its mission of reviving a sagging economy, the fashion industry received a boost from a seemingly unlikely ally: modern art. Modernism, as we have seen, is defined by its thoroughgoing commitment to the new or, more precisely, to an endless process of renewal. Since the new must always be renewed, something like planned obsolescence in art is unavoidable. What the avant-garde promotes as an aesthetic ideal that often seems utterly impractical is, for industry and the modern economy, not only practical but actually necessary. If the market were to flourish, the excessive would have to be indispensable, the frivolous essential, and the useless useful. This is not to suggest that the lines joining the avant-garde and the market are clear or direct. To the contrary, most innovative modern art struggles to escape or subvert market forces. But the market has extraordinary recuperative powers, which enable it to incorporate opposition and turn resistance to its own ends. Through unexpected reversals, the nonfunctional becomes functional and the useless becomes useful. This process of incorporation does not leave what is appropriated unchanged. As artistic resistance is translated into economic promotion, high art is popularized and commodified, and commodities are aestheticized. These developments signal the shift from industrial to postindustrial capitalism and the accompanying transition from modernism to postmodernism.

Such changes, however, were deferred for almost half a century while the industrialized world found an alternative "solution" to its economic woes: world war. It has become commonplace to insist that the First World War was the first modern war. Industrialism and its mechanical reasoning provided not only the motivation but also the means for conducting war on a scale that eventually became global. While the First and Second World Wars inflicted unprecedented suffering and economic hardship, they also enabled industrialism to survive the collapse of empire. New needs created new demands that kept factories running overtime and maintained a high rate of employment. But this solution was temporary and only served to hide the long-term problems plaguing the industrial economy.

While many modernists were horrified by Europe's catastrophic collapse into barbarism, some realized that industrialism, militarism, and modernism share a common logic. Far from a reversion to primitivism, modern warfare, enthusiasts argued, is a sign of the technological prowess of advanced industrial civilization. No one made this argument more forcefully than the Italian futurist Filippo Marinetti, who, in 1909, wrote in his First Futurist Manifesto:

> We affirm that the world's magnificence has been enriched by a new beauty; the beauty of speed. A racing car whose hood is adorned by great pipes, like serpents of explosive breath – a roaring car that seems to run on shrapnel – is more beautiful than the Victory of Samothrace.
>
> We will glorify war – the world's only hygiene....
>
> We will sing of great crowds excited by work, by pleasure, and by riot; we will sing of the multicolored, polyphonic tides of revolution in the modern capitals.

For Marinetti, the mark of modernity is speed. Claims of efficiency and functionalism notwithstanding, speed becomes an end in itself. In Marinetti's prescient vision, the quick inherit the earth.

While not everyone appreciated Marinetti's glorification of war, many modern artists, architects, and designers were religiously devoted to the machine aesthetic and the logic of industrialism. Furthermore, they were all committed to the new and thus to change. Though not immediately obvious, the veneration of speed is actually an extension of the avant-garde's long-standing dedication to innovation. As speed increases, the rate of obsolescence accelerates. Speed, in other words, is as good for the economy as it is for art. In this way, art directly and indirectly promotes industry as much as industry directly and indirectly supports art.

It is apparent, however, that the First World War also had darker economic consequences. When the war stopped, demand disappeared and factories as well as their workers fell idle. The solution to the problems created by the Great Depression was another world war. But this cycle of war-depression-war could not go on forever. Other ways to keep factories operating and people working had to be found. In the years immediately following the end of the Second World War, two closely related courses that have had lasting social, political, and economic consequences were charted. First, the alliance between industry and the military was solidified through the formation of the military-industrial complex. The emergence of the Cold War provided the rationale for sustaining a state of military preparedness for a war that, with the advent of nuclear weapons, could never be fought. With government support, the defense industry played a vital role in sustaining the nation's industrial "infrastructure." In addition to this, government-sponsored research in electronic and information technologies, initially intended for military use, laid the foundation for what eventually would become a postindustrial economy. Second, and more important in this context, consumer capitalism emerged on an unprecedented scale. While maintaining a high level of employment, the war managed to create new markets at home and abroad. On the home front, the war resulted in the accumulation of personal financial resources and generated an enormous pent-up demand. Though people had worked hard for many years, the range of products available for purchase was quite limited. When the war was over, demand exploded, creating what Thomas Hine correctly describes as "an orgy of consumption." The high level of demand helped to make the transition from a wartime to a peacetime economy relatively smooth. With mortgage-toting men home from the war and women liberated from workshops and factories, the housing industry went into high gear, and cars, household appliances, and other "necessities" could not be produced fast enough. By the early 1950s, demand had leveled off, and once again strategies for creating new markets and reviving old ones had to be fashioned. Reversing the tides of colonialism, American business invaded Europe. The devastation of Europe provided extraordinary economic opportunities for the United States. By helping to rebuild Europe, the American government was creating new markets for an economy that always needed to expand. In the postwar period, American culture and products virtually colonized Europe.

The economic situation within the United States was somewhat more complex. "The turning point," Hine explains,

> came in 1954, an eventful year by any standard. It brought not only the downfall of McCarthy and the momentous Supreme Court decision outlawing segregated schools but also the introduction of sleek, powerful, and finny low-priced cars and the emergence of a sexy, urgent new kind of popular music – rock and roll. Some 1.5 million new homes were built that year, the great majority of them outside the central cities; 1.4 million power lawn mowers were sold and 4 million babies were born. It was a year in which Americans began to feel less threatened by Communism, and more anxious to enjoy the fruits of American affluence. And it was also a year in which major corporations changed their marketing strategies in order to induce people to spend their increasing incomes.

The means by which people were encouraged to buy what they did not need was advertising. Once incited, desire can fuel the growth of the economy by becoming as excessive as the luxuries for which it longs. The task of advertising is to engender desire through a constant display of the new. The yearning for the new is, as we have seen, a longing for the fleeting, provisional, and ephemeral. The person who wants to be up to date must travel light; this year's model is passé as soon as it is purchased. Products are not made to last but are designed to be as disposable as the income with which they are purchased. In consumer culture, *everything* becomes provisional.

Inasmuch as the new is the fashionable, the advertising industry always promotes fashion even when it seems to be selling something else. In the society of spectacle, fashion is mediated by multiple media ranging from print to cinematic, telematic, video, and electronic images. While consumer society never would have prospered without fashion, fashion has been altered by the speculative society it helped to create. The most significant transformation of fashion in the postwar period was the relative decline of haute couture and ascent of prêt-à-porter. When Charles Frederick Worth established his own Parisian fashion house in 1857–58, he began what eventually became known as haute couture. It took another half century for the fashion industry to institute a regular rhythm of seasonal shows for the presentation of new designs. The practice of having two shows a year for the introduction of summer and winter collections was not established until after the First World War. In retrospect, haute couture seems to have been created to illustrate Veblen's theory of the trickle-down effect of conspicuous consumption. The social and economic importance of haute couture can be measured less by the number of garments sold than by the influence it exercised on the mass production and consumption of apparel.

This situation changed significantly in the 1960s. "The real revolution that destroyed the architecture of the hundred years' fashion," Gilles Lipovetsky points out, "is the one that overturned the logic of industrial production. This revolution corresponds to the emergence and development of what Americans were the first to call *ready-to-wear*....Unlike traditional manufacturing, ready-to-wear committed itself to a new path: an industrial production of clothing accessible to all that would nevertheless be 'fashion,' inspired by the latest trends of the day. Whereas manufactured apparel was often

*Dis*dressing

For a fashion industry in desperate search of renewal, the motto of the moment seems to be, When in doubt, appropriate! Appropriate not only other designs, eras, and cultures but above (or below) all, appropriate the street.

"Grungemania has captivated the short attention span of today's trendsetters." Word sent down from on high proclaims that haute is no longer quite so haute. Low has become high and dressing down is dressing up. "As the fin de siècle draws near, greed has gone to seed. What started out as a serfs' rebellion against aristocratic glamour has turned into a fashion revolution that champions 'revolting' for its own sake. It's pop culture through the looking glass; everything old is new, everything modern is passé, and that hideous 'glam rock' getup Mom snuck from her attic to the thrift shop has reappeared in an uptown boutique. It'll cost you a week's wage to get it back. What started out as irrelevant trend bucking is now a buck-making trend. Flannels, ratty tour shirts, boots, and baseball caps have become a uniform for those in the know, and their legions are growing."

Though it is not clear where all of this is heading, it is obvious where it all began. As so often in recent years, fashion is again following trends set in the music world. This time the scene is Seattle. "Spawned in dilapidated rock clubs and nurtured to health by intoxicated fans, the grunge phenomenon started as one city's reaction to the elitist eighties. The aesthetics that govern the moment have roots in urban bohemianism and in slacker-era schleppiness. Wary of the prissy pretension that reigned unchecked, frustrated students and minimum-wage slaves banded together and created a lifestyle, ever cynical and utilitarian, that more accurately reflected their conditions. The emphasis was on well-worn comfort, cheap beer, and high-volume rock'n'roll."

As the vibes of grunge spread from Seattle to New York and beyond to Paris, its tune was changed by crafty promoters who are turning the fashion world on its head through the transformation of trickle-down design strategies into bubble-up design strategies. Long considered unfashionable, the street now inspires much of what used to be considered haute

characterized by defective cuts, careless finishing, poor quality, and a lack of imagination, ready-to-wear sought to blend industry and fashion; it sought to put novelty, style, and aesthetics on the streets." In 1968, when Yves Saint-Laurent declared, "Down with the Ritz; long live the street!" the revolution was effectively complete. The shift from haute couture to prêt-à-porter signals a switch in the direction of the current that determines fashion from high to low (top-down) to low to high (bottom-up). Hardly a simple inversion, this change subverts the very distinction between high and low. As high becomes low and low becomes high, the only fashion that remains is the fashion of the street, which is neither high nor low.

In order to appreciate the far-reaching implications of these developments, it is helpful to place them in the context of changes that were occurring at the same time in the art world. As we have seen, the machine aesthetic, which both reflects

couture. This reversal, as Christian Lacroix realizes, is not without its problems. "I think that we are tired of 'salon' fashion, of 'ivory tower' fashion, opines the couturier who gave us the pouf. 'Even for the couture we need the impact of real life, because if you keep couture in the windows and in the museums, you will kill it. You need to have the impulse and the energy of the street.' On the other hand, cautions Lacroix, 'we have to be very, very, very careful not to do expensive fashion based on the problems of other people even if, and it's terrible to say, very often the most exciting outfits are from the poorest people.' The subject is on the designer's mind because he's just seen the January Comme des Garçons show, which he 'loved' but found unsettling. 'They looked exactly like the homeless. It's exactly the same: The poor guy sleeping in a cardboard box on the street and the guy on the runway this weekend clad exactly the same. That's very disturbing.'"

Disturbing indeed! Grunge dresses for $840, skirts for $490, sweaters for $1,400, suspenders for $140, oversized jeans for $620, and backpacks for $1,400.

The worn look has been around for some time. Ever since Ralph Lauren spread his glowing patina everywhere and Levi Strauss started acid- and stone-washing everything, the old has been declared new. Now worn is giving way to torn. Jeans are not just faded but are ripped and even blown full of holes with shotguns. Dresses and blouses are shredded, leaving frayed fringes to unravel.

The recent fascination with the street grew out of the social upheavals of the 1960s. In 1968, Yves Saint-Laurent disingenuously proclaimed solidarity with rebelling students by brazenly announcing: "Down with the Ritz; long live the street." But the street of Saint-Laurent and the street of students were heading in opposite directions. For the generation of '68, the commitment to antifashion expressed social concerns that grew out of deeply felt criticisms of the abuses of Western political and economic power so vividly displayed in the Vietnam War. The hippies of the counterculture had style and their style was protest. As the sixties gave way to the seventies, cynicism and nihilism replaced social idealism and activism. Not only the times but also the styles, they were a changin. With the harsh electric sounds of punk drowning out the gentle guitars

and promotes industrialism, privileges form and function over ornament and decoration. From this perspective, ostensibly useless embellishment is not only aesthetically inferior but is socially irresponsible and culturally retrograde. Everything that is so-called high or advanced is unabashedly elitist and strictly formal or abstract. In his classic 1939 essay "Avant-Garde and Kitsch," Clement Greenberg argues: "Where there is an avant-garde, generally we also find a rear-guard. True enough – simultaneously with the entrance of the avant garde, a second new cultural phenomenon appeared in the industrial West: the thing to which the Germans give the wonderful name Kitsch: popular, commercial art and literature with their chromeotypes, magazine covers, illustrations, ads, slick and pulp fiction, comics, Tin Pan Alley music, tap dancing, Hollywood movies, etc., etc." Greenberg's entire aesthetic is structured around oppositions like authentic/fake, genuine/

and soft voices of folk, dyed-and-spiked hair, leather, and safety pins replaced tie-dyed T-shirts, fringed skirts, and flowers. The styles changed, and the protests grew ever louder and became more pointless. Increasing defiance signaled deepening despair. When the promise of nirvana eventually ended in the death of Nirvana, one cycle had run its course and another was ready to begin.

The hippie sixties, punk seventies, and grunge eighties have become the prefabricated styles that are making headlines in the nineties.

Hippie Heaven	Punk Rocks Again	Grunge & Glory
We're heading into what promises to be a fall and winter of love, bedecked in designer bell-bottoms, peace symbols, tie-dye and beads. Eve Babitz remembers hippies then – to try to fathom hippies now.	*Safety pins, shocking pink hair, plastic jeans – punk trappings are popping up everywhere from shopping malls to couture runways, finds Janet Siroto*	*It's broken out of the clubs, garages, and thrift shops of Seattle to dominate rock radio, MTV, and the aspirations of kids all across the America. Jonathan Poneman, whose record label SubPop first signed some of the scene's seminal bands, examines the triumph of grunge, and Steven Meisel captures its impact on fashion in the repentant '90s*

counterfeit, difficult/easy, handmade/mechanically produced, original/ derivative, abstract/figurative, high/low, and elite/ popular. For Greenberg, these categories are both descriptive and prescriptive: "Kitsch, using for raw material the debased and academicized simulacra of genuine culture, welcomes and cultivates this insensibility. It is the source of its profits. Kitsch is mechanical and operates by formulas. Kitsch is vicarious experience and faked sensations. Kitsch changes according to style, but remains always the same. Kitsch is the epitome of all that is spurious in the life of our times. Kitsch pretends to demand nothing of its customers except their money – not even their time." Rarely has a critic exercised as much influence as Greenberg over the production as well as the interpretation of art. From Jackson Pollock and Barnett Newman to Mark Rothko and Ad Reinhardt, Greenberg's theories overtly and covertly contributed to the art they theorize.

Repentant nineties? Repentant of what? Protest, it would seem. But repentance hardly appears necessary because protest no longer seems possible. What's a poor kid to do when his in-your-face T-shirt appears in a boutique window before he reaches the end of St. Mark's Place? In today's world of fashion, signs of protest are immediately appropriated by the very systems they are designed to resist. Our situation once again is reminiscent of the 1960s. Just as Andy Warhol once claimed to be subverting the hierarchy between elite and popular art but ended by making the popular elite, so today's designers declare a revolution by turning from avenue to street or boulevard to rue but end by trickling down what had bubbled up.

The rapid transformation of antifashion into fashion is a ruse that defuses resistance. The strength of any system is directly proportional to its capacity to assimilate that which resists it in such a way that apparent opposition is turned to its own advantage. When measured by this standard, the power of the fashion system – if fashion is a system – seems to know no bounds. The repeated failure of resistance is what remains so distressing about disdressing.

Within Greenberg's hermeneutical circle, the only art worthy of the name is abstract.

The next generation of painters attempted to break free from the strictures of abstract expressionism by soliciting a return of what Greenberg and his followers deliberately repressed. Turning from "high" to "low," pop art valorizes precisely what abstraction avoids: the fake, counterfeit, mechanical, derivative, figurative, and, most important, popular consumer culture. Pop art extends the avant-garde's ceaseless search for the new by rejecting the elimination of figure and defiantly embracing kitsch. Having started their careers as commercial artists, window designers, and advertisers, Robert Rauschenberg and Andy Warhol refuse to distinguish "advanced" art from popular culture. Warhol freely acknowledges the inevitable commercialization of art and, with characteristic irony, insists that business has become the prevailing

*In*Vestments

MONEY IS THE MOMENT

*Appeared in a dress made
of gold cards.*

LOS ANGELES (March 28, 1995) – "Money," Andy Warhol once announced, "is the MOMENT to me." Though always associated in the world of fashion, money and the moment were joined dramatically at last night's Academy Awards. Accepting the Oscar for best costume design, which she received for work in *The Adventures of Priscilla, Queen of the Desert*, Lizzy Gardiner appeared in a dress made of American Express gold cards.

"'I was looking for an American symbol,' said Miss Gardiner in a telephone interview from Los Angeles, where she recently migrated from Australia. 'A Coca-Cola bottle or a Mickey Mouse would have been ridiculous, doing anything with the American flag would have been insulting and Cadillac hubcaps were just too uncomfortable.'

"An added bonus: the cards matched her Oscar.

"The inspiration for the dress actually came to her when she was designing costumes for the film, but American Express would not agree to give her the cards she needed, she said, adding, 'It was a small Australian film, and they really did not want to be

involved, and I didn't really blame them.'

"Two weeks before the awards ceremony, when she realized that she needed something to wear, she appealed again to the company, to send her 300 cards. She and Salvadore Perez, a Los Angeles designer, whipped the whole thing together in about 12 hours.

"'It was her idea and we made it happen,' said Maureen Bailey, a spokeswoman for American Express. 'We feel so happy that every time she uses American Express now, she'll remember this great moment.'"

A great moment for sure! But what makes this moment – or perhaps any other moment – great is that it cannot be repeated. It is

artistic style: "Business art is the step that comes after Art." To underscore the close affiliation of modernity, money, and art, he boldly declares: "Money is the MOMENT to me." In a series of works, Warhol translated money into art and art into money by rendering money in images, which were commercially very successful. In postwar consumer culture, Warhol's art became the currency of exchange.

Anticipating Robert Venturi's proclamation that "less is a bore," pop artists revel in figured surfaces. The images decorating their canvases are re-presentations of the images and icons of popular culture. Warhol parodied the modernist infatuation with industrialism and the machine aesthetic by establishing Andy Warhol Enterprises and setting up a studio named The Factory, where he and his assistants created serial silkscreens using production techniques borrowed from the assembly line. Combining the handmade with the mechanically

impossible to imagine Gardiner wearing her dress a second time. The dress is obsolete the moment she steps on stage. No sooner is it in than it is out. The only apparel that can be worn a second time is the apparel that is eminently forgettable. But apparel that is not memorable is not fashionable. Once, only once, never again.

Fashion and money meet in vestments that are momentary. If fashion is to thrive, expenditures must be made without regard to long-term returns on investments. When concerns turn practical and use becomes a value, fashion slows down and the economy becomes sluggish. To invest in fashion is to bet on the present without regard for the future. Live now, pay later. Charge, charge, and recharge it. The charge is the charge that keeps everything and everybody current. It's all so...so American. As expressly American as Coca-Cola, the flag, Mickey Mouse, and Cadillacs.

Gardiner's dress is as much an economics lesson as it is a fashion statement. When money becomes fashionable, she seems to be saying, it is as ephemeral as garments made to be instantly passé. Though infinitely important, money no longer carries the weight it once had. The charge of the card is a flickering flash that is extinguished as quickly as it is lit. Currency is no longer gold or even paper but is plastic or even light. As if mimicking fashion, which is mimicking it, currency has become a current that gives everyone a charge. Money is as lite and immaterial as throwaway dresses made of plastic. Gold has become as plastic as our idols. It's all a matter (or nonmatter) of image. While never delivered directly, the message of the Academy Awards is that image has become our God.

Last night, Gardiner's dress was the in-est vestment in town. For those with eyes to see, her spectacular dress stripped us of our illusions about both Hollywood and ourselves. Even though Lizzy might never use it again, for at least one night she did not have to be reminded that she should never leave home without it.

reproduced, Warhol simultaneously inscribed and erased the auratic mark of originality that traditionally had distinguished high from low art. But even when adopting quasi-industrial methods, Warhol questioned modernist theory and practice. He was one of the first artists to realize that the transition from industrialism to postindustrialism marked the dawning of the electronic media age. The most telling trace of this shift is TV. Warhol realized that, far from being simply another product promoted by consumer capitalism, TV has the capacity to transform our very notion of reality: "Before I was shot, I always thought that I was more half-there than all-there — I always suspected that I was watching TV instead of living life. People sometimes say that the way things happen in the movies is unreal. The movies make emotions look so strong and real, whereas when things really do happen to you, it's like watching

Jeanetic Engineering

SAN FRANCISCO (Nov. 8, 1994) — *"Levi Strauss & Co. today announced the introduction of the Levi's Personal Pair custom-fitted jeans program for women. The program is in limited distribution and is only available at four Original Levi's Stores across the country. 'While we currently make over 170 fits and sizes in our regular line of women's juniors' and petite jeans, we found that there was still a customer who required a very specific fit,' explains Annette Lim, retail marketing services manager for Levi's Only Stores. 'We see these jeans to be targeted to the woman who is discriminating about how her jeans fit or who is just a denim connoisseur in search of the 'ultimate jean.'*

"The Personal Pair jeans program is based on Levi's Jeans for Women tapered-leg jeans that are custom-fitted to the woman's body using a special computer program to assist with the fit and measurement. To participate women must go to be measured at an Original Levi's Store offering the program. Four of the customer's measurements are taken by a trained sales associate: waist, hips, rise, and inseam. These measurements are entered into a computer which generates the number of a prototype trial jean with those measurements. The sales associate retrieves that prototype and the customer tries it on. From here, modifications, as small as one-half an inch, can be made to the jean. Once those modifications are determined, the sales associate inputs the

new measurements into the computer to generate the next prototype for trial. On average, it takes two or three prototypes before a customer is totally satisfied with the fit. Once the customer is satisfied, the coordinates of the final prototype are sent via modem to the LS & Co. factory in Mountain City, TN, where a dedicated team of sewing operators constructs the jeans. In approximately three weeks, the customer can either pick up her jeans at the Original Levi's Store or, for a small extra fee, have them sent directly to her via an express mail service. "Sewn into the waistband of the Personal Pair jeans is a bar code with an individual customer number. This number is kept on computer at the Original Levi's Store to facilitate future orders. Customers can then call the store to

television — you don't feel anything." If, as Warhol insists, "the channels switch, but it's all television," nothing can escape the surface of the screen. But screening is a complex process; to screen is both to display and to conceal. Screening, therefore, is a revealing reveiling and a reveiling revealing through which the image becomes real and the real becomes image. Warhol's appreciation for the power of image led to his fascination with celebrities and constant courting of the media. When art, as well as everything else, is a matter of image, the final work of art is the conversion of oneself into nothing more than image. From his early silk-screened self-portraits to his late self-promotion in videos and the media, Warhol gradually virtualized himself until Andy became "Andy." This pursuit of celebrity status can be understood as performance art adapted to an age in which the media constitute reality. When *l'oeuvre d'art* is

order new colors and finishes. Personal Pair jeans are currently available in stonewashed, bleached, black, white and natural finishes."

According to L. S. Claudel, this most recent stage in Levi Strauss's production and marketing strategy is a logical extension of developments within both the apparel industry and American manufacturing since the late 1960s. "In the '60s," Claudel observes, "jeans moved from the factory to the street to become a fashionable expression of anti-fashion sentiments. While most baby boomers quickly gave up protesting, they were reluctant to give up their jeans." Always quick to recognize the shifting winds of change, fashion designers rushed in to transform the uniformity and anonymity of denim into a seemingly endless variety of

colors and styles. Signs of protest were translated into designer labels. By the 1980s, denim suits, dresses, and even tuxedos had become the rage. The Personal Pair program completes the journey of jeans from the world of low fashion to the world of high fashion by establishing the possibility of the personalized touch on a mass scale.

None of this would have been possible, Claudel points out, without the significant changes in manufacturing processes that have been introduced over the last thirty years. Until the 1960s, large-scale manufacturing involved mass production, which led to the standardization of products. Mass production requires mass consumption, which, in turn, presupposes market uniformity. By the late 1960s,

it was clear that the formula that had led to the postwar economic boom was no longer effective. The domestic market had become saturated with standardized products. Furthermore, changes in population generated markets that were not as uniform as they once had been. To create new demand, different production methods and marketing tactics had to be devised. While the aim of the industrial era had been to foster uniform desires for uniform products, the challenge of the postindustrial economy is to create as well as fulfill diverse desires for different products.

This challenge is being met by interfacing information and manufacturing technologies. "Perhaps the most important change to have taken place since the invention of the assembly

successful, it is impossible to tell where the image (of Andy) ends and the real (Andy) begins. Image both makes up the artistic corpus and consumes the artist's body.

Though the obsession with image is most transparent in the later years of his life, Warhol's awareness of the importance of appearance is evident even in his earliest work. As I have noted, when image reemerges in the wake of abstract impressionism, it returns as a refiguring of images drawn from popular culture. Instead of depicting so-called natural subjects,

objects, and scenes, the task of the artist in the age of electronic reproduction is to reproduce reproductions. The implications of this return of repressed figures can be effectively formulated in semiotic terms. From Rauschenberg and Johns to
Lichtenstein and Warhol, artists produce signs that are signs of
signs. If the sign is always a sign of a sign, it never represents the
thing itself but is a simulacrum that testifies to the imaginary

line," Claudel notes, "is the integration
of data processes at both the input
and output stages of production.
Increasingly sophisticated methods
of information gathering enable us to
discover what people want and to target very specific markets with something like designer advertising. While
most target marketing so far has been
limited to print, the rapid growth of
electronic and televisual media is creating new opportunities. On the output
end of the operation, information technologies are creating flexible, decentralized production networks that can
respond quickly to changing market
conditions."

These developments lead to a
paradoxical situation in which technological innovation makes possible
mass-produced individualized fashion.

In a world where fashion seems to
know no bounds, even jeans become
haute couture. "Look at it this way,"
Claudel suggests. "It's like LS & Co.
has found a way to make genetic engineering fashionable. Just as our uniform genetic code creates unique individuals, so uniform computer code
produces individualized jeans. Since
every program – whether genetic or
jeanetic – can be rewritten, we are not
only designed but are also designers.
Designer jeans for designer kids. This
is a revolution neither Lévi-Strauss nor
Levi Strauss could have anticipated."

status of the original. While Greenberg and abstract expres-
sionists struggle to avoid the fake by creating originals, Warhol
and other pop and postpop artists realize that in a world where
everything is mediaized, originality is an idle dream. On closer
inspection, what is promoted as "genuine culture" always
turns out to be "simulacra of genuine culture." In different
terms, the work of art inevitably refigures what has always
already been figured.

This endless play of appearances brings us back to the

question of fashion in a way that creates the possibility of a fashionable consideration of fashion. Fashion is always in some sense nonsense; it is a matter that is not and does not matter. In its immateriality, fashion remains a matter of facing. Every attempt to fashion is an effort to save face by repeatedly facing reality. Facing reality, however, is never simple, for every face turns out to be an interface that falls between opposites

Making It Up

The face is opaque – seductively opaque. It is covered with a translucent layer that can easily be peeled away to reveal the presence of the face proper. The revealing veil is not flawless but is marked with writing:

Now, lift away the dull, dry surface of your skin and uncover the newer, younger looking skin. Introducing Oil of Olay Renewal Cream

Our new Dual-Action Hydroxy Complex

85%   30%

improved skin clarity   reduction in the look of fine lines

It's breakthrough:
it actually lifts away the dull, dry surface of your skin – uncovering newer, clearer, more even textured skin.
It's unique:
Our Dual-Action Hydroxy Complex combines our most advanced hydroxy technology with nourishing Olay moisture.

From "primitive" body painting and tattooing to "modern" cosmetics and makeup, skin has always been close to the heart of fashion. "Presence," as the Guinot ad proclaims, "begins with beautiful skin." But how can such heavenly presence be achieved?

The foundational presence upon which fashion rests presupposes the art of makeup. The presence that is desired is never present until something is added. Presence, in other words, must be fabricated or made up. Jean Ressac, director of one of France's leading cosmetics firms, insists that "we must reverse traditional wisdom according to which clothing is a second skin, and begin to see skin as thoroughly

that once seemed fixed. Along this interface, every view is an Interview. As the site or nonsite where self meets other and body touches world, fashion is neither subjective nor objective but is liminal – irreducibly liminal. The liminality of fashion de-signs the architecture of interpretation by subverting the opposition between significance and insignificance.

In a fashion strictly parallel to Warhol silk screens, fashion recycles images. All fashion is retro even when it claims to be innovative. Since the new can only be affirmed by negating the old, the out-of-date forever haunts the up-to-date. The cycles of fashion, which attempt to naturalize artifice by appearing seasonally, form a specular system in which this year's trends take shape by rejecting, appropriating, or reforming the styles of previous years. The passé is always passing away in a fashion that eternally disrupts the "just now." The ceaseless quest for the moment is what keeps the cycles of fashion turning.

In this turning and returning, the goal of fashion is to fashion everything in its own image. There can be no fashion without mirrors, because fashion is nothing more and nothing less than a play of mirrors. This play, which is an interplay, is both specular and speculative. The specularity of fashion is its self-referentiality. By facing reality, fashion hopes to see only itself. But the realization of such specularity is impossible apart from speculation, which inevitably involves wagering, betting, and gambling. Inasmuch as it is made to be consumed, fashion necessarily speculates on consumption. This wager is, in a certain sense, a matter of faith. The consumption of fashion is the transubstantiation of image into body and body into image. As the image is incarnate, the body is virtualized. The virtualization of the body through its fashioning issues in the disappearance of the real and the realization of appearance. In this intricate process,

LUCIDITY

Light-Diffusing Makeup SPF 8
It's the rarest of things –
a true breakthrough.
A makeup that covers
flawlessly...yet looks natural.
A makeup that moisturizes
and protects your skin,
every minute you're wearing it.
Estée Lauder Research has
found a way for the color to
skim the surface of your
skin so smoothly, it reflects light away from lines
and shadows—makes them seem
to disappear. You don't
see the makeup...you see
the perfection.

When liquid makeup becomes lucid, the supplement, paradoxically, marks a return to nature. Thus, the natural, far from being natural, is an artifice made up in such a way that one seems to be wearing no makeup. In this play of supplements, addition is subtraction.

New advances in skin care, however, are also reversing the ancient art of makeup by transforming the addition that is a subtraction into a subtraction that is an addition. Since the point at which body meets world is a thin layer of lifeless cells, the presence that begins with skin is always a dead presence. In an effort to revitalize the cosmetics industry, new fast-acting lasers and extra-strength acids are now being used to eliminate blemishes and peel away the outer surface of the body as if it were nothing more than the wrinkled skin of an onion. What does this subtraction add? Nothing but more skin. Peel away one layer and you uncover another layer of skin. It's skin all the way down. Beauty might only be skin-deep but skin is undeniably profound – as profound as the unfathomable layers of an onion.

Subtraction is no less artificial than addition. The "newer, younger looking skin" that is revealed when the "dull, dry surface" of the skin is "lifted away" is every bit as made-up as the face whose mask is lucid. In the art of cosmetics – and what art is not cosmetic? – everything is made up. Fashion is an endless game of hide-and-seek in which hiding always has the last word, even when there is nothing left to hide but skin that reveals more skin.

the (body of the) real is, in effect, crucified and resurrected as simulacra. When consumption is all-consuming, everything becomes immaterial, insubstantial, and insignificant.

The virtualization of the real consumes the foundation that had appeared to secure truth and ground meaning. In the absence of any real referent, signs constantly represent other signs. This proliferation of signs eventually subverts the very architecture of signification. In classical linguistic theory, the structure of the sign presupposes a stable hierarchical distinction between the signifier and the signified. Meaning is determined by grounding the signifier in the signified. Within this scheme, interpretation is a one-way street that passes from signifier to signified. As anticipated, different hermeneutical alternatives recast the signifier/signified distinction in terms of exteriority/interiority and surface/ depth. Accordingly, exteriority is decoded as an expression of interiority and surface is

Modeling Reality

"Backstage at the recent Dolce & Gabbana show in Milan, Domenico Dolce firmly instructed a bevy of models: 'You are not models, this is not a fashion show. This is you.' No, it wasn't some kind of existentialist mind game. They are models, of course, but Dolce wanted them to forget their hip-thrusting walks and frozen smiles and be real."

No doubt it was inevitable – as inevitable as the fall of hemlines after they reach embarrassing heights: following the celebrity model, the "real" person. In recent years, models have often overshadowed the fashions they are paid to promote. No longer anonymous faces and bodies, supermodels have emerged from behind designers' veils to become instantly recognizable media figures. When Cindy Crawford hosts MTV's House of Style and George Michael features no less than five supermodels in his new music video, you cannot be sure whether fashion is following TV or TV is mimicking fashion.

But as supermodels' stars have risen, they have grown more distant from the person on the street. It is one thing to market dreams but quite another to make the dream seem unreal. In an effort to revitalize the market, models are coming back down to earth. Borrowing strategies that have made the T V show *Funniest Home Videos* immensely popular, fashion is attempting to recover what Coke has long been pushing: The Real Thing.

But not everyone is following suit. "'What does real mean, anyway?' asks Karl Lagerfeld, dismissing the phenomenon altogether after showing a street-smart, model-packed fall collection for Chanel. `Real' for Calvin Klein might well be 'faux real' to the rest of us."

The search for the real is not new. It was "Gaultier who pioneered the 'real' thing in 1977 and has continued to defy industry norms by using unknowns and oddballs like the strong-featured Spanish actress Rossy de Palma, a larger-than-life makeup artist named Stella, and, most recently, the bald model Eve. 'I wanted to show women of all ages and sizes in my clothes to prove that anyone could wear them,' said Gaultier, who still regularly plucks kids off the street and thrusts them onto the runway. 'My clothes are about the

deciphered as a symptom of depth. If, however, the signified is itself a signifier, the structure of the sign is actually reversible and the architecture of signification collapses. The one-way street of textual decoding and deciphering becomes a two-way superhighway along which hypertextual meanings multiply. The lack of a solid referential foundation leaves a void where meanings proliferate as meaning withdraws. The collapse of the signified de-signs the sign and leaves meanings to spread in their apparent insignificance. The problem, once again, is not too little meaning but too many meanings; meaning always threatens to run out of control in endless dissemination. Rather than spreading a common seed, dissemination is an "epidermic process" of metonymic dispersal, which is perpetually on the verge of becoming epidemic. There is always something excessive about fashion; its epide(r)mic process is *de trop*. Yet this too much is also too little. Never arriving here

street, and people from the street correspond to my look better than any professional model would.'

"Photographers, designers, and modeling agencies followed Gaultier's lead, scrambling to nightclubs and combing beaches to look for 'real,' 'interesting,' and 'imperfect' faces – adjectives hitherto forbidden in the fashion business. By 1982, Bruce Weber was creating a kind of primitive virtual reality for Ralph Lauren with highly stylized ads featuring photos of real-looking families lounging on Kodachrome-color-drenched lawns or struggling with the spinnakers of properly aged sailboats."

Where does this search for the real end? Perhaps not where it seems. Long before we had heard anything about data suits and head-mounted displays, fashion was virtualizing reality. "When reality is modeled," Julio Fantano points out, "it is not really 'real' but is rendered virtual. Models have never been incidental to fashion but constitute its very essence. Though usually masked, the very purpose of fashion is to model reality by transforming every body into its own image." If the model is real, Fantano suggests, the real is always (already) modeled. In the world of fashion – and what world is not fashioned? – every real is faux and every faux is "real." As Liz Claiborne advertises: "Reality is the best Fantasy of All."

and now but always already passé, fashion's point is its dis-appointment.

The dis-appointment of fashion is the lingering trace of the real's withdrawal. Fashion, we have learned, is an all-consuming spectacle that mirrors a self-reflexive play in which significance appears to be insignificant. This spectacle, as Baudrillard points out, "bears the closest resemblance to ritual—fashion as spectacle, as festival, as squandering." Such festivals are far from innocent, for they always involve what Freud describes as "obligatory excess," which inevitably leads to violence and death. Within the fatal play of the festival, the god/father dies at the hands of the believers/sons. This ritual sacrifice remains charged with ambiguity. Since violence simultaneously destroys and identifies with that against which it is directed, thanatos and eros can never be completely separated. This paradoxical

Net Effects

Nets and networking have become pervasive figures of our time. In the information age, it seems everyone is surfing the net and cruising the web. Some of the more daring are now taking net working to the next level by sporting nets and wearing webs. The results are both unexpected and vexing.

The elevation of nets and webs to iconic status owes less to burgeoning cyberculture than to the recent obsession with self-exposure that can be seen and heard from runways to talk shows. "Spinning a tale that began last season, designers add to the sexiness of transparency for spring with the textural 'spider web' looks of netting and lace, macramé and crochet. Woven into this sultry scheme: meant-to-be-seen lingerie details and eye-catching openwork stockings." The creations of Jil Sander, Marc Jacobs, and Anna Sui are suggestive, but Karl Lagerfeld's designs are obviously the most revealing. Lagerfeld effectively "deconstructs the dress, paring it down to a dramatic veil of paneled silk netting. While a lacy bra and panty take center stage here, the sheer effect can be tamed – as it was on the runway – with the addition of a thigh-length tunic." In a more modest but no less captivating contribution, Lagerfeld presents what can only be described as "the return of the spiderwoman" in which "a cobweb of guipure lace is spun over a crepe tank dress."

The ever-shifting folds of Lagerfeld's carefully fabricated webs create an effect that verges on the virtual. Bodies flicker in nets that cannot quite contain them. The new net look, Vogue's Carlyne Cerf de Dudzeele observes, "walks a fine line between revealing and concealing the body – fluid sheaths with back-baring cutouts to a curve-hugging tube of lacy crochet work." In this play of hiding and exposing, nets and webs catch the body in the act of withdrawal. Net working, it seems, allows the disappearance of the body to appear. The absent presence and present absence created by the body's withdrawal arouse the desire that is the draw of nets and webs.

coincidence of opposites is enacted in the totem meal. The festive ritual of communion involves the act of consumption through which the dead god/father becomes incarnate in the believers/sons. In this way, the death of God the father is the disappearance of the transcendent(al signified) that prepares the way for the dissemination of the word in the *imago dei*.

The spectacle of fashion restages this ancient ritual of consumption. The infinite play of signifiers dramatizes the death of the signified. This death is not a simple disappearance but a complex refiguring through which the signified returns as signifiers. Just as God dies and is reborn in the believer, so the real disappears only to reappear in fashioned images. With the recognition that the real is a fabrication, fashioning becomes all-consuming and reality is rendered immaterial. The immateriality of the real is a function of its virtualization. In the world of fashion, all "reality" is virtual reality.

Whether Donna Karan is reading cyberpunk fiction or William Gibson or is watching the runways, one thing is certain: fashion has entered the cyberage. In his recent novel, *Virtual Light*, set in near-future cyburbia, Gibson projects a world in which more than channels are surfed. Describing New Age merchandise at a wind-surfing boutique called Just Blow Me, Gibson writes: "What Kevin sold, primarily, was clothing. Expensive kind that supposedly keeps the UV and the pollutants in the water off you. He had two whole cartons full of the stuff, stacked in their room's one closet. Rydell, who currently didn't have much in the way of a wardrobe, was welcome to paw through there and borrow whatever took his fancy. Which wasn't a lot, as it turned out, because wind-surfing gear tended to be Day-Glo, black nanopore, or mirrorflex. A few of the jazzier items had UV-sensitive JUST BLOW ME logos that appeared on days when the ozone was in particularly bad shape."

As if citing Gibson, who actually might be appropriating DK designs, Donna Karan offers a futuristic vision of her own. "'The future of fashion,' she predicts, 'lies in the test tube; we'll need fabrics that protect us from the sun's rays, help retain heat, or cool the skin.' While none of these visions is department-store ready yet, Karan is among those already dabbling in decidedly nonnatural fibers. For spring, she's sculpted second-skin bodysuits and angular little skirts from a luminous, water-repellant fabric (technical name: reflective triacetate) that shimmers in the dark – a chic metaphor for modern-day body armor. Other designers looking forward to a new silver age include Jil Sander, who is crafting long, liquid metallic dresses – as well as experimenting with aluminum-coated fibers – and Liza Bruze, who cuts stretch, tunic-short tank dresses fit for intergalactic travel."

From jewelry and accessories to skirts, blouses, and dresses, fashion is going interactive. Like the hottest architects who are wrapping buildings with skins that are environmentally sensitive and responsive, designers are stretching fabrics to the limit by draping bodies in data suits

Cyberchic

Citizens of the society of spectacle implicitly or explicitly realize that there is nothing that is not fashion(ed). Absolutely nothing. The contradictory reactions to fashion reflect alternative responses to this uncanny nothing. The nothingness of fashion is a "matter" of life and death. Forever committed to the new, the duplicity of fashion is destined to trace the passing away that does not pass away. "Fashion's aggressiveness, whose rhythm is the same as that of vendettas, is thus disarmed by a more patient image of time; in that absolute, dogmatic, vengeful present tense in which Fashion speaks, the rhetorical system possesses reasons, which seem to reconnect it to a more manageable, more distant time, and which are the politeness or – the regret – of the murder it commits of its own past, as if it vaguely heard that possessive voice of the slain year saying to it: Yesterday I was what you are, tomorrow you will be what I am."

that interact with their surroundings. With clothing that breathes, sweats, and cools already commonplace, some are now predicting that bioactive self-cleaning garments soon will be available. Nanotechnology holds the promise of nanowear that will effectively hide the skin with another skin.

Though advanced cyberfibers have not yet materialized, high-tech designs are far from idle fantasies. Taking her cue from *The Terminator*, Sylvia Heisel is creating jeans and coats made from Teflon. "'I use it,' she explains, 'because of how it feels – strangely soft, like a snake –

and because of the implications. It's incredibly durable, friction- and wind-resistant, which may not be so important but will be in the future.'"

While Heisel is appropriating film for her designs, Pedro Almodóvar is enlisting designers for his films. Almodóvar has recently called on Jean-Paul Gaultier to design the costume for Victoria Abril, who plays the central character in his new film *Kika*. Gaultier responded by creating a data suit extraordinaire. "Victoria Abril, as Andrea in 'Kika,' is the personification of morbid trash television run amok. She plays the host of 'The Worst

of the Day,' a show set in Spain in which the most horrific, prurient events are glamorized after having been tracked down by Andrea herself. As she goes on patrol, her cable-crossed army green jumpsuit and breastplates act as camera lights, while hand controls on the arms move the video camera clamped on her helmet. 'Her costumes are half of the character she interprets,' Mr. Almodóvar said. 'I told Jean-Paul I wanted him to create a sort of robot, with a military aspect, like a soldier.' For Andrea's hostess gowns for 'The Worst of the Day,' he said, 'I asked Jean-Paul to imagine that she

had just been the victim of a catastrophe, but to integrate it with glamour.'" Gaultier has fashioned a wardrobe in which "gore meets glamour: Andrea's hair in a bouffant of snaking rubber wires, breasts exploding from black velvet, with shiny red appliqués of plastic dripping like blood onto red shoes. 'This was a reflection of the aesthetics of horror in fashion, of trash and post-punk and all the styles using violence aesthetically,' Mr. Almodóvar said."

But not all cyberfashion is inspired by cyborgs gone mad. At London's design house Space Time, holographers

The fear of fashion is the dread of time whose sting is death.

But since thanatos and eros are inseparable, death is not merely death but also always harbors a faint pulse of life. Eros presupposes the lack inscribed by thanatos, and thanatos inevitably turns out to be the end toward which eros indirectly strives. The disappearance of the real creates the gap that opens the time and space of desire, without which there can be

Mia Manners and Richard Sharpe are using "heat-sensitive liquid-crystal designs that change color according to your body temperature and with patterns that appear only under ultraviolet light." Their most impressive "achievement to date has been the development of the world's first holographic fabric, which the designers already use on their full collection, from jeans and jackets to organza tracksuits." In the near future, Manners and Sharpe expect to offer "4-D deep holographic clothes that change according to the angle of view."

Austin-based techno-jeweler Vernor Reed is ahead of the curve in the rapidly expanding world of memewear. "'The work I'm doing now,' he notes, 'aims to amplify the individual psyche through technological means. I can create personal cybernetic adornments that are both wearable and capable of interacting in complex ways with environmental stimuli. Rather than use Liquid Emitting Diodes, I use direct-drive, twisted nematic Liquid Crystal Displays that I design and fabricate in my own studio. The spatial and temporal configuration of these LCDs is controlled by programs stored in on-chip EPROM (the Erasable Programmable Read-Only Memory chip) of Motorola single-chip micros. I've been working with sixteen-segment LCDs because it's easy to control with two one-byte I/O ports. The programs are written in a proprietary language that I commissioned so I wouldn't necessarily have to learn assembler. The graphics are generated in realtime, and the tiny (2k) memory allows about three minutes of novel imagery. Movement and change are everything in the new jewelry paradigm.'"

Rapidly spreading from computer networks to the latest fashions, cyberspace knows no limits. Boundaries that once seemed secure are becoming permeable membranes allowing inner to become outer and outer to become inner. When clothing is a second skin that is not exactly inorganic, we can no longer be sure where bodies we once thought were "own" begin or end.

no life. The fulfillment of desire is death; when desire is satisfied, becoming ends. To remain vital, desire must always desire desire. Through its wily de-signs, fashion conspires to extend life by perpetually engendering desire. To embrace fashion is to affirm life – "not the life that shrinks from death and keeps itself untouched by devastation, but rather the life that endures it and maintains itself in it." To say *yes* to fashion

Trendy Nomads

All of a sudden, the entire world has become grandma's attic waiting to be ransacked by enterprising designers.

Fashion is going global. Styles are becoming as deterritorialized as flows of information, currency, and people ceaselessly crossing borders and circulating around the world. "'We are all nomads,' said a smiling Lacroix as he surveyed a trio of models in embroidered tweed pantsuits before his show. 'Modern technology and communication have created a kaleidoscope of cultures. And the result is a kind of nouveau folklore.'"

Perpetually in motion and always in transition, global nomads belong more to a time than a place. And the time to which they belong is the present. As transportation and communication networks speed up, distance virtually disappears. This "time-space compression" draws people together and exposes their differences. "'National boundaries are dissolving, and the environmental movement has really driven home the point that we're one planet. It's only natural that fashion should reflect that and celebrate diversity whenever possible,' says Todd Oldham, whose spring collection included a madcap mix of multicultural prints."

Indeed, on the streets of San Francisco, Paris, and Prague, where the cybertribe style is stepping out, "slick

is to affirm the inescapable eternity of time in which nothing lasts forever.

> Did you ever say "Yes" to one joy? Oh my friends, then you also say "Yes" to *all* the pain. All things are entwined, enmeshed, enamored –
>
> – did you ever want Once to be Twice, did you ever say "I love you, bliss, – instant – flash – " then you wanted *everything* back.
>
> – Everything anew, everything forever, everything entwined, enmeshed, enamored – oh, thus you love it forever and for all time; even to pain you say: Refrain but – come again! *For joy accepts everlasting flow!*

Flow...

vinyl jeans and silver down parkas are combined with the kind of handcrafted, multicultural finds seen at many flea markets – Tibetan embroidered vests, South American knits, and Guatemalan purses. Fresh from the spring runways come Issey Mijake's marriages of leotard-like Lycra knits in acid colors with primitive, raw-edged linen chaps and dusters, and Koji Tatsuno's pairings of metallic cropped tops with folkloric burlap skirts."

Even within Europe, the purity of national styles is being contaminated by emerging globalism. Trumpeting his new Eurovision in twelve languages, Jean-Paul Gaultier boldly declares: "'I love the idea of taking the traditional dress from each country and mixing it up.' Which in Gaultier-speak means an English fox-hunter look with pin-striped jodhpurs and a fire-engine-red hacking jacket or chalk-striped evening dresses topped with lederhosen straps straight out of Tyrol. 'People keep their own traditions, but then they travel to other countries and pick up new ideas along the way.'"

It's difficult to know what all this mixing without matching adds up to. For some, nomadic fashion is a badge of growing awareness of, and sensitivity to, other cultures, which holds the promise of greater global harmony. For others, designers' appropriation of traditional styles is an act of cultural plunder that perpetuates age-old patterns of exploitation. Neither side in this often heated debate is wrong; nor is either side right. Whether we see the globalization of fashion as creative or destructive, one thing seems certain: it is as impossible to halt the free circulation of styles as it is to secure borders against social, political, economic, and cultural flows that transgress every limit. Fashion is no longer merely current but has become the currency of our time.

... fleeting, transient, ephemeral, everlasting flow.

Nothing more...

nothing less.

Stripping Fashion

FASHION IS LEARNING FROM LAS VEGAS.

Less might be a bore but not on the runway!

NEW YORK (Nov. 5, 1994) – Less might be a bore in architecture but it's sure not on the runway! More than two decades after Robert Venturi and Denise Scott Brown shook the foundations of modernism by launching postmodern architecture, fashion is finally learning from Las Vegas.

"Any sociologist preparing an essay on America's complex yearning for a little nastiness would have found plenty of material in Thursday's fashion shows. What was a nice girl like Cynthia Rowley doing playing craps in Las Vegas? And what messages were the models sending who refused to pole dance in Tracy Feith's presentation at Show World's Big Top? What were they saying about the stripper fashion so many designers on both sides of the Atlantic are offering?

"Women are going to make some intriguing decisions when these collections, which have become sexy staples for television news on the very nights they are presented, make it into stores in February. No longer will Mr. Feith's presentation be divorced from what will hang on the racks. Women who see his

Nothing...

(the) nothing (that) lasts forever.

clothes in stores may have first seen them as the press and the buyers did, dancing down the mirror-lined runway of a strip joint. How appealing these shoppers find women getting dollar bills tucked into their G-strings will have a lot to do with how appealing they find these clothes."

But, as we all know, nastiness is not always nasty; bad can be good – real good, and good can be bad – real bad. "Cynthia Rowley made Las Vegas games-of-chance clothes that, yes, even good girls can wear. There were dice embedded in the heels of spike shoes or silver spurs on the backs of python stilettos. And there were witty takes on everything from slot machines (three cherries were rung up across one dress) to the club acts that occupy tourists between games (golden halter dresses with sheer stars across them)." Whether witty or not, the image of cherries on a slot machine is far from innocent!

If all of this seems a bit excessive, we should not be surprised. La Monde's Michel Richman points out that "fashion has always been about excess – excess that can never be contained." Excess, however, can be a matter of either too much or too little. Nowhere is the provocative ambiguity of excess more spectacularly displayed than on the Strip, which, we are relearning, knows no bounds. As the Strip becomes the runway and the runway the Strip, addition subtracts and subtraction adds. When fashion is stripped, neither ornament nor its removal is a crime. In this play of signs, which are not always neon, pluses and minuses do not completely cancel each other but leave a trace whose strange name is excess.

Ground Zero

Pyramid: Latin *pyramis, pyra* -funeral pyre.
Greek *puramis, pura* -funeral pyre.

The erection of the pyramid guards life -the dead -in
order to give rise to the for-(it)self of adoration. This has
the signification of a sacrifice, of an offer by which
the all-burning annuls itself; opens the annulus, contracts
the annulus into the anniversary of the solar revolution
in sacrificing itself as the all-burning, therefore guarding
itself. The sacrifice, the offer, the gift do not destroy
the all-burning that destroys itself in them; they make
it reach the for-(it)self, they monumentalize it.

Jacques Derrida

Who is sacrificed?

What is sacrificed? Is there a meaning to sacrifice? Is there a sacrifice of meaning? Does sacrifice have a point? Can sacrifice occur – if it does occur – only when the point is lost at (or on) the point of pointlessness? Can sacrifice ever be sacrificed? Does sacrifice always remain a burning question? A question of burning? Who is burnt? What is burnt? Is there an end to burning? Who is consumed? What is consumed? Who is the consumer? What is (the economy of) consumption? Is pointless consumption consuming? All-consuming as all (*holos*) – burning (*caustos*)? Is the holocaust of consumption the sacrifice of the ground that grounds? Leaving nothing? What lights do the pyramidal flames of sacrifice ignite? What darkness does the holocaust of consumption portend?

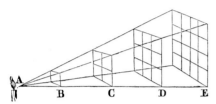

Nothing: Ground 0 = 0 Ground

The figure of the pyramid appears at one and only one point in Poe's "prose poem" "Eureka." It is represented not as a hieroglyph to be decoded but as the key that enables the detective to solve the mystery of the cosmos. Though seemingly self-contained, this pyramid is actually a section of an all-encompassing sphere that figures the rhythms of the cosmic process. In Poe's speculative poetics, the world and everything in it emerge from and return to a primordial unity that is the divine source of reality. The act of creation through which the many emerge from the One involves a process of differentiation that Poe labels "radiation": "Now a connection between these two ideas - unity and diffusion – cannot be established unless through the entertainment of a third idea – that of *radiation*. Absolute Unity being taken as a center, then the existing Universe of Stars is the result of *radiation* from that center." Unity, in other words, is an unstable nucleus that erupts in a fiery explosion, generating the world of

click

Strange lines of communication join pyramids and telephones. From the outset, there has been something ghostly about telephonic messages. In *The Telephone Book*, Avital Ronell points out:

When the French scientist Gaspard Monge followed the army of Napoleon Bonaparte into Egypt on its campaign of general decipherment, he explored the Temple of Mehmet Abn, where he made a discovery. He came upon a coil of wire in which were tangled several objects of ivory and bone, shaped somewhat in the fashion of the later drinking horn. These wires had been lying for ages in the place where they were found, a stone chamber in the temple. Later, on Monge's arrival at the pyramid of Gizeh, he discovered in a vault of about the same dimensions as the chamber in the temple some of these ivory and bone objects and more coiled wires. At the time, scientists could make nothing of the manner in which the diverse appearances. The tip of the pyramid, which is the center of the sphere, is the point at which the real is totally present. The movement from center to periphery is marked by the dispersal of reality in a play of appearances. Appearances, however, are no more stable than their origin. Having originated in lack, appearances seek reunion with the One they are missing.

> Oneness, then, is all that I predicate of the originally created Matter; but I propose to show that this *Oneness is a principle abundantly sufficient to account for the constitution, the existing phenomena and the plainly inevitable annihilation of at least the material Universe.*

The willing into being the primordial Particle, has completed the act, or more

wires and their attachments might have been serviceable. Were these funeral accompaniments, works of art, utensils of some unfathomable sort? The French publicist M. Henry Paccory has asserted that these objects were used for the transmissions of speech "and that the chambers in which they were found were nothing less than ancient telephone booths."

What Ronell does not mention is that the communication between pyramids and telephones is a two-way conversation. Always intrigued by the possibility of contacting the dead, Bell and Watson regarded the telephone as a medium with more than one message.

But Bell's unearthly interests were not limited to telephone and telepathy. Perhaps it was the haunting ghost of Râ-Atum that led to his fascination with flight and pyramids. Bell "designed kites, which finally became so large that they were capable of carrying a man into the air. To achieve this, he developed a structural

properly the *conception*, of Creation. We now proceed to the ultimate purpose for which we are to suppose the Particle created – that is to say, the ultimate purpose so far as our considerations *yet* enable us to see it – the constitution of the universe from it, the Particle.

This constitution has been effected by forcing the originally and therefore normally *One* into the abnormal condition of *Many*. An action of this character implies reaction. A diffusion from Unity, under the conditions, involves a tendency to return into Unity – a tendency ineradicable until satisfied.

Centrifugal and centripetal forces are not equal. Since unity is "normal" and plurality "abnormal," Poe insists, "the tendency to return into the *absolutely* original – into the *supremely* primitive" cannot be resisted. Within this speculative economy, there is no expenditure without return.

The dialectic of "radiation" and "concentralization" entails alternative sacrifices, which, though reciprocal, are not symmetrical. Wagering on the possibility of return, Poe longs for the sacrifice of sacrifice in which loss is lost. While it is undeniable that the realization of the many presupposes the sacrifice of the One, this loss is not fatal if the One can always be recovered. The return of,

system of relatively small frames, based on the tetrahedron. Combining an arbitrary number of these space elements in honeycomb fashion, he developed techniques for joining members at nodes, which flowed from the nature of the three-dimensional connection itself."

Not all of Bell's pyramids, however, were designed to float freely. He also used tetrahedral structural units to construct an observation tower shaped like a pyramid without a point. Occasionally, Bell went so far as to inhabit the pyramids he built. Well-known earthworks artist Robert Smithson notes that Bell "built a pyramid-shaped outdoor observation station that reminds one of the art of Robert Morris.... From inside his solid tetrahedron Bell surveyed his 'flight' projects – the tetragonal lattice-kites. A grid connection was established by him between ground and air through this crystalline system. The solid mirrored the lattice. The sight was joined to the sky in a structural equation."

to, and on the One, however, is impossible apart from the sacrifice of the many. At the tip of the pyramid is a flame, which not only radiates the sacrifice of the One but consummates the sacrifice of the many. The fire of consumption is a holocaust that consumes differences in an identity that leaves nothing but the trace of nothing. "In sinking into Unity, it [i.e., the world] will sink at once into that Nothingness which, to all finite perception, Unity must be — into that Material Nihility from which alone we can conceive it to have been evoked — to have been *created* by the Volition of God." All or Nothing? All and Nothing? All for Nothing?

Creation, fall, redemption... One, many, One... Identity, difference, Identity. The story Poe tells in "Eureka" is the metanarrative that renders all narratives meaningful. For the detective who knows this tale, nothing remains indecipherable because everything has a point. The point from which this point is visible is the point of the pyramid. In Poe's speculative poe-tic, ontology and epistemology are mirror images of each other. The tip of the pyramid is the center of vision around which everything is organized. Miming the omniscient invisible eye for which (the) all is visible, the private eye surveys the world as if it were exposed by a camera lucida. When the pyramid of perception is mapped on the pyramid of ontology, it becomes clear that pyramids are not only significant figures but figures of signification.

Since he never explains exactly what this equation adds up to, Bell's point is not clear. His pyramids seem to form something like a bridge joining earth and sky. But what (telephonic) message is Bell sending through his pyramids? What lines of connection is he attempting to draw?

While Poe was spinning his speculative tale, Hegel was constructing his speculative philosophy. No less significant for Hegel than for Poe, the pyramid is the pivot on which the system turns and the hinge on which philosophy swings. This point of turning and returning is nothing more and nothing less than the sign of the sign or, in Derrida's terms, "the semaphore of the sign, the signifier of signification." In his consideration of fantasy in *Philosophy of Spirit*, Hegel figures the sign with a pyramid: "The *sign* is a certain immediate intuition, presenting a content that is wholly distinct from that which it has for itself; — it is the *pyramid* in which the soul is ensconced and preserved." As the pivot or hinge of the system, the sign is transitional; it marks the threshold of sense, which is neither completely meaningless nor totally meaningful. At this margin, opposites are joined without being united: body/soul, corporeal/incorporeal, sensible/intelligible, material/immaterial, real/ideal, and so forth. By figuring the conjunctive disjunction and disjunctive conjunction of opposites, the pyramid functions as

> the bridge between two moments of full presence....The bridge can be lifted. The
> process of the sign has a history, and signification is even history comprehended:
> between an original presence and its circular reappropriation in a final presence. The
> self-presence of absolute knowledge and consciousness of Being-near-to-itself in
> logos, in the absolute concept, will have been distracted from themselves only for the
> time of the detour and for the time of the sign. The time of the sign, then, is the time of
> referral. It signifies self-presence, refers presence to itself, organizes the circulation of
> its provisionality. Always, from the outset, the movement of lost presence already will
> have set in motion the process of its reappropriation.

Rising above the chaotic labyrinth of experience and surveying nature and history from the tip of the pyramid, Hegel translates Poe's poetic vision into philosophical language. Hegelian philosophy is organized around binary oppositions that both articulate synchronic structures and describe diachronic processes. For Hegel as for Poe, history is characterized by the loss and recovery of unity. In Hegel's semiology, the sign constitutes the penultimate chapter of the story of exile

click

click

click

The painting is a painting of a painting, which is itself a painting of a painting. One is doubled and then redoubled to create a third that neither mediates nor synthesizes the duplicity from which it emerges. In the first painting (*The Questioner of the Sphinx*, 1863), the body is dark. A black man kneels before the Sphinx and places his ear next to its lips. Nearby a skull lies partially buried in the sand. Twelve years later, Elihu Vedder repainted this image. In the second version, the skull has disappeared and the body has changed. An old, skeletal, white man, bearded and clothed in nothing but a loincloth, kneels before the Sphinx and places his ear next to its lips. While visiting Egypt years later, Vedder recorded his response to the pyramids and the Sphinx in terms that recall Kant's use of pyramids to and return. In the sign, opposites are no longer opposite but are not yet reconciled. The association of the signifier and the signified is arbitrary rather than necessary, formal rather than integral, mechanical rather than organic. To draw out the implications of this point, Hegel suggests that the relation between the signifier and the signified is strictly parallel to the relation between the body and the soul. "Of course it is a soul deposited in a body, in the body of the signifier, in the sensory flesh of intuition. The sign, as the unity of the signifying body and the signified ideality, becomes a kind of incarnation." As long as one/One remains lost in the desert under the regime of the sign, reconciliation is incomplete and thus the body (signifier) is a tomb from which the soul (signified) longs to escape.

> Hegel knew that this proper and animated body of the signifier was also a *tomb*. The association *soma/sema* is also at work in this semiology, which is in no way surprising. The tomb is the life of the body as the sign of death, the body as the other of soul, the other of the animate psyche, of the living breath. But the tomb also shelters, maintains in reserve, capitalizes on life by marking that life that continues elsewhere. The family crypt: *oikesis*. It consecrates the disappearance of life by attesting to the perseverance of life. Thus, the

illustrate the mathematical sublime: "It is their unwritten meaning, their poetic meaning, far more eloquent than words can express; and it sometimes seemed to me that this impression would only be dulled or lessened by a greater unveiling of their mysteries, and that to me Isis unveiled would be Isis dead."

Over a century later, Mark Tansey repainted Vedder's paintings in his *Secret of the Sphinx (Homage to Elihu Vedder)*. In the interim, the monument has had a nose job and the questioner has donned a suit. More important, the listener's ear has been replaced by an electronic prosthesis. A man equipped with earphones and a tape recorder places a microphone next to the lips of the Sphinx. But the result remains the same. The Sphinx refuses to break its stony silence; its lips remain sealed, and the secret is not told.

tomb also shelters life from death. It *warns* the soul of possible death, warns (of) death of the soul, turns away (from) death. This double warning function belongs to the funerary monument. The body of the sign thus becomes the monument in which the soul will be enclosed, preserved, maintained, kept in maintenance, present, signified. At the heart of this monument the soul keeps itself alive, but it needs the monument only to the extent that it is exposed — to death — in its living relation to its own body.... The sign — the monument-of-life-in-death, the monument-of-death-in-life, the sepulcher of a soul or of an embalmed proper body, the height conserving in its depths the hegemony of the soul, resisting time, the hard text of stones covered with inscription — is the *pyramid*.

For Hegel, the story does not end with a funerary monument in a *kierkegaard*; death is never the last word. Since incarnation leads to resurrection, the body is spiritualized in such a way that the oppositions between body and soul, corporeal and incorporeal, sensible and intelligible, material and immaterial, and real and ideal are sublated. The point of history is the reconciliation of opposites through which time is effectively overcome. At the tip of the pyramid, the divine and the human become One in the all-seeing eye/I of the philosopher.

But what if this "story of the eye" is fiction? What if the eye of the philosopher

has a blind spot? What if wandering in the desert is not a passing phase but an endless condition? What if one can never reach the tip of the pyramid? What if the pyramid — as well as everything else — is pointless? Though sharing a common desire, Poe admits what Hegel denies: eros and thanatos are One.

In many of Poe's stories, tales, and poems, the figure of unity is the South Pole, which, of course, marks the end of the world. This end, however, never arrives. As (the) I approach(es), the end withdraws; where I am, it is not, and when it is, I am not. In "MS. Found in a Bottle," Poe recounts a horrifying tale of a ship wrecked while heading toward the ever inaccessible South Pole. The narrator adds a coda in which he confesses: "To conceive the horror of my sensations is, I presume, utterly impossible; yet a curiosity to penetrate the mysteries of these awful regions, predominates even over my despair, and will reconcile me to the most hideous aspect of death. It is evident that we are hurrying onwards to some

click

Hatshepsut's temple at Luxor looks like a building but it is not. It is only a façade cut in the hill.

— Michael Heizer

Route 93 heads north from Interstate 15 trough Nevada to Idaho and beyond to the Canadian border. The road cuts straight as an arrow through flat terrain covered with sagebrush and Joshua trees, and edged by rugged mountain ranges in the distance. Traveling north, the first town you hit is Alamo, which is about a hundred miles from Las Vegas. Twenty miles outside of Alamo, an unmarked dirt road heads westward into the desert. Throughout much of the year, snow, ice, and mud make this road virtually impassable. Even in good weather, rocks, ruts, and dust create endless obstacles. The treacherous road gradually ascends to a valley floor that is more than a thousand feet higher than the tallest mountain in Massachusetts. The entrance to the valley is a narrow gap that once was the plug preventing the waters of this ancient basin from draining to the distant sea. The eroding folds of the gap crowd the serpentine road, making passage almost impossible. Deeper in the desert, junipers slowly shrink until they disappear in low sage and rabbitbrush whose spring hues of lavender and yellow gently fade into the burnt browns of summer and cold grays of winter. In the distance, hills dappled with small plants slope upward, until they erupt in sheer limestone cliffs soaring toward a sky exciting knowledge — some never-to-be-imparted secret, whose attainment is destruction. Perhaps this current leads to the southern pole itself. It must be confessed that a supposition apparently so wild has every probability of favor." The consequences of this confession are far-reaching. If there is a "never-to-be-imparted secret," Poe's metanarrative unravels or becomes hopelessly tangled. A secret that is never imparted is indistinguishable from a secret that hides nothing. Instead of hiding the body that would solve every mystery, the pyramid becomes an empty tomb that marks the disappearance of the body. In the absence of a body, everything remains cryptic; detectives are condemned to blindness without insight, and hieroglyphs remain what they always have been — infinitely interpretable. To navigate the rough waters of "these awful regions," it is necessary to leave Poe and Hegel behind and follow the ever errant Bataille.

Bataille is endlessly fascinated by pyramids. Unlike Hegel, however, Bataille realizes that not all pyramids have a point. To make this point, Bataille reads Hegelianism against the grain by teasing out the implications of a fleeting observation in which Hegel notes but does not examine the explosion of the nuclear family and the economy it presupposes. "But if the universal thus easily knocks off

that knows no end yet is not infinite. At scattered points, the cliffs are decorated with petroglyphs reminiscent of the figures recorded by Poe's Pym. Between basin and range, land and sky, the desert stages a dramatic play in which clouds and land constantly mirror each other. As the moody grays and rusty pinks of scattered clouds reflect deep earth tones, the dark purple shadows cast by ever-moving clouds pattern the valley like ink splotches pressed on the surface of a tightly stretched canvas. In the opening of this space, the work of art never ceases.

At the end of the thirty-five-mile dirt road, a lonely house suddenly appears on the horizon; beyond the house, a strange form emerges in the midst of the desert. When the distant object eventually comes into focus, it appears to be a pyramid with its tip cut off. *Complex One* is part of an extraordinary earthwork, entitled *City*, which Michael Heizer has been developing for more than two decades. Uncanny echoes of

ancient Egypt fill the still air of the Nevada desert. "*Complex One*," Heizer explains,

> uses a mastaba form, which was the form of the original mound over the burial vault at Saqqara. What interests me about the Saqqara pyramid is how it was built and the use of primitive technology.... The Saqqara mastaba was eventually added to with three more mounds at 90-degree angles creating a square. The center was filled in and this unit was stacked five more times making six lifts. This was the first pyramid and the first big architecture. The original mastaba was absorbed into the pyramid. Later a ceremonial funeral complex was built beside the pyramid for Zoser's spirit. I felt this was an important source for architecture and could be one way to define the mass of *Complex One*. I modified it and re-presented it.

Architecture — big architecture — seems to begin with a pyramid or a pyramid within a pyramid.

the very tip of the pyramid and, indeed, carries off the victory over the rebellious principle of pure individuality, viz., the Family, it has thereby merely entered on a conflict with the divine law, a conflict of self-conscious Spirit with what is unconscious." What is a pyramid with its tip knocked off? Perhaps it is something like an altar – an altar of sacrifice. According to the uneconomical reflections of Bataille, a pointless pyramid figures the sacrifice of meaning. Poe's "exciting knowledge – some never-to-be-imparted secret, whose attainment is destruction" might, then, anticipate the "nonknowledge" that Bataille detects at the heart of Nietzsche's gay science.

Pyramids, Bataille repeatedly insists, are inseparable from labyrinths. The foundations of these monumental structures are not solid but are intricate networks of cryptic subterranean passages. While dark labyrinths represent the confusion of earthly life, pyramids map escape routes by pointing to the bright light illuminating the world. Long associated with solar religion, pyramids reflect the triangular pattern of the sun's rays, which radiate creative power. Spanning the heavens and the underworld, pyramids are associated with birth as well as death. In one version of the Egyptian creation myth, the world first emerges in the shape of a pyramidal mound

from Nun, who personifies the primordial ocean toward which Poe was always rushing. At the tip of this mound a lotus grows and from this lotus the sun god Râ-Atum emerges. Râ-Atum generates Geb, the earth god, and Nut, the sky goddess, whose offspring include, among others, Osiris and Isis, who prefigure the Christian drama of death and resurrection. By the Sixth Dynasty, Egyptians believed that after death the king, who is completely identified with the sun god, ascends to heaven to join Râ-Atum and travel through the night sky, struggling against forces of darkness. Like the sign, the pyramid is the bridge that simultaneously brings together and holds apart different worlds. By representing the sacred mountain where order emerges from chaos, the pyramid forms the *axis mundi*, which allows passage from earth to heaven. In a brief essay entitled "The Obelisk," Bataille summarizes the point of the pyramid:

> Each time death struck down the heavy column of strength the world itself was shaken and put into doubt, and nothing less than the giant edifice of the pyramid was necessary to re-establish the order of things; the pyramid let the god-king enter the eternity of the sky next to the solar Râ, and in this way existence regained its unshakable plenitude in the person of the one it had *recognized*.... Thus, they assure the presence that never ceases to contemplate and dominate human agitation, just as the mobile prism reflects every

To the north of *Complex One, Complex Two* is carved out of the desert floor. A vast expanse resembling an ancient plaza opens in the middle of some long-lost city that unfolds at the base of the pyramid. The slanting sides enclosing *Complex Two* are punctuated by two forms, which recall both step pyramids of Egypt and Mayan altars of sacrifice. When viewed from a distance, the entire wall surrounding *City* approximates the shape of a pointless pyramid. As you descend the side of the pyramid, the work of art becomes all-consuming. The landscape steadily disappears until it is completely absorbed; like Nietzsche's sponge, *City* "wipes away the horizon." Even though the work is undeniably material, the earth itself seems to dematerialize in art.

Deeper than the deepest ground of the desert, there is another surface that seems to be the foundation of a complex pyramid or complex of pyramids. What sacrifices — ancient or modern — echo in these forms?

How is this monumental hieroglyph to be read? What is the point? What can possibly be the point of a city built in the desert where virtually no one wanders? Nothing seems clear. Nothing but the ceaseless burning of the sun which allows nothing to live. The emptiness of the space renders it labyrinthine. In the absence of center and grid, all sense of direction disappears. At this point...in this point, the desert becomes the site of a certain desertion. This is the territory of exile without return. Calls for help go unanswered: no One is on the other end of the line. Only silence remains. In this silence nothing seems real, because the real is undeniably nothing.

one of the things that surrounds it. In their imperishable unity, the pyramids—endlessly
— continue to crystallize the mobile succession of the various ages; alongside the Nile,
they rise up like the totality of centuries, taking on the immobility of stone and watching
all men die, one after the other: they transcend the intolerable void that time opens
under men's feet, for all possible movement is halted in their geometric surfaces: IT
SEEMS THAT THEY MAINTAIN WHAT ESCAPES FROM THE DYING MAN.

The pyramid fixes time by tracing an escape from the labyrinth. "If one considers the
mass of the pyramids and the rudimentary means at the disposal of their builders,"
Bataille concludes, "it seems evident that no enterprise cost a greater amount of labor
than this one, which wanted to halt the flow of time." At the tip of the pyramid, time
is supposed to become eternity.

But not all pyramids have a point; some are decapitated. If the point of the
pyramid is to fix time by reversing temporal flow through a return to the eternal
ground or origin of being, then the absence of the point marks the impossibility of
return — or points to a different return which, though eternal, permits no escape from
temporal flux. A pyramid of sorts triggered the ecstatic vision that marked the turning
point in Nietzsche's life: "The intensity of my feelings makes me both tremble and

laugh.... I had cried too much.... these were not tears of tenderness, but tears of jubi-
lation.... That day I was walking through the woods, along the lake of Silvaplana; at a
powerful pyramidal rock not far from Surlei I stopped." At precisely this moment,
Nietzsche is blinded by the insight that *time returns eternally*. Nietzsche's notion of the
eternal return represents a recognition of the irreversibility of time and the
inescapable transience of everything once deemed unchanging. Never attempting to
overcome time by returning the temporal to the eternal, Nietzsche acknowledges
the eternity of time by collapsing the eternal in the temporal in such a way that every
possibility of recovery vanishes. For Nietzsche, there is no Isis to re-member Osiris's
dismembered body; crucifixion is not followed by resurrection. Bataille underscores the importance of Nietzsche's insight.

> In order to represent the decisive break that took place, it is necessary to tie the sun-
> dering vision of the "return" to what Nietzsche experienced when he reflected upon
> the explosive vision of Heraclitus, and to what he experienced later in his own vision
> of the "death of God": this is necessary in order to perceive the full extent of the bolt
> of lightning that never stopped shattering his life while at the same time projecting it
> into a burst of violent light. TIME is unleashed in the "death" of the One whose eterni-
> ty gave Being an immutable foundation. And the audacious act that represents the
> "return" at the summit of this rending agony only wrests from the dead God his total
> strength, in order to give it to the deleterious absurdity of time.

A pyramid with its tip knocked off is an altar of sacrifice. For Nietzsche,
this sacrificial altar is the site of the death of the One that grounds Western meta-
physics. The proper name of the One is God. In the absence of God, who "gave
Being an immutable foundation," there is no transcendental signifier to stop the
play of signs.

> For it is the *foundation* of things that has fallen into a bottomless void. And what is fearless-
> ly conquered—no longer in a duel where the death of the hero is risked against that of
> the monster, in exchange for an indifferent duration—it is not an isolated creature; it is
> the very void of the vertiginous fall, it is TIME. The movement of all life now places the
> human being before the alternatives of either this conquest or a disastrous retreat. The
> human being arrives at the threshold: there he must throw himself headlong into that
> which has no foundation and no head.

This is the threshold that marks the groundless ground where we now must
attempt to stand. The headless pyramid, which infinitely extends the labyrinth by

foreclosing every possibility of escape, figures a solar economy in which there is expenditure without return. Where Poe sees a glowing candle lighting the way back to the original matrix or primal origin, Bataille glimpses the exploding sun that temporarily gives the gift of life by burning itself out. The sun that is truly prodigal consumes itself in a holocaust that renders return impossible. The solar economy is a consumer economy in which consumption is not only a way of life but also a way of death. When consumption becomes excessive, festivals know no end. Everything...everyone is consumed with consumption. But consumption is never simple. If bound by the principles of work, consumption is a giving that is a taking; there is no investment without an expectation of return, no wager that seems unprofitable. Consumption, however, does not always work and thus is not always economical. Sometimes giving is not taking but is a letting go that expects nothing in return...nothing. For the reasonable economist, such a wager is as absurd as the time in which it is made. Why spend (yourself) for nothing? Why sacrifice (yourself) for nothing? Why bet when the odds are stacked against you? The house always wins, even — perhaps especially — when it is not a home.

But is the refusal to wager really a choice or only the semblance of choice? Bataille insists that the ceaseless search for the One, which grounds Being and secures meaning, involves a futile effort to overcome temporality by attempting to negate the negativities constitutive of human experience. To embrace the death of God is to affirm "the deleterious absurdity of time" in which meaning is eternally sacrificed in a potlatch that is as pointless as the pyramid on which it is staged. The sacrifice of God is the death of the transcendental signified, which marks the closure of the classical regime of re-presentation. Left to float freely, signs figure other signs in a play that is as endless as it is purposeless. A pyramid with its tip knocked off serves as a bridge to nothing. This nothingness is not Poe's Nihility, which is really everything, but a nothing that is nothing but nothing. The tomb, it seems, is empty — not because resurrection has occurred but because the body has disappeared or has become nothing but the semblance of a body. If the crypt is empty, the secret is that there is no secret. If the pyramid has no point, the eye of reason is blind. If the riddle of the sphinx is unsolvable, hieroglyphs remain infinitely readable signs.

Nothing remains...to hide.

The worst thing that could happen to you after the end of

your time would be to be embalmed and laid up in a pyramid.

I'm repulsed when I think about the Egyptians taking each

organ and embalming it separately in its own receptacle.

I want my machinery to disappear.   Andy Warhol

We are challenged to solve two difficult problems when
we build architecture in a simulated city. One is how we can
create a work of architecture as an entity while goods as entities are losing
their significance, and another is how we can build architecture
that endures time while local communities are nullified,
and the network of communications via media appears
and disappears instantly....
For the first problem, we are required to solve the question of how
to make fictional or video-image-like architecture;
for the second problem, we need to learn how to make ephemeral
or temporary architecture. I do not mean that architecture
should be replaced with video images or that
temporary buildings should be used.
We should rather build fictional and ephemeral architecture
as a permanent entity.

Toyo Ito

Once you uncover that which lies behind the mask,
it is only to discover another mask.
The literal aspect of the disguise (the façade, the street)
indicates other systems of knowledge,
other ways to read the city: formal masks hide socioeconomic ones,
while literal masks hide metaphorical ones.
Each system of knowledge obscures another.
Masks hide other masks and each successive level of meaning
confirms the impossibility of grasping reality.

Bernard Tschumi

It begins (again) as it always begins, with the disap

pearance of the body—not a real body but the semblance of a body, a filmic body or, more precisely, the semblance of the semblance of a body, which takes the form of a transcription of a filmic body. "They found the *Transcripts* by accident. Just one little tap and the wall split open, revealing a lifetime's worth of metropolitan pleasures—pleasures they had no intention of giving up. So when she threatened to run and tell the authorities, they had no alternative but to stop her. And that's when the second accident occurred— the accident of murder." When the crime involves modern architecture, murder is not accidental. The history of architectural modernism is a story of alternative strategies for making the body disappear. The crime of ornamentation provokes the crime of bodily violation in which materiality dematerializes. As everything becomes transparent, surface grows ever more important and nothing remains to hide. "With the new disembodied skins," Bernard Tschumi explains, "the roles of engineer and architect became increasingly separate: the engineer took care of the frame, the architect the skin. Architecture was becoming a matter of appearances." For modernists, these

The darkness of the desert is dark beyond the

superficial appearances playing on the skins of glass boxes reflect the complexities and contradictions of temporal experience, which must be overcome. Transparent buildings turn away from the fleeting world and in on themselves to become reflexive structures whose autonomy mimes a transcendence once limited to gods. For Tschumi, the figure of this ancient longing for transcendence and permanence is the pyramid. The abstraction and dematerialization of modern architecture represent the desire to escape time by securing stability in the midst of flux.

But what if, as Tschumi insists, "eternity is over?" What if time is inescapable and insecurity unavoidable? Following Bataille, Tschumi believes that a labyrinth undermines every pyramid.

> It has been implied the Labyrinth shows itself as a slow history of space, but that total revelation of the Labyrinth is historically impossible because no point of transcendence in time is available.... One can never see it in totality, nor can one express it. One is condemned to it and cannot go outside and see the whole. But remember: Icarus flew away, toward the sun. So after all, does the way out of the Labyrinth lie in the making of the Pyramid, through a projection of the subject toward some transcendental objectivity?

darkness of night. No light can illuminate the darkness whose shadow renders everything obscure. In this other darkness, disappearance appears as the trace of something that is never there but is always slipping away. The desert makes our transiency transparent. To linger in the desert—and what place is not the desert?—we must embrace the loss of what we never possess. In the fleeting moment of this impossible caress, nothing is visible. Nothing.

The straight and narrow road stretches endlessly like a fragile film along the shifting surface of the desert. In the distance, a light gradually begins to appear. As the road rolls beneath the car as if winding itself on an invisible reel, the light becomes an eerie ray, which either descends from the heavens to the earth or ascends from earth to the heavens. Like an ancient pillar of fire, this beacon glowing in the wilderness guides exiles toward the promised land.

At the edge of town near the point at which city and desert meet, a huge glas(s) pyramid as black as Memnon suddenly emerges as if out of nothing. At first it appears that the tip of the pyramid has been knocked off. But closer inspection reveals that the thirty-story pyramid is capped by the world's most powerful beam of light (315,000 watts), which, on a clear night, is visible 250 miles away. Between

Unfortunately not. The Labyrinth cannot be dominated. The top of the Pyramid is an imaginary place, and Icarus fell down: the nature of the Labyrinth is such that it entertains dreams that include the dream of the Pyramid.

The dream of modernism will not end until architecture once again becomes timely. When the pointlessness of the pyramidal fix is exposed, labyrinthine architecture becomes possible.

But how can architecture become timely? Tschumi has bet his career on the possibility of subverting architecture's preoccupation with stable forms by reconfiguring the relationship between space and event. In a 1995 interview with Isozaki Arata, he observes:

You said architecture is something that people normally see as static, as permanent. It is important, I think, that for six thousand years architecture was always the symbol of stability, of permanence, of eternity. It starts with religion. Architecture is always about stability, either structural stability or the stability of the institution. It's frozen, it's there, it never changes. As we know, it even marks our mode of thinking – one talks about the foundation of our society or the structure of thought – it's always about stability. One thing that struck me very early on was that architecture simultaneously was always challenged by the movement of bodies going through architecture, by various activities in it....You know, I like stories. When I was reading about architecture, it was always nice stories. I liked bad stories, I liked murder stories. Your question, when you place it in

the pyramid and the road stand an obelisk covered with enigmatic hieroglyphs and a sphinx twice the size of the Egyptian original. The black pyramid with its monumental ornaments is the 2,526-room Luxor Hotel,
located at the southern end of the Strip in Las Vegas.

  As one walks under the Sphinx and enters the pyramid, one does
not so much step through a looking glass as pass through an invisible
screen and enter a space that is virtually cinematic. The Luxor boasts the
largest atrium in the world – twenty-nine million cubic feet, large enough
for nine 747 airplanes. Unlike every other hotel in Vegas, the Luxor's casino
is not immediately obvious. The cavernous space, reminiscent of the pyramidal microchip structure housing the Tyrell Corporation in *Blade Runner*, is
divided into several levels. Ascending a flight of stairs, one encounters
another obelisk encircled by restaurants, gift shops, and three movie theaters with marquees announcing *In Search of the Obelisk*, *Luxor Live?* and *The
Theater of Time*. These films form *Secrets of the Luxor Pyramid*, which has been
written and directed by special-effects wizard Douglas Trumbull, whose

terms of my work, of course, goes to early
times when I was trying to learn about architecture through the cinema, through film,
because I felt that the film space was telling
me something about architecture, because
you had always movement of bodies in space.
Space was constantly activated by movement.

In *The Manhattan Transcripts* (1981),
Tschumi presents a theoretical exploration of the ways in which events and
movements can generate timely structures. Ever sensitive to the shifting currents of contemporary culture, the events
that preoccupy Tschumi are "mediaized."
"Let us return to the media," he urges. "In

our era of reproduction, we have seen how the conventional
construction techniques of frame and skin correspond to the
superficiality and precariousness of media culture, and how a
constant expansion of change was necessary to satisfy the
often banal needs of the media…. In a world heavily influenced
by the media, this relentless need for change is not necessarily
to be understood as negative." Instead of fleeing the flux of
time by searching for eternal structures, Tschumi embraces
ephemerality by creating an architecture whose "substance"
is a play of images. He situates his work by describing a trajectory that has led architecture from the real to the virtual.

  The continuing transformation of buildings from heavy to light, from dark
  to (electric) light, and possibly from classic to lite; the impulse is to move
  from material to immaterial…, from the heavy stone of the Egyptians to
  Roman vaults, then Gothic arches, then iron construction, the curtain wall,

credits include 2001: *A Space Odyssey*, *The Andromeda Strain* (1969), *Close Encounters of the Third Kind* (1976), *Star Trek: The Motion Picture* (1979), *Blade Runner* (1982), *Brainstorm* (1983), and *Back to the Future: The Ride* (1993).

The Luxor complex creates a simulated immersive environment in which the cinematic morphs into the virtual. Film layered upon film generates a space in which passive observers of cinema become active players in virtual games that know no end. Trumbull proudly declares: "You're not just looking at the movie, you're in the movie; you become a character." In theaters strategically located within a structure that is a reproduction of a movie set that has never been built, the mechanical reproductions of the panorama and diorama are transformed into the electronic reproductions of telematic media. Like every typical Western narrative, *Secrets of the Luxor Pyramid* has three parts, which are intended to weave together past, present, and future to form a coherent whole. The film portrays an advanced pre-Egyptian civilization that has been forgotten for centuries. Within the frame of the film, everything traditionally associated with ancient Egypt is reinscribed as a poor facsimile of the sophisticated technologies developed by an even more ancient

structural glass, immaterial light screens, Albert Speer's Cathedral of Light, holograms, and now virtual reality. Dematerialization in architecture cannot be separated from the development of technology. The more recent stages of dematerialization… are not only structural but they also introduce electricity and electronics as integral parts of architecture. Between the tectonic and the electronic, between the building and the billboard, between the city of places and the space of flows is a residual space that ultimately changes its own definition. This residual, nondesignated, in-between space can be designated as one of the spaces of the event.

In the residual space of the in-between, Tschumi morphs tectonics into teletonics to create what can best be described as electrotecture.

The Manhattan Transcripts anticipates the trajectory of Tschumi's later work. His fascination with film reflects what might be called the "cinematization" of contemporary experience. As

the media networks in which we are entangled become ever more intricate, images consume everything that once seemed real. The images constituting "reality" are neither stable nor secure but are constantly changing. What most intrigues Tschumi about film is the way in which its insistent sequentiality captures temporal flux. Though cinematic sequence is structured, it is not fixed and, therefore, harbors an instability that can be both creative and destructive. In the shifty structure of film, Tschumi discerns a way of smuggling time into architecture.

people. One of the secrets of the Luxor is that what has long been considered the source of civilization is actually an imitation of an original, which has left virtually no trace. In this way, the trilogy reconfigures the space of the Luxor by recasting the hotel as a simulation of a simulation. Even at the source of the Nile, only a film of the original remains. Describing his fantastic metanarrative in terms designed to promote his vision, Trumbull explains:

> Episode One: "In Search of the Obelisk," is a thrilling, four-minute simulator ride during which the audience explores a mysterious underground pyramid, escapes its terrifying booby traps, and battles a power-hungry cult leader who will stop at nothing to take possession of a "crystal obelisk," the key to the temple's power.
> Episode Two: "Luxor Live," is a multimedia presentation featuring a Showscan rear-projected film, large-screen 3-D film projection, and several large, multi-image video screens. During the fifteen-minute show, the 350 audience members participate in a live television broadcast, view a total solar eclipse in Egypt, experience an elaborate dream-like vision, and ultimately question what is real and what is illusion.
> Episode Three: "Timestorm," presented in a steeply raked 350-seat theater with a vertical screen seven stories tall. During the fifteen-minute show, the theater becomes

Tschumi develops his (re)visionary architecture by appropriating filmic techniques to extend and subvert some of the most seminal and least appreciated aspects of modern architecture. As interpreters sought an adequate theoretical framework for the articulation and defense of modernist practices, an alliance between architecture and semiotic theory developed. During the first half of this century, the linguistic turn, initiated by thinkers as different as Wittgenstein and Saussure, spread steadily until it encompassed virtually all areas of cultural analysis. By the 1960s, it seemed everything was, in Lacan's famous phrase, "structured like a language." In architecture, as in other areas of inquiry, the most important extension of linguistic theory was Lévi-Strauss's use of Saussure's structural linguistics for the interpretation of social and cultural phenomena. Influential theorists attempted to decode the "language" of architecture by establishing the isomorphism between supplemental ornamentation and essential forms on the one hand and, on the other, shifting signifiers and the deep structures or generative rules of grammar. To understand cultural phenomena, critics argued, it is necessary to uncover foundational structures by stripping away superficial appearances. Whether understood epistemologically or ontologically, structural analysis exposes the Platonism implicit a time machine transporting the audience far into the future where they witness alternative visions of how the future may unfold.

As we move back to the future, always searching for the past that was never present, which forever approaches as the future that never arrives, we are consumed by the images we consume. Consuming images create a labyrinth from which there is no exit. Descending from the heights of virtuality to foundational depths, one passes boats ferrying guests to their rooms along the Nile River, which flows gently around the interior of the pyramid. "Real" palm trees whose trunks "have been injected with a dye-preserving fluid, which also acts as a fire retardant," line the path to the casino. When interiority and exteriority as well as nature and culture become indistinguishable, filming becomes an abyss that is infinitely profound. At the far end of the casino, stairs descend to the lowest level of the structure, where King Tutankhamen's tomb and an adjoining museum gift shop are located. As if to ground simulation in reality, the entrance to the tomb is marked by a "piece from one of the stone blocks used to build the great pyramids of Giza."

in modern architecture's formalism. When the "real" is associated with pure form, temporality becomes a world of illusion to be overcome or even destroyed. All of Tschumi's work is directed against this ancient tradition, which continues to infect modernity.

Having learned the lessons of poststructuralism, Tschumi realizes that effective criticism must be subversive rather than merely oppositional. By reading structuralism against the grain, he detects faults in the foundational principles of modern architecture. Tschumi organizes his critical reflections around two pivotal insights. First, recalling an argument initially advanced by Venturi in *Complexity and Contradiction in Architecture* and *Learning from Las Vegas*, Tschumi underscores a tension between what modern architects say and what they do. While preaching a formalist doctrine in which ornamentation is

regarded as a crime, modernists appropriate industrial images and iconography for aesthetic purposes. Appearances to the contrary notwithstanding, form is ornamental. When the stylistic interests of modernism are exposed, it becomes clear that instead of form following function, form follows form. Moreover, since architectural form reinscribes stylish images, forms, which have long been declared essential, are actually images of images. This line of analysis erases what is usually regarded as the definitive difference between modern and postmodern

When wary tourists cautiously enter the dark labyrinth, they are greeted by the reassuring voice of Howard Carter, who retraces the steps that led to his original discovery: "Hello, my name is Howard Carter. On behalf of the Luxor Hotel, it is my pleasure to welcome you to this recreation of the tomb of Tutankhamen, the fabulous archeological treasure that I discovered in 1922. Please walk down the passageway. The steps you are taking now are the same that Lord Carnarvon and I took on that fateful November afternoon." The playfully forbidding tunnel leads past carefully designed displays of faux artifacts preserved in the pyramid's crypt. In the middle of the labyrinth at the base of the pyramid, the darkness is suddenly shattered by the brilliant light of glittering gold in King

architecture. Rather than overturning modernism, postmodern architecture renders its stylistic strategies transparent. Tschumi argues:

> It is significant that architectural postmodernism's challenge to the linguistic choices of modernism has never assaulted its value system. To discuss "the crisis of architecture" in wholly stylistic terms was a false polemic, a clever feint aimed at masking the absence of concerns about use. While it is not irrelevant to distinguish between an autonomous, self-referential architecture that transcends history and culture and an architecture that echoes historical or cultural precedents and regional contexts, it should be noted that both address the same definition of architecture as formal or stylistic manipulation. Form still follows form; only the meaning and the frame of reference differ.

The second pivot of Tschumi's polemic begins to emerge when his analysis of modernist formalism is translated into semiotic terms. His reading of structural linguistics is as subversive as his account of modern architecture. While traditional semiotics privileges the signified over the signifier, structural linguistics shifts from a referential to a relational theory of meaning. Instead of referring to a signified, which is prior to and the condition of the possibility of meaning, signifiers, structuralists argue, refer to other signifiers. What appears to be a signified that simultaneously escapes and grounds the play of signifiers is actually another signifier caught in an endless web of relations. A sign, therefore, never presents the thing-in-itself or represents a transcendental signified but always refigures signs of signs. Signs, of course, are not always verbal; they can also be, inter alia, visual. When representations are visual, to insist that signs are always signs of signs is to admit that images are always images of images.

It is not difficult to recognize the unsettling implications of this line of argument. If the sign is always the sign of a sign and not the presentation of the thing-in-itself or re-presentation of a transcendental signified, the foundation that secures the significance of signs and determinability of meaning disappears. In the absence of a stable ground, signs float in shifting currents

Tutankhamen's burial chamber. The walls are decorated with scenes painted in tempera, recording the king's journey from the world of the living to the world of the dead. Images of twelve baboons represent the first twelve hours of night through which both sun and king must pass to reach the dawn that is their rebirth. In the middle of the chamber, the royal coffin rests. "Carter's" hushed voice describes the scene.

> What you see here is the outermost of three coffins that enclose the body of Tutankhamen. These coffins were enclosed in the stone sarcophagus and, like the great shrines, they nested one inside the other. When we removed the lid of the stone sarcophagus, we found two sheets of linen covering an indistinct form. Slowly, cautiously, we rolled back the ancient blackened cloth. Everyone present was astonished, overcome by the sheer magnificence of the object revealed — the object you now see before you. This coffin was made of cyprus wood and was finished in gold foil. The face is that of Tutankhamen, the boy king, a face at once mournful and filled with royalty and youth. On his forehead are the symbols of royalty — the vulture and the cobra. The elongated beard and crossed arms holding the crook and flail are symbols of Osiris, lord of the afterlife with whom Pharaoh is now joined.

God and king are united by the axis mundi, which passes through the center of the pyramid. The light at the tip of the pyramid is named Râ. By ascending this eternal ray,

that cannot be fixed. Furthermore, codes, which once had been used to crack the meaning of phenomena, become reversible. Since the significance of signifiers is differential or diacritical, neither term in a relationship can be privileged. The reversibility of signifiers leads to the undecidability of meaning. When extended beyond the realm of linguistics sensu strictissimo, the switch from a referential to a relational perspective implies that meaning is contextual. If signs are irreducibly relational, meaning changes with context. In an effort to prevent the devaluation of linguistic currency, structuralists attempt to establish a fixed exchange rate among signifiers. Though meaning shifts with context, the rules of exchange remain constant. For structuralists, the codes regulating language, and, by extension, all cultural phenomena, are universal and eternal. The stability of the code implies that the mind is hardwired. If the mind displays permanence, changing relations always harbor unchanging principles, which secure significance and ground meaning.

For critics schooled in what Paul Ricoeur aptly labels "the hermeneutics of suspicion," structuralism appears to be a last-ditch effort to preserve certainties, which are slipping away. Having glimpsed ground zero, structuralists attempt to cover the abyss by inverting transcendent forms to create immutable

Tutankhamen escapes time and becomes divine.

But, of course, the tomb buried beneath the Nevada desert is empty —not because resurrection has occurred but because the body has disappeared or has become nothing but the semblance of a body that was never present in the first place. Between the darkness of the crypt and the light of Râ lies the scene of virtualization where the real becomes immaterial. If the crypt is empty, the secret of the Luxor Pyramid is that there is no secret. In the absence of the secret, nothing remains to hide.

Ascending from the depths of the structure, which now appear utterly superficial, one crosses the Nile, leaving behind camels and palm trees, and approaches the tunnel leading to the Strip. Having discovered the absence of the body at the base of the pyramid, the hieroglyphs decorating the walls now seem indecipherable. When corpus is not grounded in corpse, signs become endlessly interpretable and, thus, are either completely meaningless or infinitely meaningful. Even after leaving the tomb, everything remains irreducibly cryptic.

Though the Luxor is unlike any other hotel, there is something strangely familiar about its "crypto-Egypto" architecture. Egyptomania is not, of course, new.

foundations. But all such efforts eventually prove futile. Once faulted, foundations eventually crumble, leaving nothing, which is fraught with danger as well as opportunity. Tschumi summarizes the architectural stakes of this collapse of ground: "Not only are linguistic signs arbitrary (as Saussure showed us long ago), but interpretation itself is open to constant questioning. Every interpretation can be the object of interpretation, and that new interpretation can, in turn, be interpreted, until every interpretation erases the previous one. The dominant history of architecture, which is a history of the signified, has to be revised, at a time when there is no longer a normative rule, a cause-and-effect relationship between a form and a function, between a signifier and its signified: only a deregulation of meaning."

If "the dominant history of architecture" has been "a history of the signified," it now seems imperative to create a new departure by developing an "architecture of the signifier." The signifier upon which such an architecture would be built would not, of course, be wed to a secure signified but would float freely without any ground to secure it. For Tschumi, the absence of ground, which is our inescapable cultural condition, creates the possibility of an imaginative revisioning of architecture. In *The Manhattan Transcripts*, his exploration of this groundless terrain leads to the formulation of *le principe du cardage*, which joins linguistic theory and

From the moment Carter opened Tutankhamen's crypt, the world has not been able to get enough of Egypt. Nor is the interplay of architecture and cinema, mediated by the imagery of Egypt, without precedent. Since the second decade of this century, Egypt has not only been the subject of countless films but has also provided guiding motifs for theme theaters ranging from Meyer and Holler's Egyptian Theater in Hollywood (1921) to Sony's 3-D IMAX theater in New York (1994).

These recurrent orientalist fantasies suggest readings of modern architecture that break with conventional critical wisdom. While the architects whose names are inseparable from the history of modernism were decrying ornamentation and stripping away decoration, other architects whose names have long been forgotten were designing and constructing spectacular movie palaces in which fantasy runs wild. From the 1920s to the 1960s, imaginative architects and speculative developers spared no expense in creating immersive environments, which effectively extended the screen beyond the stage to encompass the entire theater. In some cases, the show even spilled onto the sidewalk and street. From decorated façades depicting Egyptian, Mayan, and French themes to the sleek curves of art deco and streamlined shapes appropriated from industrial design, the space of

cinematic practice. The principle of framing weaves together the structuralist insight into the diacritical character of signs with the cinematic technique of montage in a distinctive strategy for generating architectural form from temporal events. Appropriating the structuralist turn from reference to relation, Tschumi explains that "the role of the *Transcripts* is never to represent; they are not mimetic. So, at the same time, the buildings and events are not real buildings or events, for distancing and subjectivity are also themes of the transcription. Thus the reality of its sequences does not lie in accurate transposition of the outside world, but in the internal logic these sequences display." In contrast to structuralism, the logic of Tschumi's framing is not fixed but is infinitely flexible. Though sequences are always framed, images can be cut and pasted, edited and reedited, to create meanings that are in constant flux. "The principle of framing," Tschumi stresses, "permits the arrangement of elements of the sequence because each of the frames, like images of a film, can be indefinitely combined, juxtaposed." When combinatory rules are flexible, meanings proliferate and interpretation becomes endlessly revisable. "Partial control is exercised through the use of the frame. Each frame, each part of a sequence qualifies, reinforces, or alters the parts that precede and follow it. The associations so formed allow for a plurality of interpretations rather than a singular fact. Each part is both complete and cinema became a riot of supplements in which ornament is not a crime. With the return of the repressed, the pure forms, white skins, and transparent walls of modernism no longer seem quite so functional and rational. Nor do the decorated sheds of postmodernism seem quite so innovative. If modernism has lessons to learn from Las Vegas, it is because Las Vegas has always understood modernism better than modernists themselves. Like the desires circulating through it, ornament never disappears even when it is denied. The Strip strips bare the pretenses of modernism by exposing structure as ornament and form as figure rather than ground. If ground is figure and figure ground, foundations collapse. The site of this implosion is ground zero.

The Vegas of the 1990s is not the same as the Vegas Robert Venturi, Denise Scott Brown, and Steven Izenour discovered in the 1960s. Resolutely rejecting the sterile

incomplete.... Indeterminacy is always present in the sequence, irrespective of its methodological, spatial, or narrative structure." Resisting the struggle to resolve contradictions, Tschumi cultivates the creative potential of opposition. Simultaneously determinate and indeterminate, complete and incomplete, an architecture of the signifier rejects every analysis that claims to be final.

In the first major project he realized, Parc de La Villette, Tschumi puts into practice the theory presented in *The Manhattan Transcripts*: "The Park is a series of cinegrams, each of which is based on a precise set of architectonic, spatial or programmatic transformations. Contiguity and superimposition of cinegrams are two aspects of montage. Montage, as technique, includes other such devices as repetition, inversion, substitution

and insertion. These devices suggest an art of rupture, whereby invention resides in contrast – even in contradiction." To appreciate the implications of the play of signs at work in La Villette, it is important to understand the way in which moving images generate architectural structures. As I have noted, in *The Manhattan Transcripts* images from a film that does not exist are reinscribed to create patterns that retain traces of movement. La Villette, in turn, re-presents the Transcripts in structures that appear to be timely. As the image of the transcription of images

purism, which characterizes much modern architecture, Venturi and his colleagues call for a more "tolerant" architecture that accepts "existing conditions" rather than negates what is for the sake of what ought to be. The defining feature of the 1960s Strip and its architecture, they argue, is the circuit joining car and sign.

> But it is the highway signs, through their sculptural forms or pictorial silhouettes, their positions in space, their inflected shapes, and their graphic meanings, that identify and unify the megatexture. They make verbal and symbolic connections through space, communicating a complexity of meanings through hundreds of associations in a few seconds from far away. Symbol dominates space. Architecture is not enough. Because the spatial relationships are made by symbols more than by forms, architecture in this landscape becomes symbol in space rather than form in space. Architecture defines very little: The big sign and the little building is the rule of Route 66. The sign is more important than the architecture.

From this perspective, the Strip is the expressive embodiment of postwar American automobile culture. The structure and location of buildings determine and are

that figure nothing, Tschumi's park stages the collapse of meaning.

To overcome architecture's longing for permanence, Tschumi undertakes the seemingly impossible task of introducing time into formal structures. Two elements govern the design of La Villette: a classical modernist grid, punctuated by a series of Follies, and a "promenade cinématique," which winds its way through the park. Each Folly is created by deconstructing a red cube, reminiscent of Russian constructivism, and reassembling its fragments to create heterogeneous structures that provide space for cafés, galleries, cinemas, a post office, a day-care facility, and an information center. In these Follies, form does not follow function. Moreover, meaning is neither intrinsic to structure nor imposed upon

determined by patterns of traffic flow. For Venturi, these developments mark a decisive break with the foundational tenets of modern architecture.

Ever sensitive to complexity and contradiction, Venturi correctly maintains that modernists affirm in practice what they deny in theory. While insisting that form follows function, modern architects implicitly appropriate the iconography of industrialism in a way that transforms structure into ornament. "Modern ornament," Venturi points out, "has seldom been symbolic of anything non-architectural." Since the symbolism of modernism refers to other architectural symbols, it is reflexive or self-referential. By contrast, in Strip architecture, Venturi argues, signs point beyond themselves by communicating information necessary for orientation in an ever more complex world. "From the desert town on the highway in the West of today, we can learn new and vivid lessons about an impure architecture of communication. The little low buildings, gray-brown like the desert, separate and recede from the street that is now the highway, their false fronts disengaged and turned perpendicular to the highway as big, high signs. If you take the signs away, there is no place. The desert town is intensified communication along the

structure by a master architect. Each Folly is "une case vide" – "an empty slot or box in a chart or matrix, an unoccupied square in a chessboard, blank compartment: the point of the unexpected." The board of the grid creates the space for "the game of architecture," which according to Tschumi,

> is neither function – usage – nor form – style – nor even the complete adequation between function and form, but rather the ensemble of possible combinations and permutations between different categories of analysis – space, movement, event, technique, symbol, etc. To make architecture is not to "compose" or "to make a synthesis" of opposites, but is to combine, permutate.... This game of permutations is not gratuitous. If one searches for a new model, a new form of architecture or urbanism, a new social model, it is imperative to study all possibilities, in the manner of matrices of scientific research or certain structural diagrams where the principle of the empty slot demonstrates that all signification is a function of position

highway." Elsewhere Venturi underscores the communicative function of signs in a text that suggests the source of the design feature that distinguishes both his own Vanna Venturi House (1963–65) and Philip Johnson's AT&T Corporate Headquarters (1979–84).

> The sign for the Motel Monticello, a silhouette of an enormous Chippendale highboy, is visible on the highway before the motel itself. This architecture of styles and signs is anti-spatial; it is an architecture of communication over space; communication dominates space as an element in the architecture of the landscape.... A driver 30 years ago could maintain a sense of orientation in space. At the simple crossroad a little sign with an arrow confirmed what was obvious. One knew where one was. When the crossroads becomes a cloverleaf, one must turn right to turn left.... But the driver has no time to ponder para-doxical subtleties within a dangerous, sinuous maze. He or she relies on signs for guid-ance — enormous signs in vast spaces at high speeds.

But are we sure signs still communicate? Can signs provide orientation and direction? Do signs point the way out of the labyrinth or take us even deeper into it? Can signs

and surface, produced by the circulation of the empty slot in the series of a structure.

The site where the meaning inscribed in empty slots is con-stituted and reconstituted is the cinematic promenade. As one follows the twists and turns of the filmic path, the Follies are repeatedly reframed. According to le *principe du cardage*, when frames shift, meaning changes and significance alters. La Villette actually appears to accomplish the impossible: though structures remain stable, everything is in motion. Simultaneously complete and incomplete, closed and open, the park forms a stage set for interactive media in which all production is repro-ductive co-production. Far from passive viewers, people who stroll along the cinematic promenade actively participate in the construction of the imaginative spaces in which they dwell.

Within these spaces, meaning is sacri-ficed and nothing is fixed. In a certain sense, the point of Parc de La Villette is nothing other than *la mise en oeuvre* of nothing. "La Villette," Tschumi concludes, "aims at an architecture that *means*

be trusted?

Venturi's postmodernist critique of modern architecture is, paradoxically, constructed around the quintessential modernist invention: the automobile. This is its strength as well as its weakness. Any theory or architecture that remains bound to the car cannot escape the regime of Fordism and everything it represents. "Postwar Fordism has to be seen," as David Harvey insists, "less as a mere system of mass production and more as a total way of life." In a circuit of exchange mirrored by the reflexivity of the work of art, mass production produces mass consumption, which, in turn, reproduces mass production. The automobile is, in effect, the incarnation of the structure of self-referentiality that informs both modern and modernist practices of production and reproduction. Automobility is, of course, self-movement. Like an ancient Unmoved Mover who descends from heaven to earth, the automobile is moved by nothing other than itself. The dream of automobility is autonomy. To inhabit the automobile machine is to be integrated within a closed circuit in which all production is auto-production. The very proximity of self and machine creates an insurmountable distance between self and world.

nothing, an architecture of the signifier rather than the signified – one that is pure trace or play of language. In a Nietzschean manner, La Villette moves towards interpretive infinity, for the

effect of refusing fixity is not insignificance, but semantic plurality." The endless play of semantic plurality erupts when meaning is deregulated. In subsequent projects, Tschumi refines the grave levity that haunts his baseless work by developing an architecture that is increasingly light.

Not content with an architecture that means nothing, Tschumi experiments with an architecture that is created out of nothing. In the Glass Video Gallery (Groningen, Holland, 1990), structure virtually disappears in a spectacular play

When automobility becomes a way of life, *machines à habiter* become glass houses whose windshields function like screens of noninteractive TV and nonimmersive cinema. To drive down the Strip in such a glass machine is to watch passively as the film unwinds and the spectacle unfolds.

But the Strip of the nineties, unlike the Strip of the sixties, is no longer built around the automobile. While cars do, of course, remain, Las Vegas Boulevard has become a pedestrian promenade. The shift from driving to walking reflects broader changes that have taken place in Las Vegas during the past three decades. The early years of postwar Vegas were dominated by two legendary figures: Bugsy Siegel and Howard Hughes. It was Bugsy Siegel, Los Angeles representative of the Chicago mob, who first had the extraordinary vision of creating a spectacular oasis in the midst of the Nevada desert. Though the bosses remained suspicious of Bugsy's ambitions, his relentless pursuit of his dream eventually led to the completion of the first major casino resort hotel. In the years after Bugsy's murder, the crackdown on illegal gambling in California made Las Vegas increasingly attractive to mobsters. There were intermittent efforts to clean up Vegas, but mob ruled the

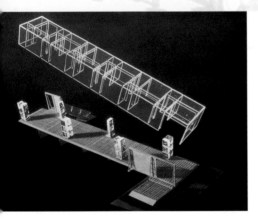

of images. Though reminiscent of the glass boxes of Mies van der Rohe and Philip Johnson, the Video Gallery represents a significant departure from the tenets of modernism. Ever suspicious of the simplicity and transparency of glass architecture, Tschumi layers superficial images to create spaces that are suggestively opaque. The gallery measures 3.6 x 2.6 x 21.6 meters and is tilted in such a way that it rises above the ground. Since the walls, beams, and partitions are held together by glass clips, there appear to be no supporting structures; this building is all skin and no bones. During the day, the surfaces of glass reflect the surrounding tress in a way that makes it unclear where nature ends and artifice begins. At night, the building dematerializes, leaving only flickering video images and insubstantial bodies, which seem to drift aimlessly in the air. Tschumi poses the questions his gallery raises: "Floating several feet above the ground, its floor is slightly tipped horizontally and vertically so as to challenge the visitor's sense of balance. At night, one's sense of imbalance becomes even more extreme as the endlessly reflected town until the late 1960s. All of this changed when, in 1966, Howard Hughes stole into Vegas in the dead of night and took up residence in the isolated penthouse of the Desert Inn.

Hughes is best known for the idiosyncratic paranoia that dominated the later years of his life. Paul Virilio goes so far as to describe Hughes as a "techno-logical monk" whose life is a grotesque embodiment of the dystopic possibilities of contemporary culture: "Speed is nothing other than a vision of the world, and for me Hughes is a prophet, a monstrous prophet, moreover, and I'm not really at all crazy about the guy, but he's a prophet of the technical future of society. That absolute inertia, that bedridden man, a universal bedridden man as I called him, that's what we're all going to become." This reading of Hughes not only represents a one-sided view of technology but also overlooks his important contributions to the transformation of Las Vegas. From his early involvement with Hollywood to his innovative development of flight simulators and high-tech amusements, Hughes projected a future for Vegas that broke with its seedy past. The realization of this future, however, required legislative actions,

images of the video screens cease to define the transparent surfaces of the glass envelope. Reality or mirrorlike simulation? Appearance of the image, disappearance of the real?" Since such questions are unanswerable, every conclusion is suspended.

While the Glass Video Gallery obviously extends the inquiry begun in La Villette, the shift from film to video represents a note-worthy development. Film is a transitional medium bound to the mechanical means of reproduction characteristic of industrialism; video, by contrast, takes advantage of the electronic means of reproduction at the heart of postindustrialism. Of the many differences separating the electronic from the mechanical, the most important in this context is the way in which electronic environments obscure the line between word and image. When information is the medium of exchange, the verbal and the visual are different inscriptions of the same "stuff." The translatability of words into images and images into words engenders an all-consuming mediascape. Tschumi is one of the few who realizes that this new cultural situation changes the condition of architecture. "The movement of lights, combined with the visual display of information systems, suggest new spatial perceptions. Whether they take the form of electronic environments...or the form of electronic liquid-crystal media screens hovering weightlessly in some abstract televisual which could only be initiated by someone with Hughes's power and influence. Prior to the 1960s, Nevada state law limited gambling licenses to individuals. This restriction created enormous financial difficulties for anyone who wanted to construct a casino. In most cases, individuals did not have the necessary capital to invest in an uncertain venture in the middle of the desert. Consequently, this state law had the unexpected effect of encouraging the illegal financing of casinos. One of the few organizations with enough money to bet on Vegas was the mob. Ever the canny businessman, Hughes recognized the financial opportunity created by legalized gambling. But he also realized that Vegas could not prosper as long as the mob ruled and legitimate business could not invest in the city. To create more favorable conditions for investment, Hughes developed a two-pronged strategy: first, he started buying hotels and casinos and, second, he began lobbying state legislators to enact a law that would permit corporations as well as individuals to secure gambling licenses. When the Nevada legislature eventually succumbed to Hughes's pressure, the Las Vegas of the nineties became not only possible but virtually inevitable.

space, this activity becomes the main event, the main program in such a space, its functional raison d'être. For centuries the program of architecture used to be the activities of humans. Could it be replaced by the electronic spectacle?" In his proposal for the Center of Art and Media Technology (ZKM) in Karlsruhe, Germany (where, we have discovered, Franz Joseph Gall presented his famous lectures on phrenology), Tschumi responds to his own question with another question: "How can architecture, whose historical role was to generate the

As major corporations moved in, it immediately became obvious that financial viability required an expansion of Vegas's customer base. If there were to be any justification for the expenditure of funds necessary for the construction of new casinos and hotels, gambling would have to be made attractive to a broader range of people. To achieve this end, the new Vegas had to distance itself from its corrupt past. In devising strategies for developing Vegas, "legitimate" investors looked to Hollywood.

While Venturi and his colleagues recognized certain similarities between Disneyland and Las Vegas, they never could have anticipated the extent to which the thematization of urban space characterizes the city today. From frontier villages and tropical oases to Mississippi riverboats and Mediterranean resorts, from medieval castles and the land of Oz to oriental palaces and the New York skyline, every hotel-casino is organized around a theme. Fantasies fold into fantasies to create worlds within worlds. The spectacular MGM Grand Hotel, whose 5,005 rooms make it the largest hotel in the world, "literalizes" the thematization of Vegas by replicating Disney World. Though ostensibly miming Disney's "original," MGM's theme park is significantly different from its prototype. While the Disney "imagineers" who

appearance of stable images (monuments, order, etc.) deal with today's culture of the disappearance of unstable images (twenty-four-image-per-second cinema, video and computer-generated images)?" His solution to this dilemma is to make ephemeral images the "substance" of his architecture. The construction of a center for art and media technology provides an unusual opportunity for an exploration of the ways in which images and information are transforming contemporary experience. Tschumi's proposal confounds oppositions like surface/depth, exteriority/interiority, and public/private. The building is organized around a central core with balconies permitting access to all parts of the center. In addition to providing a passageway to the train station, the ground floor serves as a space for performances, exhibitions, and seminars. One of the distinctive features of Tschumi's proposal is the building's façade. The surface of the structure is a constantly changing photo-electronic computer-animated skin, which reacts to external light and sound. In this way, the exterior of the building simulates the screen of an interactive video terminal.

But Tschumi's "electronic spectacle" is not limited to the skin of the building. When you peel away one surface, you find nothing but another surface. "Skin rubbing at skin, skin, skin, skin, skin" creates a structure that is profoundly superficial. The "interior" of ZKM is a large televisual designed EPCOT Center take pride in accurately representing our "small world," the architects of MGM flaunt artifice by openly imitating an imitation for which there is no original. None of the nostalgia that pervades Disney World haunts Las Vegas. In the simulated environment of Vegas, the real becomes blatantly hyperreal. The primary motivation for thematizing Las Vegas is economic. As we have seen, to attract people who never considered gambling, illegitimate vice had to be turned into legitimate entertainment. Moreover, the city had to be made hospitable to middle-class families. The Disneyfication of Vegas is intended to sanitize the city by washing away its sin and corruption. Far from a den of iniquity, Vegas creates the façade of a user-friendly amusement park. When New York, New York puts a Coney Island roller coaster between the hotel-casino and the Strip, the strategy guiding recent development is put on display for everyone to see.

Shifting financial incentives bring changes in architectural programs. To create an environment appealing to a new clientele, architects had to develop design tactics that would convincingly integrate the fantastic and familiar. Between the 1960s and the 1990s, the pedestrian space of malls displaced the automobile space of the suburban strip. By the early 1980s, there were over 28,500 malls in

hall generated by huge video screens, suspended passerelles and stairs, a tensile glass elevator, TV monitors, liquid-crystal screens, and two rooms floating in midair. By mixing and (mis)matching, Tschumi transforms architectonics into teletonics to generate vertiginous spaces from moving signs referring to nothing. If it were possible to enter ZKM, it would be like passing through a video screen and becoming totally immersed in a virtual-reality chamber. But one cannot enter this strange space

because ZKM has not been built.

When Tschumi won the competition for Le Fresnoy National Studio for Contemporary Arts (1991), he finally had the chance to realize the electronic spectacle he had long been imagining. This opportunity brought with it a growing appreciation for the complexities and contradictions of the information revolution. While continuing to insist on the creative potential of electronic media and information systems, Tschumi acknowledges certain dangers they pose. Most important, he sees in emerging technologies a potential for programming experience in a way that determines events. When media and information networks prescribe behavior, they become the latest version of the formal structures architecture has always presupposed. In an effort to preserve the aleatory, without which life becomes the eternal

North America. While most of these malls combined predictable design elements from arcades and department stores, which can be traced to the glass architecture that emerged in Europe during the nineteenth century, more venturesome developers sought to construct new environments for consumption by creating spaces in which shopping becomes spectacular entertainment. The 5.2 million-square-foot West Edmonton Mall, for example, boasts 800 shops, 11 department stores, 20 movie theaters, 13 nightclubs, 110 restaurants, a 360-room hotel, an ice-skating rink, nineteenth-century Parisian boulevards, and New Orleans's Bourbon Street. Vegas's new hotel-casino megaplexes borrow the most outlandish features of contemporary cathedrals of consumption and, as always, up the ante. Nowhere is this more obvious than in Caesar's Palace, where outside is brought inside to create an enormous mall that imitates an Italian village within the hotel-casino. Under an ever-changing Mediterranean sky, upscale shops line streets with quaint Italian restaurants and open-air cafés. In the middle of the piazza, there is a dramatic "marble" fountain whose figures are automatons, which come alive every hour to tell the story of Bacchus and his drunken festivals. In

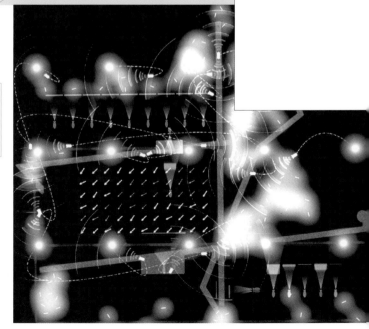

return of the same, Tschumi fashions what he describes as "a non-programmed in-between." This marginal space is an interface where events are "matters" of chance.

In approaching Le Fresnoy, Tschumi decides to preserve the "rather strange and derelict entertainment center" already on the site. Around existing structures he develops space for a school, a film studio, a mediathèque, spectacle and exhibition halls, two cinemas, laboratories for research and production (sound, electronic image, film, and video), administrative

Caesar's Palace, the "bacchanalian in which no member is sober" erupts in excessive rituals of consumption.

The Vegas mallscape, however, is not limited to the public interiors of giant hotels. In a certain sense, the entire Strip has become one big arcade or mall. No longer separated from the street by large parking lots, casinos crowd the sidewalk with façades, which dissolve the boundary between inside and outside. Most of the casinos that are still set back from the street are framed by simulated movie sets depicting everything from erupting volcanoes and warring pirate ships to Italian lakes and New York skyscrapers. As the car is left behind and pedestrians roam the set, the cinemascape changes. No longer separated from the screen by a thin film of glass, viewers are consumed by a spectacle that knows no bounds. In this way, today's Strip creates an immersive environment in which the virtual becomes real and the real becomes virtual. In Vegas, as one of its leading citizens, Andre Agassi, proclaims from signs and screens, "It's all a matter of image." As display screens dissolve into display screens to reveal endless dataspace, images become consuming, and "realities" are virtualized. Nowhere is the virtualization of

Chapter 5

offices, housing, and a bar/restaurant. The overall aim of this project is to create something like an "electronic Bauhaus" where old and new are associated but not integrated. The device linking past and future is a massive electronic roof (75 x 90 meters), which serves as an artificial sky where media events can be projected. This "artifi-ciel" recalls nineteenth-century Paris arcades and anticipates the computerized canopy enclosing Las Vegas's Freemont Street. Unlike his modernist precursors and postmodernist successors, however,

Tschumi is less interested in the new or old as such than in elusive interface between them. Only at this in-between point does chance have a chance. If there is no chance and everything is predetermined, time is nothing more than an illusory appearance of eternity. Describing his plan for Le Fresnoy, Tschumi stresses the importance of what cannot be anticipated or programmed: "A multimedia center for the arts located so as to constitute a heterogeneous assemblage of old and new constructions; all under a gigantic electronic roof. Between the old roofs and the new one lies the in-between: a nonprogrammed space for experiments and inventions. Video gardens, suspended cinemas, a computer-generated skybar activate the in-between, together with the superimposed reflections of catwalks, supporting columns, and hanging stairs." Bringing reality more obvious than on the new Freemont Street. Long associated with the seedy side of old Vegas, Glitter Gulch recently has been transformed into what is, in effect, a gigantic computer terminal or virtual-reality machine. Vegas city planners have converted the train terminal, which inspired the glass architecture of the Parisian arcades, into a computer terminal to create the new space of the virtual arcade. Freemont Street is now covered with a 1,500-foot computerized canopy with 1.4 million synchronized lights and lasers. To roam through Glitter Gulch is to discover the timely timelessness of terminal space.

The teleonics of Freemont Street suggest previously inconceivable architectural possibilities. If, as Toyo Ito suggests, the challenge of building in a simulated city — and what city today is not simulated? —can be met only by making "fictional or video-image-like architecture," which is undeniably "ephemeral or temporary," then it

together opposites that cannot be synthesized, Tschumi creates a labyrinth, which resembles Piranesi's Carceri as much as cyberspace. Floating signifiers, ephemeral images, and graphic information transform architecture into electrotecture whose significance is its insubstantiality. Completing the situationists' project by putting the society of spectacle on display, Le Fresnoy finally screens reality.

When reality is screened, the real becomes virtual and the virtual becomes real. In his current work – especially the Columbia University Student Center – Tschumi extends the processes of mediaizing and virtualizing reality by transforming bodies into images. The in-between space where media events are staged is folded into the building in such a way that screens screen other screens. Infinite screens render the real imaginary and images real. In the student center, images are no longer generated by computer programs and video projectors but are created by bodies moving along convoluted surfaces. Screens are not simply outer façades but are layered in such a way is once again necessary to learn from Las Vegas. But the lessons Vegas currently teaches are not the same as the lessons Venturi learned three decades ago. The issue is no longer modernism versus postmodernism; nor is it simply a question of form versus ornament or structure versus sign. Something else —something that, in many ways, is far more unsettling—is occurring. And this occurrence—this event as it were—involves a certain slipping away. Though Venturi no longer believes in the foundational structures of modernism, he still has faith in signs. In a world without foundations, he insists, signs provide orientation, direction, even meaning. But along today's Strip, even this faith becomes questionable. When signs consume the bodies that lend them weight, everything becomes (a "matter" of) light. The ground, which once seemed stable, becomes ground zero where nothing fixes meaning.

The more deeply one ventures into the superficial space of the Strip, the more it

INTERFACING

that the building becomes an intricate assemblage of superimposed surfaces. As bodies move across skins that run deep, the material becomes immaterial and the immaterial materializes. Along the endless boundary of the interface, nothing is hiding.

From his earliest theoretical writings to his most recent projects, Tschumi relentlessly pursues the implications of electronic media and information technologies for architectural theory and practice. As materiality appears to be symptomatic of our current cultural condition. Las Vegas illuminates the ephemerality that is our "reality." People go to Vegas hoping to win and leave having learned how to lose. They wager expecting a return on their investment but discover that in the long run their expenditure is without return. In the casino economy, even when one "wins," loss cannot be amortized.

The loss the Strip displays is the strange loss of something we never possess. As reality is virtualized, we gradually are forced to confess that real has always been imaginary. The bright lights of the Strip stage a virtual potlatch of meaning. Instead of communicating meaning, which can be read at a distance, dematerializes and virtuality is realized, the fabric of life and structure of experience are transformed. "Today in our media world," Tschumi observes, "we are constantly asking ourselves what is real, what is virtual, what is 'unmediaized' and what is 'mediaized.' Maybe architecture is really the place where that question is always present." The abiding presence of the question reflects the lingering absence of an answer. Having forsaken eternal forms and secure foundations, Tschumi realizes that the dilemma we face is not to find answers but to learn to live with the impossibility of solutions. Convinced that there is no escape from time, his architecture leaves us abandoned in a labyrinth from which there is no exit. Fleeting images and

If there is nothing material, there is
also nothing immaterial. The concept
no longer contains anything.
Friedrich Nietzsche

proliferating signs immerse us in a superficial flux that never ends. Monuments built to stop the flux turn
out to be glas(s) pyramids where the pointlessness of ancient sacrificial rituals becomes transparent. By simulating simulations, which have long been mistaken for real, the substance of our dreams is stripped away to expose the

HIDING | 266

Each surface is an interface between two environments
that is ruled by a constant activity in the form of an exchange between the
two substances placed in contact with one another.

This new scientific definition of substance demonstrates the
contamination at work: the "boundary, or limiting surface"
has turned into an osmotic membrane, like a blotting pad.
Even if this last definition is more rigorous than earlier ones,
it still signals a change in the notion of limitation. The limitation of space has become commutation: the radical separation, the necessary crossing, the transit of a constant activity, the activity of incessant exchanges, the transfer between
two environments and two substances. What used to be
the boundary of a material, its "terminus," has become an
entryway hidden in the most imperceptible entity. From
here on, the appearance of surfaces and superficies conceals
a secret transparency, a thickness without thickness, a volume without volume, an imperceptible quantity.

Paul Virilio

inescapability of time and unavoidability of death. This insight need not lead to unhappy consciousness and ceaseless mourning but can nourish a gay wisdom that freely accepts lack and embraces loss. In the game of life, it is necessary to wager everything with the expectation of receiving nothing in return. Absolutely nothing.

After (the) all has been said and done, the question that remains is not "What is virtual reality?" but "What is not virtual reality?" This query, however, is duplicitous because it raises at least two seemingly contradictory questions. The first is a statement cast as a question: "Is there anything that is not virtual reality?" suggests that there is no reality that is not virtual. The second assumes that not all reality is virtual and asks: "How can we define nonvirtual reality?" The question within the question, therefore, poses an alternative: virtuality or reality? But the term virtual reality resists every such opposition and implies something that simultaneously eludes and refigures the contrasts that structure our thought and define our worlds. To think virtuality is to think reality differently.

Such thinking inevitably must be indirect. Thus, we can only ask "What *is not* virtual reality?" by first asking the question we seek to avoid: "What *is* virtual reality?" On the most obvious level, virtual reality is, of course, a widely advertised technology, which relies on sophisticated hardware and software, whose range of applications is rapidly expanding. The far-reaching significance of virtual reality, however, remains obscure if this particular technology is not placed within the context of the philosophical, aesthetic, and technological developments from which it has emerged. When traced genealogically, it becomes clear that virtual reality effectively figures our current cultural condition. As modernity gives way to postmodernity, reality is virtualized and virtuality is realized. To comprehend the worlds into which we are ever more rapidly being thrown, it is necessary to understand complex techno-socio-cultural processes of virtualization, which have been under way for several centuries. The speed and extent of technological innovation lend a certain urgency to this interpretive task. It seems as if scientists, engineers, and technicians have been gripped by the avant-garde's obsession with making it new. From media, entertainment, and telecommunications to artificial life, neuroscience, and electronic money, virtual technologies are transforming what was once called "reality." At the precise moment that critical analysis is imperative, interpretive strategies that have proved extremely effective for the past several decades no longer seem adequate.

To overcome this impasse, it is necessary to reconsider certain determinative oppositions that continue to haunt critical reflection. The most productive debates

in recent critical theory have grown out of poststructuralist criticisms of overt and covert versions of structuralism. While poststructuralism does not constitute a unified movement, writers as different as Jacques Derrida, Jacques Lacan, and Michel Foucault on the one hand, and on the other Hélène Cixous, Julia Kristeva, and Michel de Certeau devise alternative tactics to subvert the grid of binary oppositions with which structuralists believe they can capture reality. Leading poststructuralists realize that, since they remain unavoidably entangled in the systems and structures they resist, the task of criticism is endless. From a poststructural perspective, criticism aims to undermine binary and dialectical oppositions, which are supposed to ground thought and reality, by soliciting a return of the repressed that every system or structure explicitly excludes but implicitly includes. The nondialectical mean between which extremes are suspended constitutes something like an *interface*, which is the condition of the possibility and the impossibility of seemingly seamless systems and structures. When radically conceived, this interface extends beyond every margin of difference to "contaminate" opposites that once seemed fixed. By approaching techno-socio-cultural processes of virtualization through the strange notion or nonnotion of interfacing, it becomes possible to reconfigure rather than merely reinscribe structures of difference and systems of oppositions. As a result of this reconfiguration, contrasts like mind/body, self/other, human/machine, nature/culture, natural/artificial, material/immaterial, and reality/virtuality no longer appear to be what they once were. This recasting of differences as interfaces creates new interpretive and critical possibilities.

   While poststructuralism resists every form of oppositional

thinking, critics have long insisted that it remains plagued by contrasts it claims to overturn. Though often misguided, such criticisms are not always unjustified. Many proponents of poststructuralism leave themselves open to attack by effectively repeating antitheses in their haste to avoid syntheses. This tendency is particularly evident in debates that have focused on three contrasting polarities: theory/theorized, aesthetics/politics, and system-structure/difference-other.

Resistance to theory runs deep. As criticism has become more theoretical, responses to it have become more hostile. Often blissfully unaware of the theoretical presuppositions of their assaults on theory, critics frequently dismiss new interpretive strategies as ephemeral Parisian fashions that are guaranteed to fade as quickly as they appear. Since it is usually impossible to find common ground for responsible discussion, poststructuralists all too often have ignored their critics and proceeded as if no response were necessary. This self-isolation is not without consequences. In the absence of informed exchange, previously inventive tactics lose their critical edge and are regularized and institutionalized. In this way, theory is transformed into a *method* or *technique*, which is mechanically applied to different works and imposed on diverse objects. When thus standardized, the critique of system negates itself by becoming effectively systematic. This eternal return of the same violates the very singularity poststructuralists claim to evoke.

As theory withdraws from that to which it is supposed to apply, it becomes increasingly irrelevant. Instead of engaging the "real," theory seems caught in a hall of mirrors from which "reality" is "systematically" excluded. The growing separation of theory from theorized points to the rise of a second opposition: aesthetics/politics. The interplay between the aesthetic and the political has been repeatedly subjected to critical analysis in debates surrounding postmodernism and poststructuralism. One of the most persistent charges brought against postmodern culture and poststructural criticism is that they are nothing more than reflections of postindustrial capitalism, which involve an aestheticization of experience that renders them inescapably apolitical. To break out of the self-enclosed sphere of aesthetics, it is argued, one must engage in concrete actions in the "real" world. Recent preoccupation with "the political" and "the ethical" reflect this recurrent criticism of postmodern aesthetics and poststructural theory. This line of argument obviously presupposes conventional oppositions like theory/praxis, art/life, and symbolic/real, which poststructuralism calls into question. In pressing their case, critics insist that the privileging of theory, art, and the symbolic must give way to a recovery of praxis, life, and the real. Far from effecting significant change, this reversal simply mirrors the mistake it is intended to overcome. To move beyond oppositional criticism, it is necessary to recast differences as interfaces. It is, after (the) all, possible for art to be effective politically and the political to harbor an aesthetic dimension.

LES OISEAUX CHANTANTS

The politicizing of art and aestheticizing of the political imply a refiguring of the constitution and function of structures and systems without which criticism is destined to repeat mistakes of the past. Yet it is precisely at this point that the shortcomings of poststructuralism become painfully obvious. It is clear that the defining characteristic of poststructuralism in all of its guises is a sustained critique of the totalizing and repressive propensities of comprehensive systems and all-inclusive structures. At the time poststructuralism emerged, the sociopolitical situation in postwar Europe made its critique not only understandable but necessary. Faced with totalitarianism on the Right (i.e., fascism) and the Left (i.e., Stalinism), there was a compelling need to resist every principle of totality as well as to find a nontotalizable mean that allows oppositional extremes to be negotiated. By soliciting the return of repressed differences and outcast others, poststructural criticism calls into

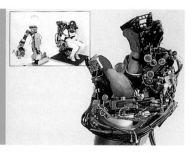

ROBOT HAND, HAND JOB

question the integrity of every intellectual, social, political, and cultural system that claims to be all-encompassing.

While this sustained critique has been enormously important, little is to be gained by ceaselessly repeating gestures of resistance that have lost their historical necessity and have become utterly familiar and predictable. It is no longer sufficient to expose the repressive character of social and cultural systems. The question that is now pressing is whether the polarity of system-structure/difference-other can be reconceived in a way that is intellectually effective, culturally creative, and socially productive. The importance of this problem increases daily as the result of political tensions to which poststructural criticism has directly and indirectly contributed. In far too many cases, the philosophy of difference has issued in a politics of identity that is indistinguishable from the divisive foundationalism and fundamentalism it is supposed to subvert. While hegemonic systems surely have not been eliminated, it is our differences that increasingly are tearing us apart. Social and cultural survival depends upon our ability to conceive and realize complex structures that can function holistically but not totalistically. Poststructuralists will not or cannot conceive of a structure that does not totalize and is not repressive. In what follows, I will attempt to think what poststructuralism leaves unthought by showing how nontotalizing structures, which nonetheless act as a whole, are beginning to emerge in the tangled networks and webs through which reality is virtualized and virtuality is realized.

The term *virtual reality* was coined by Jaron Lanier, who in 1989 invented the DataGlove, which since has become an important part of virtual-reality technology. While particular interfaces vary considerably, there are three basic types of virtual-reality devices: (1) small TV screens and earphones mounted in a helmet and a data glove or joystick (i.e., six-dimensional mouse); (2) video cameras that trace the movements of the user in a virtual graphic world; (3) 3-D modeling projected on a flat or curved screen and 3-D glasses. One of the primary goals of current virtual-reality research is to create virtual environments that are not only visually convincing but engage senses other than sight. Considerable progress has already been made in generating worlds that are tactilely and kinesthetically responsive. In 1987, Lanier's VPL Research, Inc., extended the technology of the DataGlove to create a hidelike DataSuit, comprising a network of sensors that monitor fifty bodily sites that feed data to computers, which, in turn, generate images calculated to correspond to the user's movements. As prostheses become more complex, every effort is made to keep the interfaces as inconspicuous as possible. In some of the most advanced work in interface development, researchers are experimenting with replacing the head-mounted display with retinal imaging. "This would put a picture directly onto the retina from a pinpoint source, a retinal scanner, using low-density lasers. This is not a matter of pixels; it is a matter of eye physiology, of rods and cones. There would be no screen of any description, no helmet, just spectacles, perhaps without the sort of glass we know today. And, by varying focal lengths, it should be possible to have mixed virtual and real images, at one and the same time." As this remarkable project suggests, researchers are convinced that, if virtual worlds are to be convincing, users must forget they are "inside" computers.

The intricate computer graphics required for virtual reality are created in real time by high-speed computers capable of generating thousands of polygons per second. In order to produce the speed of computation necessary for high-resolution graphics, computers use parallel rather than serial processing. The degree of verisimilitude is a function of available bandwidth, the speed of the computers, and the number of polygons produced. The worlds constructed by virtual-reality engines are completely artificial and thoroughly informational; in virtual environments, all space is dataspace.

What distinguishes virtual-reality machines from other computer graphic displays is the *interactivity* they facilitate. Scientists and engineers have finally created the world anticipated decades ago by Paul Klee when he declared: "Now objects perceive me." The reality effect of simulated environments is a result of the capacity of the virtual-reality apparatus to perceive the perception of the user and to respond accordingly. As Paul Virilio explains, "After *synthetic images*, products of the info-graphic software, after digital image processing of computer-aided design, we are on the verge of *synthetic vision*, the automation of perception." Automated perception is perception without a perceiver, or perception in which the perceiver is a machine. When the circuit is complete, the perception of the machine and the perception of the user interface in a way that makes it virtually impossible to be sure where the human ends and the machine begins.

The technological developments leading to the creation of virtual-reality machines grew primarily out of the military, aerospace, and entertainment industries. During the 1970s and early 1980s, the Department of Defense sponsored extensive research that was aimed at interfacing computer hardware and software, stereoscopy, and simulation to form artificial environments that could be used for a variety of purposes. The most useful product that grew out of this early research was the flight simulator. For NASA, virtual reality created the attractive possibility of developing telerobotic systems that could be used in space-station construction and repair. The military and NASA were also interested in the potential of interactive stereoscopic display for virtual and televisual exploration. Howard Rheingold summarizes these developments:

> The field of VR began to crystalize when the right combination of sponsors, visionaries, engineers, and enabling technologies came together at NASA's Ames Research Center in Mountain View, in the mid 1980s. It was there that a human interface researcher, a cognitive scientist, an adventure-game programmer, and a small network of garage inventors put together the first affordable VR prototypes. It was there that a generation of cybernauts donned a helmet-mounted display and glove input device, pointed their fingers, flew around wire-frame worlds of green light-mesh, and went back to their laboratories to dream up the VR applications of the 1990s.

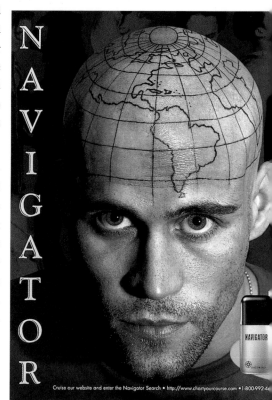

Cruise our website and enter the Navigator Search • http://www.chartyourcourse.com • 1-800-992-4

As Rheingold suggests, high-level public and private research should not overshadow the important contributions of early visionaries. Most people working in the field trace the original conception of virtual reality to a paper entitled "The Ultimate Display," published in 1965 by Ivan Sutherland, who at the time was a graduate student of Claude Shannon, the inventor of information theory. With uncommon prescience, the precocious Sutherland wrote:

> We live in a physical world whose properties we have come to know well through long familiarity. We sense an involvement with this physical world, which gives us the ability to predict...where objects will fall, how well-known shapes look from other

angles, and how much force is required to push objects against friction. We lack corresponding familiarity with the forces on charged particles, forces in non-uniform fields, the effects of nonprojective geometric transformations, and high-inertia, low-friction motion. A display connected to a digital computer gives us a chance to gain familiarity with concepts not realizable in the physical world. It is a looking glass into a mathematical wonderland.

If the task of the display is to serve as a looking glass into the mathematical wonderland constructed in a computer memory, it should serve as many senses as possible. So far as I know, no one seriously proposes computer displays of smell or taste. Excellent audio displays exist but unfortunately we have little ability to have the computer produce meaningful sounds. I want to describe for you a kinesthetic display.

The force required to move a joystick could be computer controlled, just as the actuation force on the controls of a Link Trainer are charged to give the feel of a real airplane. With such a display, a computer model of particles in an electric field could combine manual control of the position of a moving charge, replete with the sensation of forces on the charge, with a visual presentation of the charge's position.... By use of such an input/output device, we can add a force display to our sight and sound capability.

NAVIGATOR, DANA PERFUMES

GLOBAL PHRENOLOGY

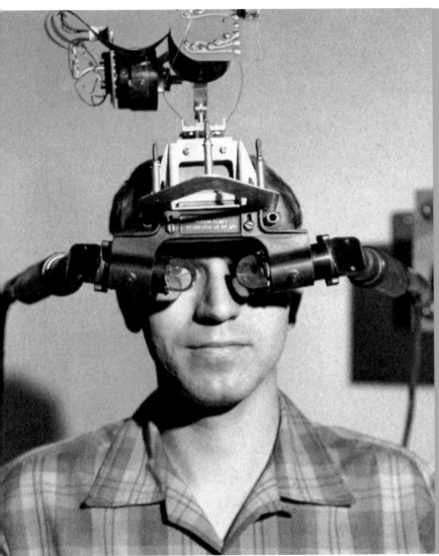

IVAN SUTHERLAND, HEAD-MOUNTED
COMPTER-GRAPHICS DISPLAY SYSTEM
DOUBLE VISION

In 1965, Sutherland's remarks sounded more like science fiction than scientific theory. But by the early 1990s, research conducted by Frederick Brooks and his colleagues at the University of North Carolina at Chapel Hill had resulted in the development of haptic display systems that fulfill Sutherland's predictions to a remarkable degree. Brooks describes the way in which his system augments visual with kinesthetic display: "Haptic displays give the user the ability to feel objects or force-fields in a virtual environment. The forces exerted on the user's hand or finger are usually expressed as a function of the user's hand position and orientation. Thus, the haptic display hardware and software repeatedly determine the user's hand position and orientation and then apply the appropriate force. Our haptic displays are designed to provide kinesthetic feedback, felt via the muscles and tendons, rather than tactile feedback, which is felt as 'touch' by the skin."

Sutherland did not merely project brave new worlds but actually wrote programs and developed technologies that helped to make virtuality a reality. In 1969, he invented the first head-mounted display, which served as the prototype for all later variations

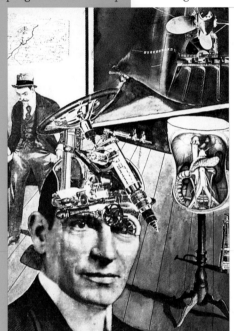

RAOUL HAUSMANN, TATLIN AT HOME, 1920

"MECHANISMS OF MEANING"

of this device. His most significant contribution, however, involved software rather than hardware. As early as the 1950s, Douglas Eagelbart was conducting research under the auspices of the military's Advanced Research Projects Agency (ARPA), which had been formed in the wake of the Soviet Union's successful launching of Sputnik. Eagelbart dreamed of creating interactive computers that would be constructed around the visual display of data. While the hardware difficulties with the interface were resolved relatively quickly by the invention of the mouse in the 1960s, a solution to the software problem proved considerably more elusive. The challenge was to create software that would make it possible to use bits of information to control the appearance of pixels on the terminal display screen. Sutherland solved this problem with his revolutionary program Sketchpad, described by Ted Nelson, the inventor of hypertext, as "the most important computer program ever written." "Sketchpad allowed a computer operator to use the computer to create sophisticated visual models on a display screen that resembled a television set. The visual patterns could be stored in the computer's memory like any other data, and could be manipulated by the computer's processor.... But Sketchpad was much more than a tool that enabled computers to translate abstractions into perceptually concrete forms. And Sketchpad was a powerful model of a totally new way to operate computers; by changing something on the display screen, it was possible to change something in the computer's memory." With the invention of interfaces that allow interactivity and visual-display programs, the very character of computers and nature of computing were thoroughly transformed. Virtual reality would not have been possible without Sutherland's revolutionary work.

But not all contributions to the emergence of virtual reality were made by mathematicians and computer scientists. Entertainment entrepreneurs and artists also played significant roles in imagining and developing what eventually became virtual reality. Three years before Sutherland projected "the ultimate display," little-known photographer and cinematographer Morton Heilig patented his Sensorama Simulator. Describing the purpose of his device, Heilig writes:

The present invention, generally, relates to simulator apparatus and, more particularly, to apparatus to stimulate the senses of an individual to simulate an actual experience realistically....

Accordingly, it is an object of the present invention to provide an apparatus to simulate a desired experience by developing sensations in a plurality of the senses.

It is also an object of the invention to provide an apparatus for simulating an actual, predetermined experience in the senses of an individual.

A further object of the invention is to provide an apparatus for use by one or more persons to experience a simulated situation.

Another object of the invention is to provide a new and improved apparatus to develop realism in a simulated situation.

Though Heilig touted the educational potential of his invention, he found its entertainment possibilities much more intriguing. His work in TV and film had convinced him that televisual technology was only in its infancy. In 1960, nine years before Sutherland developed his head-mounted display, Heilig created and patented what he described as a "Stereoscopic Television for Individual Use." Two years later he expanded his vision to construct the Sensorama Simulator, which brought together 3-D movies, stereophonic sound, and controlled motion. Though the entertainment industry was not impressed, it is clear that Heilig's creation anticipated both arcade versions of virtual reality and cinematic devices like Douglas Trumbull's astonishingly popular Back to the Future: The Ride, which has drawn more than thirty million people since it opened in Disney World in 1993. Deeply impressed by efforts in the 1950s to extend the filmic format in Cinerama and 3-D movies, Heilig devoted himself to developing a genuinely multisensory immersive environment.

> "I recognized right away why Cinerama and 3D were important," Heilig recalled. "When you watch tv or a movie in a theater, you are sitting in one reality, at the same time you are looking at another reality through an imaginary transparent wall. However, when you enlarge that window enough, you get a visceral sense of personal involvement. You *feel* the experience, you don't just *see* it. I felt as if I had stepped through that window and was riding the roller coaster myself instead of watching somebody else. I felt vertigo. That, to me, was significant. I thought about where the technology might go in the future, and I was convinced on the spot, sitting in that Cinerama theater on Broadway, that the future of cinema would mean the creation of films that create the total illusion of reality."

This future would not be realized for more than three decades. By the time Trumbull projected Heilig's dream inside the glass walls of Las Vegas's Luxor Hotel, the Sensorama Simulator as well as its inventor had long been forgotten.

Chance also played a significant role in the career of visionary artist and engineer Myron Krueger. In his 1983 book, whose appearance was delayed for years because no publisher expressed interest in the work, Krueger coined the term *artificial reality* to describe the "responsive environments" he had been developing for a decade and a half. In a series of projects dating from the late 1960s (e.g., Glowflow, 1969; Metaplay, 1970; and Psychic Space, 1971), Krueger carried performance art to a new level by interfacing artist and viewer by means of video, electronic display, and computer graphics. His most ambitious project was Videoplace, in which he used a two-way telecommunication link for the exchange of information to generate a third "place" that visitors could inhabit electronically. In *Artificial Reality*, Krueger describes the possibilities and limitations of the space he created:

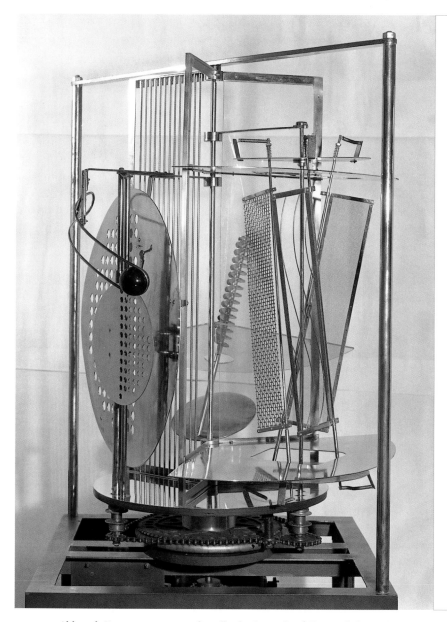

Although VIDEOPLACE cannot literally duplicate the fullness of the real world, it invents a new model of reality with methods of interacting that are equally compelling. Thus, although some aspects of reality are abridged in VIDEOPLACE, others are enhanced, since many of the constraints and limitations of reality can be overcome.

Interactions within the environment are based on a quest to understand the rules that govern this new universe. A person's expectations can be teased, leading to a startled awareness of previously unquestioned assumptions, much like the experience one has when viewing a Magritte painting.

Though nameless in the mid-1970s, by the 1990s this placeless place was known as cyberspace. As both an engineer and an artist, Krueger was acutely aware of the commercial potential of new technologies yet unusually sensitive to their philosophical significance and aesthetic promise. "We are incredibly attuned," he remarks, "to the idea that the sole purpose of our technology is to solve problems. It also creates concepts and philosophy. We must more fully explore these aspects of our inventions, because the next generation of technology will speak to us, understand us, and perceive our behavior. It will enter every home and office and intercede between us and much of the information and experience we receive. The

MOHOLY-NAGY, LIGHT-SPACE-MODULATOR

"TECHNOLOGY WILL SPEAK TO US, UNDERSTAND

US, AND PERCEIVE OUR BEHAVIOUR..."

design of such intimate technology is an aesthetic issue as much as an engineering one." In the years since Krueger's pioneering work, the philosophical implications and artistic potential of telematic technologies have rarely been analyzed. Before turning to an examination of certain developments in nineteenth-century philosophy and twentieth-century art that help to clarify the significance of virtual reality, a final unexpected influence on the emergence of contemporary technoculture deserves consideration.

The computer revolution of the 1970s and 1980s is inseparably bound to the countercultural revolution of the 1960s. It is no accident that Silicon Valley is just down the (information) superhighway from Haight Ashbury. Describing his first experience with virtual reality, the late Jerry Garcia, lead guitarist for the Grateful Dead, observed:

> What the Acid Test really was was formlessness. It's like the study of chaos. It may be that you have to destroy forms or ignore them in order to see other levels of organization. For me, that's what the Acid Test was – that's what it was a metaphor for. If you go into a situation with nothing planned, sometimes wonderful stuff happens. LSD was certainly an important part of that for me. I also think there's an electronic hinge like computer cybernetics that's going to take us to interesting places and may work the way psychedelics do without the idea of substance.... You can see where this is heading: You're going to be able to put on this thing and be in a completely interactive environment. There is not going to be any story, but there's going to be the way you and it react.... And it's going to take you places as convincingly as any other sensory input. These are remnants of the Sixties. Once you've been to some of those places, you think, "How can I get myself back there again but make it a little easier on myself."

The psychedelic revolution was, of course, part of a broader social upheaval that continues to shape the political and cultural landscape. Just as baby boomers were entering colleges and universities, the United States was in the midst of a contentious civil rights movement and was caught in the Vietnam War. When asked to give their lives for a cause they believed immoral and a war they thought was wrong, young people in unprecedented numbers answered with a resounding "No!" This response to the war gave rise to a more thoroughgoing sociopolitical critique, which, in turn, fed the resistance from which it had grown. Though ostensibly disorganized, in retrospect it is clear that the counterculture was centered on two distinct poles. While sharing a commitment to social change, youthful critics differed on how best to accomplish it. One camp argued that social renewal presupposes an alteration of human consciousness, and the other insisted that society had to be transformed before consciousness would change. Norman O. Brown and Herbert Marcuse emerged as the intellectual gurus of these contrasting positions. But for anyone whose historical vision extends beyond a decade, it is obvious that the debate between these alternative points of view runs throughout the Western tradition. The counterculture arguments of the 1960s reenact the nineteenth-century debate between Hegel and Marx, which is an extension of the ancient religious controversy between mystics and militants. For the latter-day mystics of the 1960s, the preferred vehicles for transforming consciousness were non-Western religions and drugs. From this idealistic perspective, to see differently is to be different; *seeing is believing and believing is being*.

When the counterculture faded, the concerns that had motivated it did not disappear but took different forms. With the failure of the revolution, new ways to effect change had to be found. Some of the most imaginative social critics discovered in burgeoning technoculture a new means for altering consciousness. Speaking for many of his generation, technoguru and lyricist for the Grateful Dead, John Perry Barlow, observes: "The problem is the same today as it was in the 60s: How can consciousness be changed? We had the right vision but the wrong stuff. It's not acid and Buddhism but computers and cyberspace." This conviction was one of the primary motivations for many early leaders of the personal computer revolution. Computers, they believed, are not simply calculating machines but can be vehicles for changing consciousness and redistributing power. Several years prior to his crucial participation in the development of the Apple and Macintosh computers, Steve Jobs roamed throughout India in search of wisdom. When enlightenment finally came, the knowledge it brought was anything but ancient. If knowledge is power, then what could be more radical than putting information in the hands of the people? The attempt to overthrow the authority of centralized government through social protest and the effort to disrupt the power of centralized control of information by replacing mainframes with personal computers appear to be two versions of the same reform program. With the spread of personal computers, the focus of this struggle has shifted to the control of Internet. Acutely aware of the far-reaching consequences of losing control of information technologies, the federal government is engaged in a growing effort to monitor and regulate computer networks. This intervention is being vigorously resisted by critics on the Left as well as the Right who harbor undying suspicions of the centralized authority. One of the most effective groups in this critical conflict is the Electronic Frontier Foundation, founded by Barlow and his colleague Mitch Kapor, who is a longtime devotee of transcendental meditation and founder of the spectacularly successful software company named, appropriately, Lotus. EFF's mission statement summarizes the purpose of the organization: "The Electronic Frontier Foundation has been established to help to civilize the electronic frontier; to make it truly useful and beneficial not just to a technical elite, but to everyone, and to do this in a way which is in keeping with our society's highest tradition of the free and open flow of information." Though the language has become more judicious and measured, the social agenda of the 1960s remains largely intact.

This transition from the counterculture to technoculture has been acted out in cyberspace. During the early stages of computer-aided communication, one of the most popular and influential bulletin boards was the WELL, an acronym for Whole Earth Lectronic Link. Created by one of Ken Kesey's erstwhile Merry Pranksters and founder of *Whole Earth Review*, Stewart Brand, the WELL is where psychedelics meet electronics to forge a revolution of consciousness that promises to change the world. One of the leading figures in the world of the WELL is none other than virtual-reality pioneer and leading media spokesperson for new technologies, Jaron Lanier. Remaining firmly committed to the spiritual and mystical principles of the counterculture, Lanier summarizes his understanding of the significance of virtual reality in a 1989 *Whole Earth Review* interview:

> It will bring back a sense of the shared mystical altered sense of reality that is so important in basically every other civilization and culture prior to big patriarchal power. I hope that this might lead to some sense of tolerance and understanding. But there's more to it than that. I often worry about whether it's a good technology or a bad technology: I have a little benchmark I use for that. I believe if a technology increases human power or even human intelligence and that's its sole effect, then it's simply an evil technology at birth.... If the technology, on the other hand, has a tendency to increase human communication, human sharing, then I think it's a good one overall, even though there might be ways in which it could be used badly.... I do hope that Virtual Reality will provide more meeting between people. It has a tendency to bring up empathy and reduce violence, although there's certainly no panacea ultimately....Virtual Reality starts out as a medium just like television or computers or written language, but once it gets to be used to a certain degree, it ceases to be a medium and simply becomes another reality we can inhabit. When it crosses over that boundary, it becomes another reality. I think of it as acting like a sponge where it absorbs human activity from the physical plane into Virtual Reality planes. To the degree that this happens there is a very beneficial asymmetry that comes into play. When Virtual Reality sponges up good energy from the physical plane, then what you get in Virtual Reality is beautiful art, beautiful dance, beautiful creativity, beautiful dreams to share, beautiful adventures. When Virtual Reality soaks up bad energy from the physical plane, what we get is some decrease, however small, in violence and hurt on the physical plane in exchange for events on the Virtual plane.

For Lanier and his fellow believers, there is no social restoration without spiritual renewal; virtual reality is promoted as one of the most powerful vehicles for such renewal.

But is Lanier's sponge so new? Where did it come from? Have others used this sponge? In the depths of what sea did it grow? Ever ahead of his time, Nietzsche anticipates such questions.

The madman jumped into their midst and pierced them with his eyes. "Whither is God?" he cried; "I will tell you. We have killed him – you and I. All of us are his murderers. But how did we do this? How could we drink up the sea? Who gave us the sponge to wipe away the entire horizon? What were we doing when we unchained this earth from its sun? Whither is it moving now? Whither are we moving? Away from all suns? Are we not plunging continually? Backward, sideward, forward, in all directions? Is there still any up or down? Are we not erring as through an infinite nothing?... Do we not need to light lanterns in the morning? Do we hear nothing as yet of the noise of the gravediggers who are burying God? Do we smell nothing as yet of the divine decomposition? Gods, too, decompose. God is dead. God remains dead. And we have killed him."

This is a remarkably apt description of the experience of cyberspace, where all reality seems to be virtual. Nietzsche's telling insight grew out of intellectual and cultural developments that had been unfolding for more than a century. Though rarely recognized, the terms of cultural debate in the modern Western world were set during the pivotal decade of the 1790s in the small German town of Jena. The artists, poets, philosophers, and theologians gathered in Jena defined the philosophical and theological agenda for the nineteenth century and articulated what would become the guiding principles of twentieth-century art criticism and practice.

The situation at the end of the twentieth century is, in many ways, remarkably similar to the state of affairs at the end of the nineteenth century. Then as now, the most pressing question of the era was how personal, social, political, and religious fragmentation could be overcome and oppositions joined in a sustainable unity that does not repress differences. In the late eighteenth century, as in the late twentieth, the apparent failure of social revolution led to an inward turn of consciousness. With the collapse of the French Revolution, the locus of expected change shifted from the outer to the inner world. Anticipating countercultural criticisms voiced over two hundred years later, poets and philosophers argued that, if sociopolitical structures were to be changed, consciousness would first have to be transformed. Art, religion, and philosophy, they believed, could effect an inward conversion that would reach completion in outward revolution. The pivotal figure in these developments was Immanuel Kant.

For members of the Jena circle, Kant's critical philosophy was both a symptom of the problems to be overcome and a prefiguration of the solution they sought. In an effort to build upon yet go beyond Kant, his followers concentrated on aspects of his epistemology and aesthetics. Kant sought to secure the possibility of knowledge by bringing together strands of British empiricism and Continental rationalism. Knowledge, he argues, presupposes the synthesis of given manifold of sensation and a priori forms of intuition and categories of understanding. These forms and categories function as something like the grid or matrix through which experience is unified, organized, and, thus, rendered intelligible. Since it is prior to and independent of experience, this matrix is universal. The mind is preprogrammed or, in different terms, hardwired. Since all experience is mediated by this grid, reality as such or the thing-in-itself remains forever inaccessible. The real, in other words, has always already disappeared. While insuring the possibility of a certain kind of knowledge, Kant's transcendental analysis absolutizes the opposition between subject and object and thereby reinscribes the fragmentation, division, and opposition he sought to overcome. The task of *The Critique of Judgment* is to resolve this contradiction.

The third Critique is intended to reconcile the oppositions that plague the first and second Critiques as well as to mediate the theoretical and practical faculties of the mind. The central idea around which Kant organizes his analysis is the notion of inner teleology. In contrast to mechanical relations in which means and end, cause and effect, and part and whole are external to each other, inner teleology defines a condition in which such differences are internally and reciprocally related in a self-organizing structure. "The parts of the thing combine of themselves into the unity of a whole by being reciprocally cause and effect of their form. For this is the only way in which it is possible that the idea of the whole may conversely, or reciprocally, determine in its turn the form and combination of all the parts, not as cause... but as the epistemological basis upon which the systematic unity of the form and combination of all the manifold contained in the given matter become cognizable for the person estimating it." Kant explores two instances of this "systematic unity": the living organism and the beautiful work of art. Vitality and beauty presuppose the integral relation of parts in a comprehensive totality that is self-generating and self-sustaining. Since the end or telos of the organism and the beautiful work of art is internal, neither the organism nor l'oeuvre d'art points to anything beyond itself. They are, in other words, autotelic and thus, in a certain sense, purposeless or, in Kant's paradoxical formulation, are characterized by a "purposiveness without purpose." When fully articulated and completely deployed, the structure of inner teleology is supposed to reconcile opposites that sunder thought and life.

But the strictures of Kant's epistemology prevent him from pushing his insight to its logical conclusion. Since we can never know the real, we cannot be certain that the concept of inner teleology is objectively true. Kant concludes that the notion of an internally differentiated reciprocal structure is a regulative idea or heuristic principle that is useful for organizing experience but that cannot be regarded as constitutive of reality. By setting the ideal against the real, Kant reinscribes the very opposition he struggles to overcome. The writers and philosophers gathered in Jena undertook the task of translating ideality into reality, and vice versa, by rendering Kant's regulative idea constitutive. According to one of the most influential members of the group, Friedrich Schiller, the work of art comes to completion in an organic sociopolitical structure. "It is through beauty," Schiller maintains, "that we arrive at freedom:... If in the dynamic state of rights man encounters man as force and restricts his activity, if in the ethical state of duties he opposes him with the majesty of law and fetters his will, in the sphere of cultivated society, in the aesthetic state, he need appear to him only as shape, confront him only as an object of free play. *To grant freedom by means of freedom* is the fundamental law of this kingdom." Such social change becomes possible only when consciousness is changed by artists who provide the necessary aesthetic education. In his *Letters on the Aesthetic Education of Man*, Schiller outlines what eventually becomes the agenda of the twentieth-century avant-garde.

For Hegel, by contrast, art, left to its own devices, is not up to the task of psychosocial transformation. Aesthetic education, therefore, must be translated into philosophical speculation. Hegel attempts to complete the Kantian revolution by developing an absolute idealism in which the ideal and the real are reconciled in natural and historical processes. To accomplish this mediation of opposites, Hegel historicizes, systematizes, and ontologizes Kant's epistemology and aesthetics. While Kant maintains that the forms of intuition and categories of understanding are universal, Hegel contends that perceptual and conceptual matrices develop historically. Moreover, cognitive categories are not arbitrarily associated but are integrally related in a system that conforms to the organic structure of Kant's beautiful work of art. The Hegelian Notion, whose structure is fully articulated in the *Science of Logic*, is the outworking of Kant's aesthetic idea. The principle of systematic unity that reconciles opposites without destroying differences is for Hegel, as for Kant, inner teleology or purposiveness without purpose. Hegel effectively extends Kant's analysis by arguing that the Idea is not merely logical but also ontological. The Idea, in other words, is constitutive rather than regulative and, therefore, forms the structure of both thought and being. When fully deployed, the Notion becomes an Idea that is all-comprehensive and transparently comprehensible. Since the end is in the beginning, the world, as well as the mind, is wired, and, consequently, the matrix is objective as well as subjective.

In Hegel's philosophical rendering of Kant's aesthetics, the "systematic unity" of the Idea appears as a self-reflexive or self-referential totality, which, though implicit from the beginning, unfolds gradually in space (nature) and time (history). Within this dialectical process, everything becomes itself in and through its own other and, thus, there is nothing outside or beyond the whole. Hegel's insistence that the Idea is not only comprehensible but also comprehensive spells the death of Kant's thing-in-itself. The thing-in-itself, Hegel argues, is nothing more than a concept constructed to establish the limitation of all concepts. Within Hegel's ontologic, there is nothing outside the concept. Appearances, which are particular, constitute the manifestation of the underlying essence that forms the universal substance of all things. If knowledge is not to remain superficial, it is necessary to penetrate the depths by discerning the infrastructure that grounds every suprastructure. Within Hegel's dialectical vision, there can be no appearance without essence, particular without universal, suprastructure without infrastructure, or surface without depth, and, of course, vice versa.

Hegel's philosophical reconciliation of opposites harbors implications that become explicit in twentieth-century artistic practices and sociocultural developments. In Hegel's dialectical vision, differences are not only different but are also identical. As we have discovered, when appearance and reality as well as surface and depth are not merely two but also one, *appearances are real and reality is apparent*. Furthermore, depth is but another surface, and *surface is inescapably profound*. In his lifelong attempt to surmount the dualisms and oppositions plaguing Western thought and society, Hegel is more intent on demonstrating the necessity with which reality appears and depth becomes transparent on surfaces than on exploring the consequences of the implosion of these opposites. It was left for Nietzsche to work out the radical ramifications of Hegel's thought.

Approaching his subject with characteristic indirection, Nietzsche suggests: "Whatever is profound loves masks." Nietzsche transfigures Hegel's search for profundity into an interplay of surfaces that hide nothing. Against Hegel's pursuit of thoroughness and completion, Nietzsche poses fragmentary reflections that are resolutely nonsystematic and open-ended. "Any insistence on profundity and thoroughness," according to Nietzsche, "is a violation, a desire to hurt the basic will of the spirit that unceasingly strives for the apparent and superficial." These important disagreements between Hegel and Nietzsche should not obscure how much they share. Rather than the ardent anti-Hegelian critics usually take him to be, Nietzsche is better understood as working out implications of the Hegelian system that Hegel failed or refused to recognize. AGFA, PLATINUM PRINT BY DENNIS MANARCHY

While Hegel historicizes, systematizes, and ontologizes Kant's aesthetic idea, Nietzsche fictionalizes, relativizes, and desystematizes the Hegelian concept. Nietzsche agrees with Hegel's criticism of Kant's thing-in-itself. Since determinate identity is relational or is a function of a play of differences, Nietzsche argues, there is no thing-in-itself. "The 'thing-in-itself' is nonsensical. If I remove all the relationships, all the 'properties,' all the 'activities' of a thing, the thing does not remain over; because thingness has only

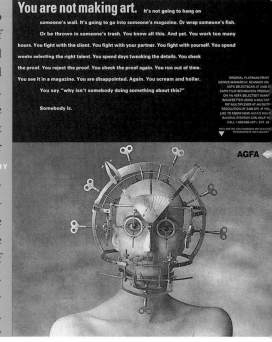

been invented by us owing to the requirements of logic, thus with the aim of defining, communication (to bind together the multiplicity of relationships, properties, activities)." As this remark makes clear, the absence of the thing-in-itself does not disclose the presence of a securely established ontological structure but points to the inescapably *fictive* character of what is usually regarded as real. "The 'real world,' however one has hitherto conceived it," Nietzsche concludes, "has always been the apparent world *once again*."

> *Critique of the concept "true and apparent world."* – Of these, the first is a mere fiction, constructed of fictitious entities.
>
> "Appearance" itself belongs to reality: it is a form of its being; i.e., in a world where there is no being, a certain calculable world of identical causes must first be created through appearance: a tempo at which observation and comparison are possible, etc.
>
> Appearance is an arranged and simplified world, at which our practical instincts have been at work; it is perfectly true for *us*; that is to say, we live, we are able to live in it: proof of its truth for us –
>
> the world, apart from our condition of living in it, the world that we have not reduced to our being, our logic and psychological prejudices, does not exist as a world "in-itself"; it is essentially a world of relationships; under certain conditions it has a differing aspect from every point; its being is essentially different from every point; it presses upon every point, every point resists it – and the sum of these is in every case quite incongruent.

"Skin rubbing at skin."... Hides hiding hides... hiding...

The fictionalization of the real is, in effect, the virtualization of reality. In a manner reminiscent of Kant and Hegel, Nietzsche argues that reality is always already mediated by schemata of perception and structures of cognition. But in contrast to his predecessors and in anticipation of his successors, Nietzsche deconstructs rather than reinscribes the real by arguing that even the limits placed upon the mind's constructive activity are practical constructions. Furthermore, Nietzsche realizes that the mind is not hardwired; perceptual and conceptual matrices are in a state of constant flux. Never existing in isolation, these matrices form something like a *web* or *network* within which "reality" apparently is fabricated. Unlike the closed structure of the Hegelian system, the open fabric of the Nietzschean web creates a fragmentary field in which aleatory associations generate unexpected patterns that disorganize as much as they organize.

The fabrication of the real is a work of art. In one of his most provocative statements, Nietzsche claims: "Only as an aesthetic product can the world be justified to all eternity." For a thinker who is primarily associated with the death of God, Nietzsche's language is sometimes surprisingly theological. Nowhere is this more evident than in *The Birth of Tragedy*.

> Throughout this book, I attributed a purely aesthetic meaning – whether implied or overt – to all process: a kind of divinity if you like, God as the supreme artist, amoral, recklessly creating and destroying, realizing himself indifferently in whatever he does or undoes, ridding himself by his acts of the embarrassment of his riches and the strain of his internal contradictions. The world was made to appear, at every instant, as a successful *solution* to God's own internal tensions, as an ever new vision projected by that grand sufferer for whom illusion is the only possible mode of redemption.

Nietzsche's "theology" of art reverses Hegel's translation of art and religion into philosophy by recasting the theological-philosophical idea as an aesthetic activity. For neither Hegel nor Nietzsche is the death of God the mere negation of the divine. To the contrary, divine creativity disappears from the heavens only to reappear on earth in a process that Hegel interprets logically and Nietzsche views aesthetically. Through this death and resurrection, the locus of creativity shifts from the transcendent Creator to the immanent web of relations in and through which everything arises and passes away.

The work of art

Nothing more?

The work of art

Nothing more.

This nothingness continues to haunt postmodernism. When art is real and the real is aesthetic, *there is nothing outside the image*. With characteristic irony, Warhol writes:

"You're saying that you're wiser this year than you were last year?" B asked me.

I was, so I said, "Yes."

"How? What did you learn this year that you didn't know before?"

"Nothing. That's why I'm wiser. That extra year of learning more nothing."

B laughed. Damian didn't.

"I don't understand," she said. "If you keep learning more nothing, that makes it harder and harder to live."

Learning about nothing doesn't make it harder, it makes it easier, but most people make Damian's mistake of thinking it makes it harder. That's a big mistake.

The culture of simulacra figured by Warhol and refigured by his postmodern successors indirectly realizes the avant-garde's dream of transforming the world into a work of art. As we have seen, the fulfillment of the aesthetic idea is inseparable from an aestheticization of the real through which reality is virtualized. While this virtualization of the real presupposes the philosophical and aesthetic tendencies we have been considering, it is no less important to acknowledge the indispensable role played by specific social and technological developments. Their enormous contributions notwithstanding, Kant, Hegel, and Nietzsche, as well as their artistic successors, do not adequately consider the complex relays between the ways we shape experience and process information and knowledge and the technologies of production and reproduction that characterize different societies and historical periods. The Kantian categorical grid and Hegelian systematic logic, which reflect and reinforce processes of industrialization, are ill-suited to a postindustrial environment governed by global currents of information and flows of images. While previous technologies do not simply disappear, the overlay of electronic networks transforms the very conditions of the possibility of experience and knowledge in ways that analysts have not yet carefully considered.

On a broad sociocultural level, virtualizing reality presupposes the specularization of experience, which accompanies modernization and postmodernization. Such specularization comes about in protovirtual environments that stage a *practical* aestheticizing of reality. As nineteenth-century train terminals, greenhouses, arcades, and department stores become twentieth-century cinemas, theme parks, malls, and video arcades, reality becomes more and more a matter or nonmatter of image.

It has become commonplace to associate postmodernism with the commodification of art and the symbolic order that accompanies postindustrial or multinational capitalism. Less often acknowledged but no less important is the recognition that this commodification of aesthetics assumes as its necessary condition the aestheticization of the commodity. As exchange value supplants use value, currency shifts from things to signs, which are, in effect, images of images. While things are intended to meet needs, signs and images are designed to create as well as (partially) satisfy desires. Like a signifier that has lost its mooring in a signified, desire is endlessly displaced and thus floats freely. The mobilization of desire is promoted by the circulation of commodities whose substance has become imaginary.

The scene for this stage in the virtualization of reality is set by the vitrification of architecture. Though usually associated with the glass boxes of Walter Gropius, Mies van der Rohe, and Philip Johnson, what Bruno Taut labels "glass architecture" actually begins with construction of arcades in major European cities during the opening decades of the nineteenth century. While Hegel was developing his speculative philosophy in Germany, Parisians were staging a spectacle of their own by building seventeen arcades between 1800 and 1830. The modern arcade was made possible by technological advances in the production of glass and the development of steel-and-glass architecture. Large sheets of glass suitable for construction purposes had been produced as early as the mid-1700s. By the latter part of the eighteenth century, merchants were using glass for large shop windows in which goods could be displayed. This seemingly innocent innovation actually represented a significant change. By splitting the space of production from the space of consumption, the store window becomes a scene for a specularization of the commodity that previews what would take place on TV screens two centuries later.

The enclosure of many shops under one roof created public interiors that confounded long-established oppositions like outside/inside and public/private. This new space provided the setting for new activities and the occasion for new experiences. The writings of Baudelaire and Benjamin have made the flâneur an emblematic figure who captures the rhythms of urban life. Forever going with the flow, the flâneur lives a life in which everything is as fleeting and ephemeral as a passing image. Commenting on Berlin's Lindenpassage, Siegfried Kracauer writes: "But now, under a new glass roof and decked out in marble, the former passage reminds me of the vestibule of a department store. The shops still exist, but picture postcards are the standard fare; the world Panorama has been overtaken by the film and the Anatomical Museum has long ceased to be a famed attraction….In fact, as a passage, the thoroughfare is also the place where, as in no other journey, the departure from the near into the distant, can be portrayed: body and image become united." As the site where body and image become one, the arcade is something like a proto-virtual-reality machine where reality is virtualized. BARBARA KRUEGER, I SHOP THEREFORE I AM

While the early arcades were undeniably revolutionary, their far-reaching significance does not become evident until the invention of the department store. Recognizing that consumption was rapidly becoming not merely a way of life but a religion, Émil Zola dubbed les grands magasins of the nineteenth century "cathedrals of modern commerce." Changes in production necessitated changes in marketing and distribution. Assembly lines were kept fully operational by creating what were, in effect, conveyor belts of consumption on which an endless flow of commodities captured the fancy of mobile buyers. Mass production, in other words, produced mass consumption.

One of the first to recognize the implications of emerging consumer culture, Zola uses Bon Marché, which opened in 1852, as the setting for his prescient novel The Ladies' Paradise. More than two decades later (1876), this hugely successful department store moved into a new building conceived by the architects L. C. Boileau and Gustave Eiffel. The prototype for department-store architecture was Joseph Paxton's Crystal Palace, constructed in 1851 for London's Great Exposition honoring the achievements of Victorian civilization. Paxton, who had been a builder of popular greenhouses and botanical gardens, combined greenhouse design with the latest innovations in steel-and-glass construction to create what is arguably the first example of modern architecture. His plan was quickly adapted not only to other department stores but also to exhibition halls (Les Halles, 1853)

and train stations (King's Cross Station, 1851). These new spaces were all sites of transport where everything and everybody remained in perpetual motion. The distinctive feature of this new architectural style was the effective interplay of the material and immaterial in steel and glass. The dematerialization of the building in its diaphanous façades mirrors the growing absorption of the commodity in its promotional image.

While distinctively transparent, the spaces of Bon Marché were nonetheless strangely reminiscent of Piranesi's *Carceri*. Zola's fictional description is more telling than any so-called firsthand account.

POPULAR MECHANICS, NOVEMBER 1994

HEAD(Y) HOUSE

Just at that moment Madame Desforges, after having nearly had her mantle carried away in the crowd, at last came in and crossed the first hall. Then, on reaching the principal gallery, she raised her eyes. It was like a railway span, surrounded by the balustrades of the two storeys, intersected by hanging staircases, crossed by flying bridges. The iron staircases developed bold curves, multiplying the landings; the iron bridges suspended in space, ran straight along, very high up; and all this iron formed, beneath the white light of the windows, an excessively light architecture, a complicated lace-work through which the daylight penetrated, the modern realization of a dreamed-of palace, of a Babel-like heaping up of the storeys, enlarging the rooms, opening up glimpses on to other floors and into other rooms without end.

This labyrinth from which there seems to be no exit expands both vertically in stories that follow no narrative line and horizontally in an endless serial dispersion.

Zola exposes display strategies devised by early merchants of the society of spectacle: "mirrors, cleverly arranged on each side of the window, reflected and multiplied the forms without end." In this hall of mirrors, images extend metonymically to other images; as the shopper descends from floor to floor, she discovers that beneath every image there is another image.

By allowing *flâneurs* and *flâneuses* to step through the looking glass and into the display window, the department store creates a new space in which consumption becomes a consuming spectacle and the spectacle is commodified. In this spectacle of consumption, where thing is transmuted into image, the currency of exchange is imaginary rather than real. As exchange value displaces use value, the image becomes the reality that counts. But the tran-

PAUL VAN HOEYDONCK, CYB HEAD AND ARM, 1969

"THE DISPERSION AND MOBILITY OF THE GAZE..."

substantiation of the real into the image is not limited to displayed objects. The looking-glass world of consumption recasts the very shape of subjectivity by transfiguring the forms of perception and altering the structure of the body. The gaze of the shopper turns back on itself, creating a reflexive circuit of exchange that refigures body as image. In the arcades and on the boulevards of what was once Descartes's Paris, "Cogito, ergo sum" becomes "I shop, therefore I am" (Barbara Kruger).

The phantasmagoria of consumption transforms the very structure of the perceptual and conceptual apparatus. The arcade and department store, as Christoph Asendorf observes, demand "completely new perceptual maneuvers from the potential buyer, a readiness to shift continually between diffused and concentrated attention." The dispersion and mobility of the gaze are not limited to the activity of shopping but characterize multiple forms of modern awareness. Postindustrial technologies and postmodern experiential and cognitive practices accelerate these tendencies. As speed increases, change and the mobility it brings become both daunting and exhilarating, even intoxicating. The proliferation of commodities triggers an experience of something like what Kant describes as the mathematical sublime. If, as Baudelaire insists, modernity involves "the ephemeral, the fugitive, the contingent, the half of art whose other half is the eternal and the immutable," then two of the primary spaces where the modern emerges are the arcade and department store. When the impressionists dissolve things into a fleeting play of light captured in paint, they reflect the virtualization of the real that is already well under way in store windows.

The play of light through which reality is virtualized is not, however, limited to display windows; it spreads to a variety of display screens. When taken together, the modern arcade and department store anticipate what is perhaps the quintessential postmodern topos – the mall. As Kracauer stresses, there is an important connection between the arcade and the cinema. The point is not simply that many early cinemas were located in arcades; the relation between arcade, department store, and mall on the one hand, and cinema on the other, is more subtle and complex. Anne Friedberg goes so far as to insist that the shopping mall is actually a "cinematic apparatus." Display windows rolling before the gaze of the shopper recall the frames of film passing before the eyes of the spectator. There is, of course, an important difference between these two modes of virtual transport. While flâneur and flâneuse are mobile and window frames are fixed, the cinema spectator is immobile and filmic frames roll by.

The evolution of cinema roughly parallels the development of glass architecture in arcades, department stores, and eventually the curtain walls of high modernism. The Lumière brothers' premiere of *The Arrival of a Train at La Ciotat Station*, screened at the Grand Café in Paris on December 28, 1895, marks the culmination of technological advances that had been unfolding for two centuries. Their camera-projector-printer, named a cinematograph, extends developments begun in panoramic painting, patented by Robert Barker in 1787; the diorama, invented in 1823 by Louis-Jacques-Mandé Daguerre (who also created the photographic process known as the daguerreotype); and, most important, the kinetoscope, introduced by Edison in 1893. From dioramas and panoramas to kinetoscopes and nickelodeons, images come to life and life passes into image. As the modern arcade becomes the postmodern mall, the cinematic is supplemented by the telematic. It is not sufficient for today's mall to have multiplex cinemas showing the latest films; it

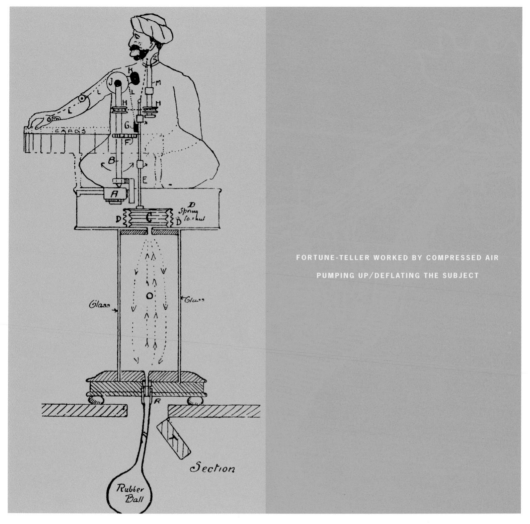

FORTUNE-TELLER WORKED BY COMPRESSED AIR
PUMPING UP/DEFLATING THE SUBJECT

must also be equipped with a state-of-the-art video arcade. The telematic simultaneously expands and reverses the cinematic by creating virtual environments that
are immersive and interactive. As the cinematic arcade becomes the telematic video
arcade, department stores and shopping malls give way to home shopping networks. In the course of this transition, the public display windows of arcades and
department stores are transformed into TV screens and liquid crystal displays scattered in private homes. While the arcade, department store, and mall obscure the
opposition between interiority and exteriority by creating public interiors, televisual networks and electronic webs turn everything inside out by bringing the

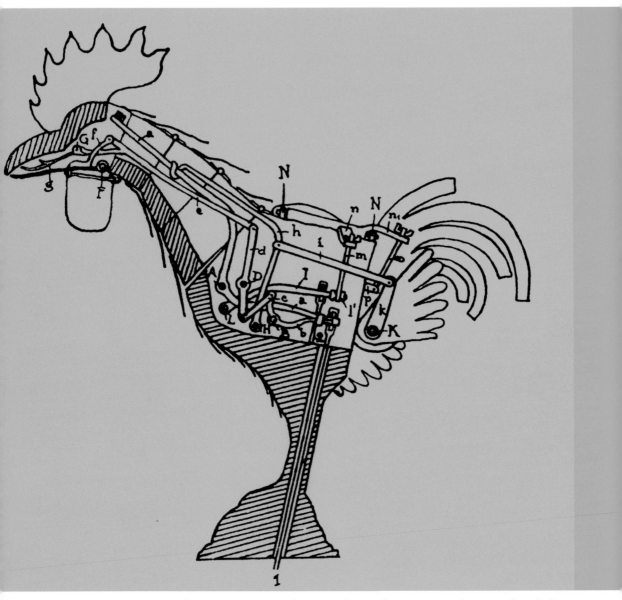

outside in, and wiring inside to outside. Rendering images electronically, teleshopping exponentially expands the virtualization of the real.

Though hardly adequate to trace all the influences contributing to the development of virtual technologies, these remarks should suggest the complexity of the genesis of the worldwide webs now entangling us. If the ways in which we constitute experience and process information are bound to changing technologies of production and reproduction, then newly emergent networks not only alter how we experience and think but also transform the very structures of self and world. In this way, nets and webs form a cultural a priori or genetic template, which, though constantly in flux, is the only reality engine we have. By weaving together the philosophical, aesthetic, and sociotechnological threads in this genealogy of virtual reality, it becomes possible to wire Kant's categories, Hegel's logic, and Nietzsche's perspectives to the electronic webs and networks constituting our world. The intricate electronic matrix that is our milieu serves as something like an expanded head-mounted display or wrap-around goggles that render reality virtual and virtuality real.

MÉCANISME DU COQ

As the infosphere and dataspace steadily expand, virtual technologies become ever more pervasive. The response to these developments has been predictably mixed. For some, virtual reality is a nightmare in which isolated subjects sit in front of computer terminals, alienated from their bodies, other people, and the environment. For others, virtual reality creates the possibility of escaping the limitations of time and space, and holds

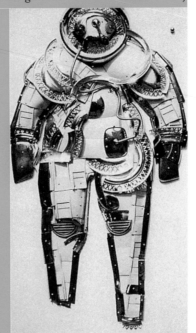

PAUL VAN HOEYDONCK, ROBOT 1968
PRÊT-À-PORTER

the promise of realizing the ancient dream of global unity and harmony. It should be clear by now that these antithetical assessments of virtual reality share mistaken assumptions and presuppositions. First, by failing to contextualize their analyses, supporters as well as critics make the mistake of representing virtual reality as a specific technology rather than an effective figure of the postmodern condition. Second, previous responses to virtual reality reinscribe oppositions like mind/body, human/machine, natural/artificial, and material/immaterial, which the long process of virtualizing

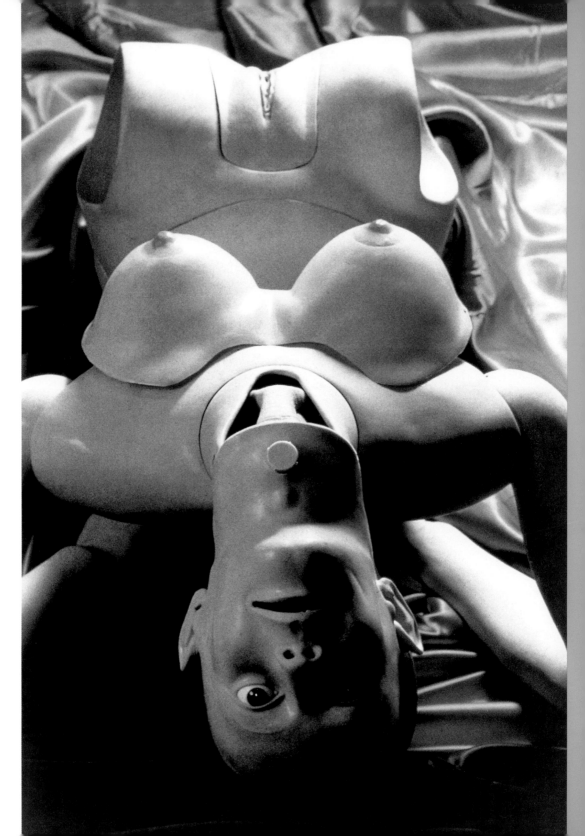

CINDY SHERMAN

reality subverts. What once seemed to be hard-and-fast oppositions now appear to be interfaces in which neither term remains the same. Virtual reality involves neither the synthesis of opposites nor the suppression of one term by the other but gives rise to a different order of "reality" that eludes traditional classificatory structures. When virtual reality is understood as a process rather than a product, ostensibly stable oppositions become oscillating interfaces that are constantly reconfigured. As the material becomes immaterial and the immaterial materializes, binary structures like human/machine, mind/body and natural/artificial are thoroughly transformed. A consideration of the changes wrought when binary or dialectical opposites are reconstrued as intricate interfaces suggests the novelty and complexity of virtual environments.

No opposition seems more fundamental than the contrast between living and nonliving. But are we any longer sure that we know how to define life? Some of the most revolutionary work now being done in computer science is in the field known as *artificial life*. The desire to animate the inanimate is, of course, ancient. From the earliest times, various automata have played important roles in religious rituals. In Egypt, Ka, representative of the deceased, was the soul that breathed life into statues, thereby enabling them to perform remarkable feats like moving mechanically, giving oracles, and pouring wine from golden goblets. In two extraordinary treatises, *Pneumatica* and *Automata*, Hero of Alexander left detailed descriptions and diagrams for complex automatic theaters that operated by hidden networks of cisterns and hydraulic conduits. These theaters, which were very popular in the second century B.C.E., were used in religious festivals. Centuries later, during the Middle Ages, automata became more complicated and their actions more sophisticated. Clocks with moving figures and altarpieces with weeping madonnas and bleeding crucifixes were not uncommon. The most intriguing medieval automaton was the golem, which is the ancestor of Mary Shelley's infamous Frankenstein monster. Formed in alchemists' ovens, the golem played a vital role in the ancient Hermetic tradition that lies behind Jewish cabalism. Provoking fascination and fear, the golem, created to serve its master, always threatens to run out of control and destroy the one it is supposed to protect. In this way, the story of the golem both reflects the history of humankind's relation to God and expresses abiding anxieties accompanying promethean inventions.

Not until the modern era, however, do the far-reaching philosophical and social implications of automata become clear. When Descartes split the world by opposing *res cogito* to *res extensa*, he effectively transformed human bodies, as well as all other biological organisms, into mechanical automata. From the outset, it proved difficult to restrict the principles of Cartesian mechanism to the "material" domain. Pascal's invention of an arithmetic calculating machine (1642) suggested that the mind might also be mechanical. The 1747 publication of La Mettrie's *L'homme-machine* brought together Descartes's philosophical musings and Pascal's ingenious invention in an argument that depicts human beings as qualitatively indistinguishable from the automata they create. No eighteenth-century automaton had a greater impact than Jacques de Vaucanson's famous *Canard*. In contrast to his predecessors, Vaucanson applied mechanistic principles to internal organs as well as to external movements. His duck was capable of moving, drinking water, eating grain, and even excreting. As if reading La Mettrie's *L'homme-machine* as a blueprint, Vaucanson undertook a secret project, sponsored by Louis XV, to create a mechanical man with functioning internal organs. Unlike others, Vaucanson realized that his experiments with artificial life were both philosophically suggestive and socially revolutionary. In his capacity as state inspector of silk manufacturing, he introduced a series of innovations that improved production techniques. This important invention was a machine for producing cloth, which was regulated by punch cards and driven by donkeys. By the end of the eighteenth century, most of western Europe had caught up with Vaucanson; automata were transformed from intellectual curiosities into social realities. Machine-as-man became man-as-machine. Realizing the fears embodied in the golem, the mechanization of production processes made people the extensions of, and slaves to, the machines they had created. The work of art in the age of mechanical production became nothing other than human beings. When Karel Capek coined the term robot in his 1921 play R.U.R. (i.e., Rossum's Universal *Robots*), his vision was as much a historical survey as a futuristic prediction. R.U.R. serves as a useful reminder that modern-day robots, humanoids, androids, and Terminators are descendants of earlier generations of automata, homunculi, and golems.

While differing in many ways, mechanical robots all display a common architecture: they are subject to centralized control, structured hierarchically, and operate serially. However, as modern industrial assembly lines are supplemented or replaced by postmodern data networks, organizational architecture shifts from centralized, hierarchical, and serial to decentralized, lateral, and parallel. This transformation actually reflects a change in the understanding of life. No longer merely mechanical, living organisms now appear to be complex information systems. In the information age, automata and robots are no longer restricted to science fiction but are rapidly invading a world that no longer seems as real as it once did.

> The humanoid known as Cog is composed of black and chrome metal beams, canister-like motors, and lots of wire and cable. Its torso is mounted on an electronics-crammed pedestal. Cog has one arm with a three-fingered hand. Special compliant joints give its moveable body parts a less rigid, more life-like feel than conventional robot parts; if you push on Cog, Cog gives a little, but pushes back. Its skull doesn't resemble a human's, though it does have two eyes; each consists of a pair of cameras, one a fisheye lens to give a broad view of what's going on around Cog, and one normal lens to give this humanoid a higher-resolution of what's happening directly in front of it.

NAM JUNE PAIK, GLOBAL ENCODER

Cog was created by Rodney Brooks and his colleagues at MIT's Mobile Robot Laboratory. Today's most advanced robotic devices look nothing like either the humanoids in *Blade Runner* or indestructible Terminators. The differences between the present generation of "robots" and earlier automata are more a matter of "mental" life than physical appearance. Cog is not controlled by a central computer but is run by up to 256 microchips, each of which can be linked to a Mac II. Though operating independently and in parallel, these chips nonetheless constantly interact. Interactivity is not, however, limited to the internal operating systems of the machine. Cog is not governed by prescribed software and thus is not completely preprogrammed. Its activity results from multiple miniprograms that continually interact with each other as well as with the surrounding environment. By constructing flexible and adaptable robotic devices, Brooks is attempting to build machines that can "learn" and "evolve." In other experiments, he and his associates are carrying decentralization, lateral organization, and parallel processing even farther by creating "insect robots" that are no bigger than a shoe box. These creatures coordinate their functions like bees in a hive, birds in a flock, or ants in a colony. In this work, research in artificial intelligence and artificial life is coming together to form creatures, which, though not conscious, seem to "know" what they are doing.

Two of the guiding principles of research and development in electronic technology are miniaturization and speed: ever smaller and ever faster. While

Brooks's insectoids are smaller and faster than their humanoid ancestors, some investigators working in the field of robotics insist that the insectoids are neither small nor fast enough. Nanotechnology extends the process of miniaturization by producing cellular automata (i.e., CAs), which exhibit most of the characteristics of living organisms. Though anticipated in the late 1940s by John von Neumann in a paper entitled "The General and Logical Theory of Automata," neither the hardware nor the software necessary to create cellular automata was available for several decades. During the 1970s, researchers at the University of Michigan revived interest in von Neumann's cellular automata when they began using biological organisms as prototypes for electronic systems. Tommaso Toffoli, a member of Michigan's Logic of Computers Group, explains that

> "the importance of cellular automata lies in their connection with the physical world." Particularly that of complex dynamical systems, where behavior arises as an emergent property of a number of variable forces. Because, unlike so many things simulated on the computer, CAs do not merely reflect reality — they are reality. They are actual dynamical systems. While they can be used to model certain physical systems, with the validity of each model to be determined by how well the results match the original theory, they can also be used to understand complex systems in general.

Cellular automata "do not merely reflect reality – they are reality": this is the central claim of artificial-life research. In a manifesto issued on the occasion of the first conference devoted to artificial life, held at Los Alamos in 1987, Chris Langton, a leading investigator in the field, declares:

L'ÉCRIVAIN

> Artificial life is the study of artificial systems that exhibit behavior characteristic of natural living systems. It is the quest to explain life in any of its possible manifestations, without restriction to the particular examples that have evolved on earth. This includes biological and chemical experiments, computer simulations, and purely theoretical endeavors. Processes occurring on molecular, social, and evolutionary scales are subject to investigation. The ultimate goal is to extract the logical form of living systems. Microelectronic technology and genetic engineering will soon give us the capability to create new life forms in silico as well as in vitro.

Langdon's claim becomes considerably more plausible when one recognizes his most basic presupposition. "The leap you have to make," he stresses, "is to think about machineness as being the logic of organization. It's not the material. There's nothing implicit about the material of anything – if you can capture its logical

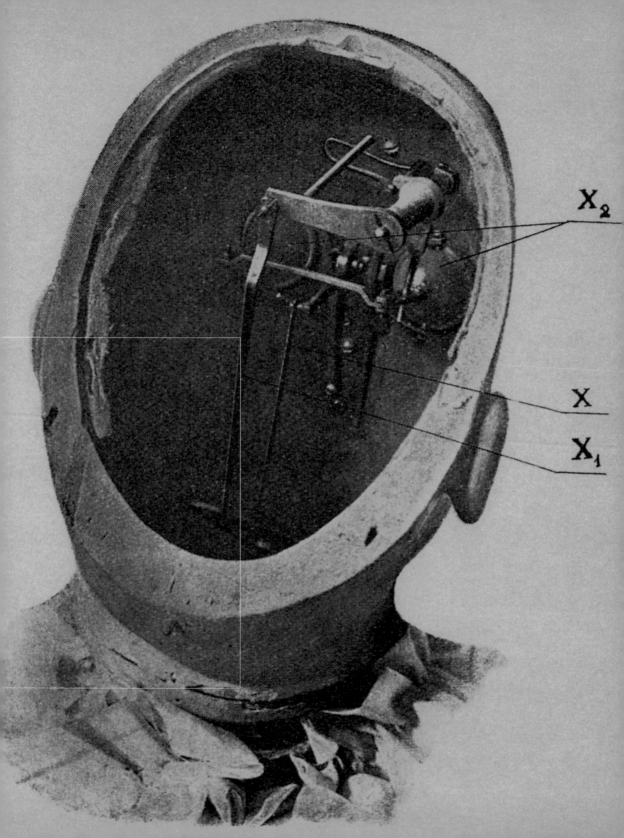

X_2

X

X_1

organization in some other medium you can have the same 'machine' because it's the organization that constitutes the machine, not the stuff it's made of." What Langdon is suggesting is that life is more immaterial than has been recognized. Life, in other words, is defined as a property of the organization of matter rather than a property of the matter that is organized. From this point of view, "the stuff of life is not stuff. Life is a dynamic physical process, and, if you can duplicate those processes – enable them to 'haunt' otherwise inanimate material — you have created life. This can be done regardless of the materials. It could even be done on a computer."

If life is understood in terms of the pattern and communication of information instead of the presence or absence of material, then computer-generated information organisms might be alive in more than a trivial sense. Within the space of the computer, virtual organisms are born, reproduce, and die. Like other living organisms, these creatures are self-organizing and self-replicating. Furthermore, through the use of genetic algorithms, it is possible for these information organisms actually to "mate" and "evolve." Virtual organisms, or what Kevin Kelly aptly

MONTY PYTHONS, 7TH LEVEL

IS IT POSSIBLE FOR THESE VIRTUAL

ORGANISMS TO "MATE" AND "EVOLVE"?

POSNER AND RAICHLE, IMAGES OF MII

GRAY MATTERS?

names "vivisystems," distribute information functions beyond the body of the insectoid to the dispersed "body" of the entire insect community. Redrawing the boundaries of bodies so that margins of difference become interfaces, vivisystems confound every clear demarcation between inside and outside. Far from closed hierarchical systems, virtual organisms are weblike structures governed from the bottom up "with the collective power of small actions rippling upward, combining with other small actions, often recursively so that action begets reaction – until a recognizable pattern of global behavior emerges." In the absence of centralized

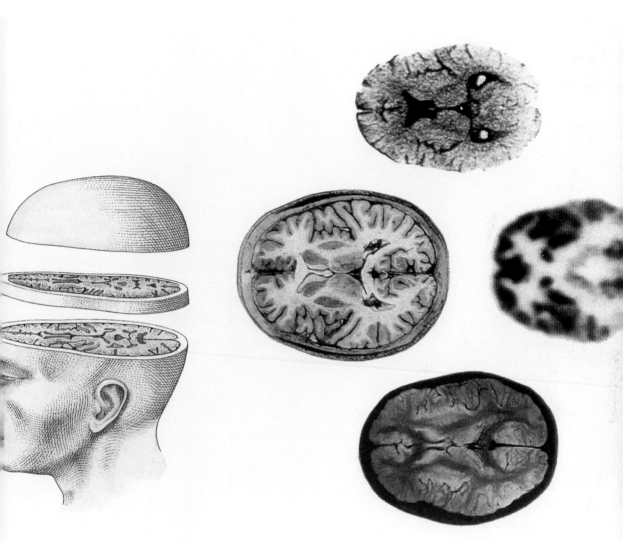

control, the operation of inforganisms emerges from the interplay of members following the principle of allelomimesis according to which action is conditioned by, and responsive to, the behavior of neighbors and the environment.

The more one probes virtual organisms, the more obscure the line between organism and mechanism, natural and artificial, body and mind, and material and immaterial becomes. Langdon and many of his colleagues are convinced that their work with artificial life proves "*that the forces of biology can be reproduced in machines.*" But is it possible to demonstrate the converse? Can the forces of

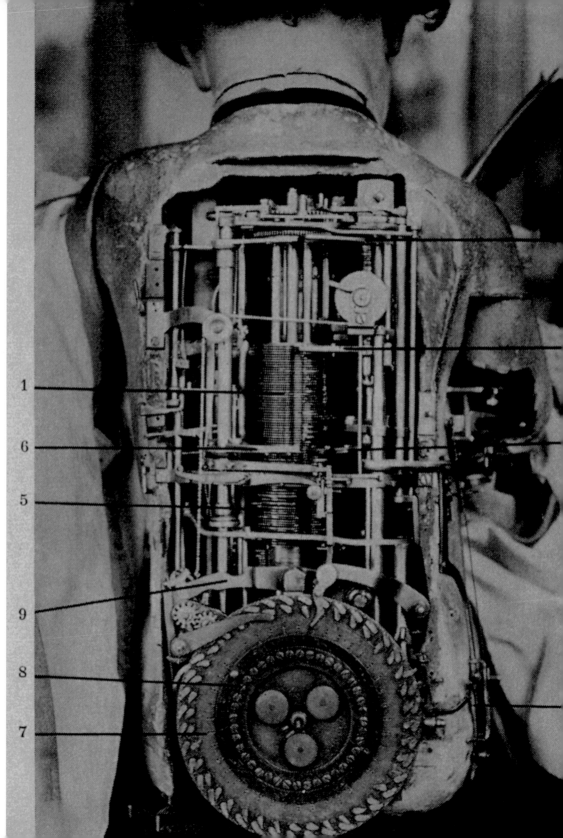

computers be reproduced in biological organisms? If animate organisms function as computers and computers produce inforganisms, then it would seem that life is informational and information is living.

On November 11, 1994, Leonard Adleman, a leading computer theorist from the University of Southern California, published "Molecular Computation of Solutions to Combinatorial Problems" in the influential journal *Science*. Adleman reported the results of an extraordinary experiment in which he used the genetic codes of DNA as a computer to calculate the shortest path linking seven cities. While electronic computers code information as zeros and ones and program it to travel along logical circuits, molecular computers represent information in terms of the chemical units of DNA, which are manipulated and synthesized to perform calculations. "Molecular computers," Adleman observes, "are breathtakingly fast and efficient, and they have unheard of storage capacities.... [T]hey can perform more than a trillion operations per second, which makes them a thousand times as fast as the fastest supercomputer. [Molecular computers] are a billion times as energy efficient as conventional computers. And they can store information in a trillionth of the space required by ordinary computers." The speed of biocomputers is a function of extensive parallel processing. In contrast to electronic computers with anywhere from 100 to 1,000 independent processors, a molecular computer in a small test tube can have as many as 10^{20} DNA molecules all performing calculations simultaneously.

In a single bold stroke, Adleman created the new field of biomolecular computers. His accomplishment has provoked both widespread interest and considerable skepticism. Pointing out that the problem Adleman solved was carefully chosen and particularly well-suited to this kind of computational machine, critics immediately expressed doubts about the capacity of molecular computers to perform more complex calculations. But when scientists gathered at Princeton University five months later, preliminary research results were very encouraging. In a paper entitled "DNA Solution of Hard Computational Problems," Richard Lipton demonstrated that Adleman's techniques can be used to solve a broad range of problems that conventional computers have difficulty handling. Summarizing the consensus reached at the Princeton meeting, the *New York Times* reported: "Researchers explain that they now realize that in DNA nature has created an extraordinary, special purpose computing system. DNA and the genetic machinery that processes it store and retrieve a prodigious amount of information — all that is needed to design and maintain every kind of living organism. Scientists think they can make DNA work for them by using the same genetic machine that generates living organisms to solve mathematical problems." Adleman is persuaded that his discovery is only the beginning of what promises to be a vast new area for research and development. "There might be a lot of computers out there," he speculates, "and I suspect there are."

The way was prepared for Adleman's revolutionary breakthrough by James Watson and Francis Crick's cracking of the genetic code in 1952. With the discovery of the manner in which genetic material is replicated and transmitted, the inherent immateriality of matter and informational character of biological processes become undeniable. Subsequent research has demonstrated the extraordinary significance of Watson and Crick's findings. As the Human Genome Project is making clear, deciphering genetic codes creates the possibility of genetic engineering, which thoroughly confounds the boundary between the "natural" and "artificial."

The growing appreciation for the interfacing of information and biological processes is not limited to the cellular level. It now appears that operational principles at work in nanotechnology and biomolecular computers are also responsible for brain functioning and mental activity. The notion of the brain and its operations as centralized and hierarchical is currently as outdated as the claim that mind and body are dualistic opposites. Synthesizing and summarizing results of recent research, Daniel Dennett concludes:

> There is no single, definitive "stream of consciousness," because there is no central Headquarters, no Cartesian Theater where "it all comes together" for the perusal of a Central Meaner. Instead of such a single stream (however wide), there are multiple channels in which specialist circuits try, in parallel pandemoniums, to do their various things, creating Multiple Drafts as they go. Most of these fragmentary drafts of

"narrative" play short-lived roles in the modulation of current activity but some get promoted to further functional roles, in swift succession, by the activity of a virtual machine in the brain. The seriality of this machine (its "von Neumannesque" character) is not a "hardwired" design feature, but rather the upshot of a succession of coalitions of these specialists.... The result is not bedlam only because the trends that are imposed on all this activity are themselves the product of design. Some of this design is innate, and is shared with other animals. But it is augmented, and sometimes even overwhelmed in importance, by microhabits of thought that are developed in the individual, partly idiosyncratic results of self-exploration and partly the predesigned gifts of culture. Thousands of memes, mostly borne by language, but also by wordless "images" and other data structures, take up residence in an individual brain, shaping its tendencies and thereby turning it into a mind.

Dennett's remark suggests the possibility of rethinking the epistemological issues raised by Kant, Hegel, and Nietzsche in light of the insights of current computer science, cognitive science, and neurophysiology. In contrast to Kant's a priori categorical grid and Hegel's universal logical structure, the brain, it seems, is not hardwired; nor is it a *tabula rasa* passively awaiting impressions. Rather, the structure of the brain is multidimensional and malleable. Organized performance *emerges* from ostensibly chaotic behavior through something like a phase-state shift or quantum leap. While partly preprogrammed, the matrices of perception and conception are also culturally constituted and thus historically emergent and constantly changing. Not only words but also images and data structures contribute to the formation of templates that screen thought and experience. As we have discovered, these patterns of mediation are themselves mediated by changing media and technologies of production and reproduction. From this point of view, the interrelation of body and mind or nature and culture does not involve the interaction of two qualitatively different substances but entails the endless interplay of information that knows no depth. The brain is something like a virtual machine, which, paradoxically, has always already been produced by the virtual worlds it has produced.

So understood, the virtual machine forming the human brain bears an uncanny resemblance to Cog. In the absence of any centralized control mechanism, brain activity is generated by multiple semiautonomous agencies arranged in a bottom-up architecture and operating by parallel distributed processing. According to this model, "information processing takes place through the interactions of a large number of simple processing elements, each sending excitatory and inhibitory signals to other units." Though each processing unit has direct connections with only a small number of other units, the workspace of the brain is nonetheless "global." "It is global," Dennett explains, "not only in the functional sense (crudely put, it is a 'place' where just about everything can get in touch with just about everything else), but also in the anatomical sense (it is distributed throughout the cortex, and no doubt involves other regions of the brain as well). That means, then, that the workspace has to avail itself of the very same neural tracts and networks that apparently play a major role in long-term memory."

Much effort is currently being devoted to determining the precise location of psychic and mental processes in the brain. For the historically informed, this work bears the traces of the discredited "science" of phrenology. Charting the emergence of neuroscience, Michael Posner and Marcus Raichle noted that "phrenology was based not only on an idea about cognition, but also on one about the brain: that similar types of computation are performed in the brain in contiguous locations. This old idea has received dramatic confirmation in studies of awake, behaving laboratory animals complemented by detailed anatomical studies." With the aid of the most advanced imaging technologies, researchers are trying to translate nineteenth-century nescience into twentieth-century neuroscience by coordinating different mental activities with specific areas of the brain comprising neural networks that are directly and indirectly linked.

What is emerging from research in a variety of fields is a picture in which the brain is structured like a network or web. More precisely, the brain is a network of networks or web of webs whose "global" operations mirror and are mirrored by the circuits of the worldwide webs that now circle the globe. Neural networks, however, are no more seamless than electronic and telecommunication networks. There are gaps even in webs that appear to be all-encompassing. These irreducible fissures and faults break the grip of determinism and create the space and time for chance.

Orderly brain activity, I have noted, emerges from the apparently disorderly interaction of local neural networks. The phase-state transition involved in such emergent behavior can be understood in terms of the chaotic action characteristic of turbulent systems. It seems that the complex recursive loops linking neural networks create a sensitivity to initial conditions that conforms to the principles of chaos theory. Yet chaos theory is not chaotic enough to account for all the gaps in the networks of the brain. According to the tenets of chaos theory, apparent disorder inevitably harbors a more profound order. Chaos, therefore, is order that has not yet been adequately comprehended or computed. While the complexity of a chaotic system might make measurement practically impossible, there is nothing in such systems that is intrinsically unmeasurable or incalculable.

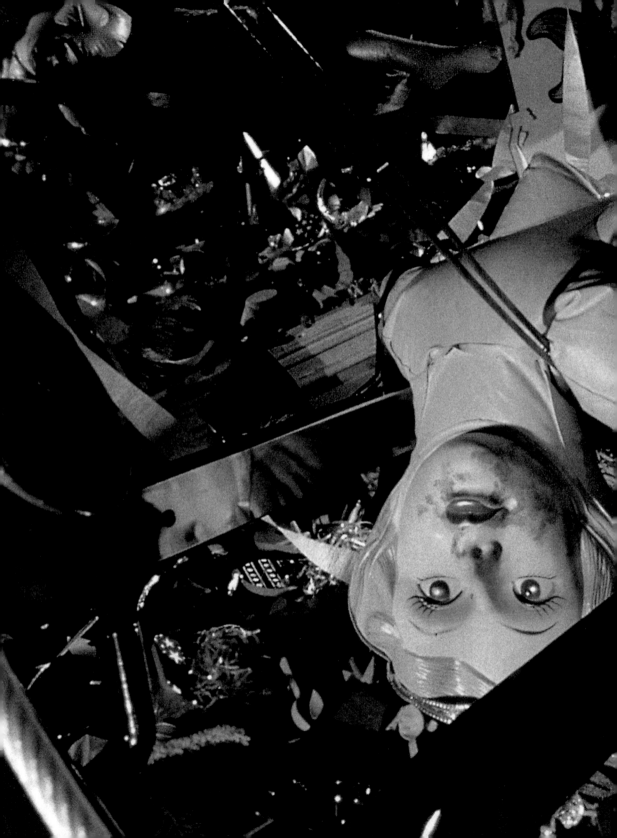

CINDY SHE

Roger Penrose, professor of mathematics at Oxford, contends that the indeterminacy of brain functions and mental activity is irreducible. "The phenomenon of *consciousness*," he argues, "can arise only in the presence of some noncomputational physical processes taking place in the brain." By weaving together a brilliant rereading of Gödel's theorem with quantum mechanics and neuroscience, Penrose discloses irreducible gaps in neural networks. While at the macrolevel brain activity appears to be governed by digital logic and the laws of classical physics, at the microlevel the indeterminate and probabilistic rules of quantum mechanics seem to be at work. According to Penrose,

> the chemical forces that control the interactions of atoms and molecules are indeed quantum mechanical in origin, and it is largely chemical action that governs the behavior of the *neurotransmitter* substances that transfer signals from one neuron to another — across tiny gaps that are called *synaptic clefts*. Likewise, the action potentials that physically control nerve-signal transmission itself have an admittedly quantum-mechanical origin. Yet it seems to be generally assumed that it is quite adequate to model the behavior of neurons themselves, and their relationships with one another, in a completely classical way. It is widely believed, accordingly, that it should be entirely appropriate to model the physical functioning of the brain as a whole, as a *classical* system, where the more subtle and mysterious features of quantum physics do not significantly enter the description.

To overcome the difficulties that research on the relation between the brain and mind has encountered, Penrose inserts "the subtle and mysterious features of quantum physics" into the interface or synapse between neurons. Messages traveling along central neural axons are digitally coded in a way that is strictly parallel to electronic computers. But each axon branches into dendrites and ends in synapses that must be bridged if messages are to arrive at their destination. The delivery of the message depends on chemicals known as neurotransmitters. Each neuron is encased in something like a cytoskeleton made up of microtubules that secrete neurotransmitters. The effect of the impulse traveling along the neuron is directly proportional to the strength of the synapse, and the strength of the synapse, in turn, is a function of the strength or weakness of the neurotransmitters produced by the neuron's microtubules. The activities of these microtubules are not, however, explainable in terms of classical physics but follow rules that approximate the principles of quantum mechanics. "Our picture," Penrose concludes, is of some kind of global quantum state which coherently couples the activities taking place within the tubes, concerning microtubules collectively across large areas of the brain. There is some influence that this state... exerts on the computations taking place along the microtubules – an influence which takes delicate and precise account of the putative, missing, non-computational OR [objective reduction] physics that I have been strongly arguing for. The "computational" activity of the conformational changes in the tubulins controls the way that the tubes transport materials along their outsides and ultimately influences the synapse strengths at the pre- and postsynaptic endings. In this way, a little of this coherent quantum organization *within* the microtubules is "tapped off" to influence the changes in the synaptic connections of the neural computer of the moment.... On the view that I am tentatively putting forward, consciousness would be some manifestation of this quantum-entangled internal cytoskeletal state and of its involvement in the interplay between quantum and classical levels of activity.... Accordingly, the neuron level of description that provides the currently fashionable picture of the brain and mind is a mere *shadow* of the deeper level of cytoskeletal action – and it is at this deeper level where we must seek the physical basis of *mind*!

While Dennett claims that the brain is a virtual machine, Penrose is suggesting that it functions like a postal system in which the arrival or nonarrival of messages is a function not only of calculable operations but also of incalculable interruptions. The destructured structure of synaptic clefts is the site of chaotic operations that produce neurotransmitters necessary for the delivery of messages. Since the production of these chemicals does not conform to any known calculus, communication through neural networks is made possible by something that remains incalculable. The incalculable is incommunicable. Thus, the circuits of exchange are never complete because something is always lacking. This lack creates unavoidable interference that delays or even interrupts the flow of communication. In this way, neurotransmitters facilitate whatever communication occurs while at the same time communicating a certain lack of communication. At the most rudimentary stage of biomental activity, the condition of the possibility of communication is also the condition of the impossibility of communication. Moving from the micro- to the macrolevel, we are led to conclude that thinking inevitably entails the unthinkable. As Derrida constantly reminds us, some letters never arrive at their destination or arrive by not arriving, thereby both breaching and bridging the circuits with and without which thought and communication are impossible. Far from accidents or mistakes, faults in the delivery system make arrival possible and nonarrival unavoidable. This insinuation of the incalculable in the calculable insures the play of chance, which is both reassuring and unsettling. Though we are increasingly entangled in webs, not everything is preprogrammed and not all scription is prescription. Furthermore, the interfacing of the biological and the informational in the interaction of brain and mind need not necessarily lead to a reductionism in which everything mental becomes the epiphenomenon of a material base. "*Quantum indeterminacy*," Penrose insists, "might be what provides an opening for the mind to influence the physical brain." What materialists and idealists see as a one-way street is actually a two-way superhighway, which, like a Los Angeles expressway, is riddled with detours and delays.

Even this radical recasting of the operation of the brain and mind does not, however, do justice to the implications of the thoroughgoing refiguring of the interface between biological and information networks. The decentralization and distribution of information processes extends beyond genes, the brain, and nervous system to the body as a whole. The body, as Donna Haraway maintains, is "a coded text, organized as an engineered communications system, ordered by a fluid and dispersed command-and-control-intelligence network."

An account of the biomedical, biotechnical body must start from the multiple molecular interfacings of genetic, nervous, endocrine, and immune systems. Biology is about recognition and misrecognition, coding errors, the body's reading practices...and billion-dollar projects to sequence the human genome to be published and stored in a national genetic library....The biomedical-biotechnical body is a semiotic system, a complex meaning-producing field, for which the discourse of immunology, that is, the central biomedical discourse of recognition/misrecognition, has become a high-stakes practice in many senses.

> In relation to objects like biotic components and codes, one must think, not in terms of laws of growth and essential properties, but rather in terms of strategies of design, boundary constraints, rates of flows, system logics, and costs of lowering constraints. Sexual reproduction becomes one possible strategy among many, with costs and benefits theorized as a function of the system environment. Disease is a subspecies of information malfunction or communications pathology; disease is a process of misrecognition or transgression of the boundaries of a strategic assemblage called self.

As Haraway suggests, the understanding of bodily processes as data processes has been greatly advanced by the investigation of autoimmune diseases like psoriasis, diabetes, and AIDS. The importance of Haraway's analysis is reinforced by the widespread description of immunology as "the science of self-nonself discrimination." Irun Cohen begins an informative and suggestive paper entitled "The Self, the World, and Autoimmunity" by explaining that "it is generally assumed that the main job of the immune system is to distinguish between what is 'self' and what is 'not self.' Once the distinction has been made, 'self' is preserved and 'not self' is destroyed. At the most general level, of course, this is true, and human beings remain alive and healthy only because of it. Recently it has become clear, however, that at a finer level of detail the distinction between self and other is not absolute." Health presupposes self-recognition in which the self knows itself as not other, and, correspondingly, disease arises from the failure of self-recognition that results from the inability to distinguish self from nonself. The medium of healthy self-recognition is *information* distributed throughout the body. Agents by which immunological information is sent, transmitted, and received include, inter alia, antigens, antibodies, hormones, lymphocytes, and macrophages. In this way, multiple intelligence agents create communications networks that extend beyond the brain and central nervous system and run throughout the entire body.

In order to appreciate the significance of these insights, it is necessary to distinguish intelligence from consciousness. Bodily activities as well as the "material" workings of nature require immaterial information processes that are undeniably intelligent. As we have seen, such intelligence does not completely exclude unintelligibility. To the contrary, there can be no intelligibility without a certain unintelligibility. Nor should intelligence be confused with consciousness or self-consciousness. The relation between intelligence and consciousness is asymmetrical rather than reciprocal: while consciousness and self-consciousness presuppose intelligence, not all intelligence entails consciousness or self-consciousness.

HIDING | 322

Besides the cellular compartment, the immune system comprises a vast array of circulating acellular products, such as antibodies, lymphokines, and complement components. These molecules mediate communication among components of the immune system, but also between the immune system and the nervous and endocrine systems, thus linking the body's multiple control and coordination sites and functions. The genetics of the immune system cells, with their higher rates of somatic mutation and gene product

The notion of *distributed intelligence* redraws the boundaries within the body, between mind and body, and between self and world. While the mind is not a mind, but a network of networks, the body is not a body but, in Donna Haraway's terms, a "network-body."

Far from being circumscribed units, bodies are societies in which every body is also an antibody. Boundaries are never secure but are interfaces whose folds make it impossible to be sure what is inside and

323 | INTERFACING

splicings and rearrangings to make finished surface receptors and anti- bodies, makes a mockery of the notion of a constant genome even within "one" body. The hierarchical body of old has given way to a network- body of truly amazing complexity and specificity. The immune system is everywhere and nowhere. Its specificities are indefinite if not infinite, and they arise randomly; yet these extraordinary variations are the critical means of maintaining individual bodily coherence.

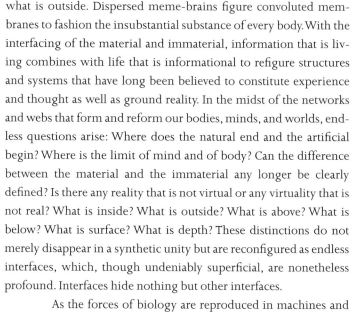

what is outside. Dispersed meme-brains figure convoluted membranes to fashion the insubstantial substance of every body. With the interfacing of the material and immaterial, information that is living combines with life that is informational to refigure structures and systems that have long been believed to constitute experience and thought as well as ground reality. In the midst of the networks and webs that form and reform our bodies, minds, and worlds, endless questions arise: Where does the natural end and the artificial begin? Where is the limit of mind and of body? Can the difference between the material and the immaterial any longer be clearly defined? Is there any reality that is not virtual or any virtuality that is not real? What is inside? What is outside? What is above? What is below? What is surface? What is depth? These distinctions do not merely disappear in a synthetic unity but are reconfigured as endless interfaces, which, though undeniably superficial, are nonetheless profound. Interfaces hide nothing but other interfaces.

As the forces of biology are reproduced in machines and the forces of computers are reproduced in bodies, the interplay of "ideality" and "reality" anticipated in philosophical theories and artistic practices can be discerned throughout what was once called "nature." This transfiguration of the material and immaterial infinitely extends processes through which reality is virtualized and virtuality is realized. The interfacing of the informational and the biological leaves nothing unchanged. *Nothing.* Everything that once seemed substantial and material is insubstantial and immaterial.

At the outset of this discussion, I indicated that virtualizing reality refigures distinctions and oppositions in a way that makes it possible to overcome the critical impasse in which we are currently mired. This impasse, I argued, can be traced to two primary difficulties: First, the poststructuralist insistence that systems and structures necessarily totalize and, thus, inevitably exclude differences and repress otherness has led to a fragmentation in which our intellectual, social, and cultural differences are tearing us apart. Second, the growing self-reflexivity of theory seems to entail an aestheticizing of politics that makes cultural analysis and criticism increasingly irrelevant. Our consideration of the long and involved processes through which reality is virtualized and virtuality is realized suggests responses to the challenges posed by both of these difficulties.

Neither totalizing structures that repress differences nor oppositional differences that exclude commonality are adequate in the plurality of worlds that constitute the postmodern condition. To think what poststructuralism leaves unthought is to think a nontotalizing structure that nonetheless acts as a whole. Such a structure would be neither a universal grid organizing opposites nor a dialectical system synthesizing opposites but a seamy web in which what comes together is held apart and what is held apart comes together. This web is neither subjective nor objective and yet is the matrix in which all subjects and objects are formed, deformed, and reformed. In the postmodern culture of simulacra, we are gradually coming to realize that complex communication webs and information networks, which function holistically but not totalistically, are the milieu in which everything arises and passes away. These webs and networks are characterized by a distinctive logic that distinguishes them from classical structures and dialectical systems. Though always eluding classificatory schemes constructed to capture them, webs and networks never-theless display certain rules that guide their operation. The articulation of these rules defines the contours of nonto-talizing structures that function as a whole.

1. *Rule of association:* Webs and nets are not all-encompassing structures but consist of associations and strategic coalitions of nodes, cells, modules, and circuits. The rule of association characterizes patterns of relation that fall between the externality of mechanisms and the internality of organisms. Never permanent or fixed, lines of association are subject to constant reformulation and revision. The net or the web is nothing more than the ever-shifting interaction of local nets and webs.

2. *Rule of distribution:* The architecture of webs and networks is bottom-up rather than top-down, and parallel rather than serial. Never centralized, functions are distributed among multiple circuits that operate in paral-lel. Parallel distributed processing issues in decentered and nonhierarchical networks. The organization of such webs is lateral and dispersed instead of hierarchical and consolidated.

3. *Rule of allelomimesis:* Nonintegral connections create the possibility of global processes that do not inevitably totalize. Nodes interact through networks of influence and constraint, which coordinate without nec-essarily unifying. Thus, while networks allow for a certain

proximity, they also maintain critical distance in which presence and absence, as well as positivity and negativity, mingle without becoming one.

4. *Rule of nonlinearity:* Networks are complex non-linear structures in which intricate feedback loops create an extreme sensitivity to initial conditions that leads to effects that are disproportionate to their ostensible causes. The recursivity inherent in nonlinearity makes it possible for simple interactions to generate complex behavior. Forever incomplete, such nonlinear networks do not exhibit a circularity that is self-reflexive or self-referential.

5. *Rule of emergency:* Webs are not preprogrammed but are in a state of constant emergency. Instead of pre-scribed foundational principles, the rules at work in non-linear networks emerge from the interactivity of local networks. Following axioms of parallel rather than serial processing, no part of a network controls the whole, yet the structure can function as if it were a whole. The emer-gency of networks renders them open rather than closed. Context-sensitive and endlessly adaptable, networks are flexible without being indeterminate.

6. *Rule of the aleatory:* While there is nothing that is not caught in interwoven webs, networks are riddled with gaps where the incalculable leaves room for the unexpect-ed. Necessity is no more possible apart from chance than chance is apart from necessity. As a result of the aleatory,

control is always insecure and knowledge uncertain.

7. *Rule of volatility:* The aleatory fosters disaster as well as novelty. Never stable structures, networks are characterized by an inescapable volatility. Since stability is indirectly proportional to speed, an increase in the speed with which networks operate tends to lead to a decrease in their stability and vice versa. The more networks expand in order to restrain volatility, the more complex they become. Complexity, in turn, breeds the very volatility it is designed to control.

8. *Rule of vulnerability:* The volatility of networks exposes their vulnerability. Vulnerability is a function of interrelation or connectivity. The more interconnected networks become, the more vulnerable to viral disruption they are. Contrary to expectation, the stronger the connections, the greater the network's weakness. Volatility and vulnerability combine to pose opposite threats. On the one hand, the recognition that networks can run wild provokes efforts to seize control through tactics of surveillance, administration, and management. On the other hand, the awareness of the fragility of networks creates the prospect of subversive or even terrorist activity.

9. *Rule of contestation:* Far from organisms whose unity borders on beauty, networks are sites of

contestation that sometimes turns violent. Consequently, increasing connections does not necessarily enhance unity and harmony. All too often closer association sharpens disagreements and increases conflict. Settlements are inevitably disputed and, therefore, must be negotiated and renegotiated. Since negotiation is always unpredictable, results can never be anticipated with certainty.

10. *Rule of interfacing:* Within webs and networks, every facing is an interfacing. Nothing exists in itself and no one exists by herself or himself. Interfacing realizes virtuality by transforming all that once seemed solid and secure into liminal transitions in networks that know no end and yet remain finite.

Associative, distributed, allelomimetic, nonlinear, emergent, aleatory, volatile, vulnerable, contested, interfacing – networks and webs are not controlled by principles that are either integrative or disjunctive but are regulated by rules displaying the strange logic of the neither/nor. When so understood, webs and networks are neither hegemonic nor fragmenting, though they are undeniably haunted by tendencies in these contradictory directions. These nontotalizing structures that nonetheless act as a whole are allelomorphs. Allelomorphs mark the site of intersection between the

biological and the informational. An allelo-morph is, in the strict sense of the term, an allele, which, in turn, is "any of a group of possible mutational forms of a gene." Genes, we have discovered, are data structures that constitute the programs of biological organisms. Since these genetic programs are not completely prescribed, biological organisms are not hardwired. The connective wiring of the body extends beyond its ostensible limits to the cultural networks within which it is inscribed. With lines of communication that turn everything inside-out and outside-in, bodies are prostheses of machines as much as machines are prostheses of bodies. The interfacing of the so-called natural and artificial creates forms that are always mutating. In the lexicon of current telematic technologies, the process by which one shape (morphe) is transformed into an

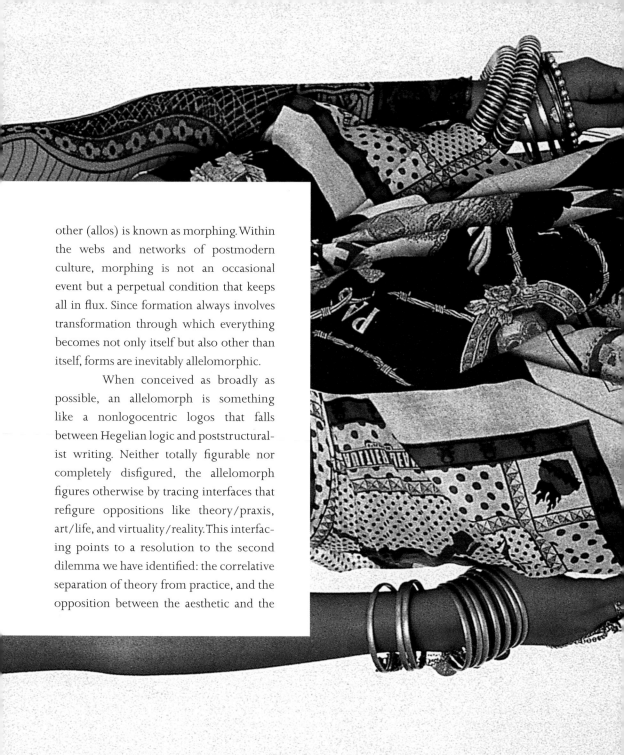

other (allos) is known as morphing. Within the webs and networks of postmodern culture, morphing is not an occasional event but a perpetual condition that keeps all in flux. Since formation always involves transformation through which everything becomes not only itself but also other than itself, forms are inevitably allelomorphic.

When conceived as broadly as possible, an allelomorph is something like a nonlogocentric logos that falls between Hegelian logic and poststructuralist writing. Neither totally figurable nor completely disfigured, the allelomorph figures otherwise by tracing interfaces that refigure oppositions like theory/praxis, art/life, and virtuality/reality. This interfacing points to a resolution to the second dilemma we have identified: the correlative separation of theory from practice, and the opposition between the aesthetic and the political. Allelomorphs are the condition of the possibility of the effectiveness of images and symbols. The symbolic order and reality are not inherent opposites but are different inscriptions of distributed information. As a result of this interfacing of the immaterial and the material, images and symbols have concrete effects in the "real" world. Conversely, biological, technological, and sociopolitical "reality" transforms the symbolic order. If the virtual is real and the real is virtual, theory and practice are no more separable than art and life.

When the philosophical, aesthetic, and technological strands of our genealogy of virtual reality are woven together, it becomes clear that allelomorphs are networks of networks in which the imaginary becomes real, thereby constituting the real imaginary. Because the symbolic and the real are not simply identical, the practical implementation of artistic vision is necessary; because the symbolic and the real are not merely different, artful practice is possible. When everything is caught in webs and networks that comprise subjects as well as objects, the political is aesthetic and art is inescapably political.

At the end of the twentieth century, the site of social and political contestation is increasingly the symbolic order. Far from being a limited technology, virtual reality, we have discovered, is a trope for our current cultural condition. In the multiple worlds of postmodernity, there is nothing that

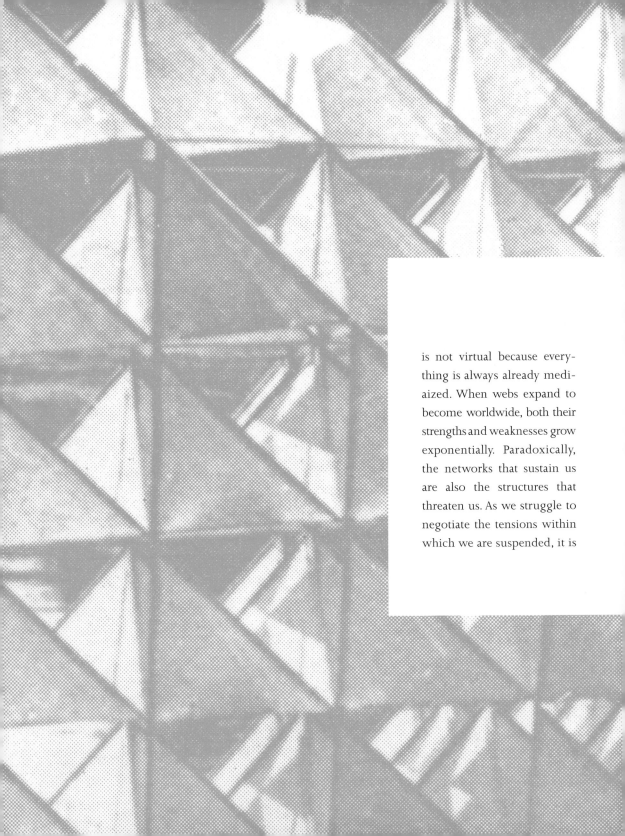

is not virtual because everything is always already mediaized. When webs expand to
become worldwide, both their
strengths and weaknesses grow
exponentially. Paradoxically,
the networks that sustain us
are also the structures that
threaten us. As we struggle to
negotiate the tensions within
which we are suspended, it is

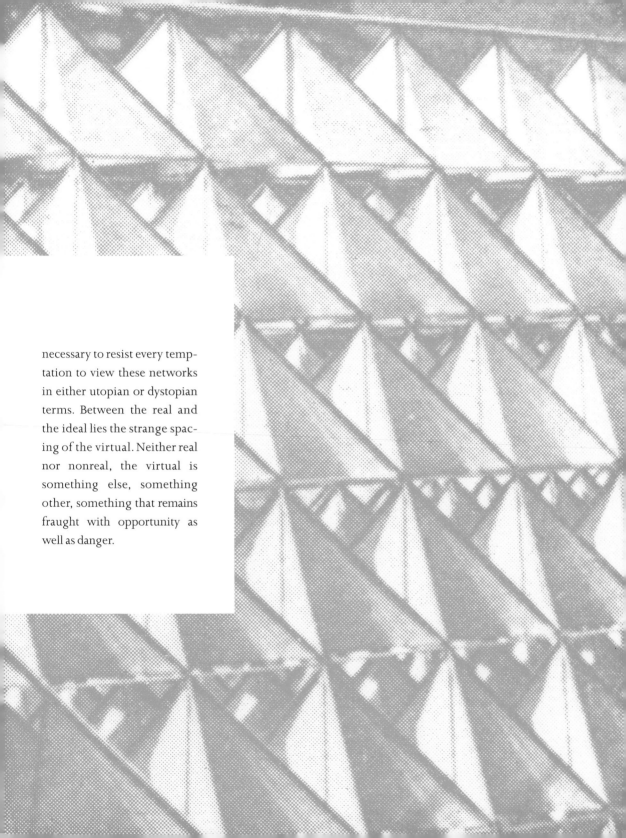

necessary to resist every temptation to view these networks
in either utopian or dystopian
terms. Between the real and
the ideal lies the strange spac-
ing of the virtual. Neither real
nor nonreal, the virtual is
something else, something
other, something that remains
fraught with opportunity as
well as danger.

To err
amidst
shifty
interfaces
that know
no end is to

ive an
rreducible
nigma :
othing
s
iding.

Notes

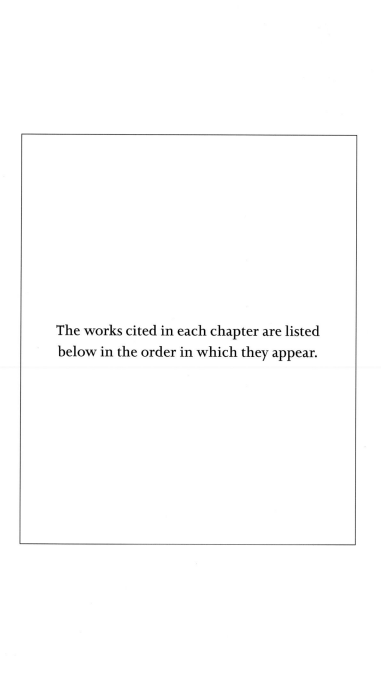

The works cited in each chapter are listed
below in the order in which they appear.

Skinsc(r)apes

Dennis Potter, *The Singing Detective* (New York: Random House, 1988)

Wallace Stevens, *Opus Posthumous*, ed. Samuel French Morse

(New York: Random House, 1982), p. 163

Dennis Potter, *Potter on Potter*, ed. Graham Fuller (London: Faber and Faber, 1993), pp. 30 – 3 1

Paul Auster, *City of Glass* (New York: Penguin Books, 1985)

Maurice Blanchot, *Vicious Circles: Two Fictions & After the Fact*, trans. Paul Auster

(Barrytown, NY: Station Hill Press, 1985), p. 67

Edgar Allan Poe, *Narrative of A. Gordon Pym*, Poe: *Poetry and Tales*, ed. Patrick Quinn [NB]

(New York: The Library of America, 1984), p. 1167

Maurice Blanchot, *Death Sentence*, trans. Lydia Davis (Barrytown, NY: Station Hill Press, 1978)

Paul Auster, *The Invention of Solitude* (New York: Penguin Books, 1982), p. 128

Auster, *The Art of Hunger: Essays, Prefaces, Interviews* (Los Angeles: Sun and Moon Press, 1991)

Francis Galton, *Inquiries into Human Faculty and Its Development*

(New York: Macmillan and Co., 1883), p. 354

Lynn M. Herbert, *Faces: Nancy Burson* (Houston: Contemporary Arts Museum, 1992), pp. 9 – 10

Theology at the End of the Century: A Dialogue on the Postmodern with Thomas J. J. Altizer, Mark C. Taylor, Charles E.

Winquist, Robert Scharlemann, ed. Robert Scharlemann

(Charlottesville: University of Virginia Press, 1990), p. 137.

Marginal inserts throughout "Skinsc(r)apes" are from: Friedrich Nietzsche, *The Gay Science*, trans. Walter Kaufmann

(New York: Random House, 1974), pp. 123, 38, 116

Friedrich Nietzsche, *The Will to Power*, trans. Walter Kaufmann (New York: Random House, 1968),

pp. 301, 267, 327

Friedrich Nietzsche, *Beyond Good and Evil*, trans. Walter Kaufmann

(New York: Random House, 1966), pp. 46 – 47

John Updike, "At War with My Skin," in *Self-Consciousness* (New York: Knopf, 1989),

pp. 48, 61, 75, 76, 78

Joseph Shipley, *The Origin of English Words* (Baltimore: Johns Hopkins University Press, 1984), p. 209

Lombroso, *L'homme criminel* (Paris: Ancienne Librairie Germer Bailliére et Félix Alcan, 1897), p. iv.

Dermagraphics

Tattoo Time, ed. Ed Hardy (Honolulu: Hardy Marks Publications), vols. 1 – 5

Marks of Civilization: Artistic Transformations of the Body, ed. Arnold Rubin

(Los Angeles: Museum of Cultural History, 1988), pp. 190 – 34

Arkady G. Bronnikov, "Telltale Tattoos in Russian Prisons," *Natural History*, November 1993, p. 53 – 54

Michael Mason, "Every Picture Tells a Story," *Newsweek*, January 7, 1991, p. 60

Michel Thévoz, *The Painted Body* (New York: Rizzoli, 1984), p. 21

John Carswell, *Coptic Tattoo Designs* (Beirut: The American University of Beirut, 1958), p. xii

Adolf Loos, "Ornament and Crime," in *The Architecture of Adolf Loos* (New York: Arts Council, n.d.)

G. W. F. Hegel, *Aesthetics: Lectures on Fine Art*, trans. T. M. Knox
(New York: Oxford University Press, 1975), vol. 1, pp. 7–8

Clement Greenberg, "Modernist Painting," in *Modernism with a Vengeance, 1957–1969*,
ed. John O'Brian (Chicago: University of Chicago Press, 1993), p. 87

Charles Harrison, *Essays on Art and Language* (Cambridge, MA: Basil Blackwell, 1991), p. 47

Kate Linker, *Vito Acconci* (New York: Rizzoli, 1994), p. 23

Donald Kuspit, "Chris Burden: The Feel of Power," in *Chris Burden: a Twenty-Year Survey*
(Newport Beach, CA: Newport Harbor Museum, 1988), p. 37

Chris Burden, *Chris Burden 74–77* (Los Angeles: Burden 1978)

Ed Hardy, *Modern Primitives: An Investigation of Contemporary Adornment & Ritual*, ed. V. Vale and Andrea Juno
(San Francisco: Re/Search Publications, 1989), p. 53

Stelarc, Obsolete Body / Suspensions / Stelarc, ed. James D. Paffrath
(Davis: CA: JP Publications, 1984), pp. 24, 76

Paul McCarthy, "The Body Obsolete," *High Performance*, no. 24 (1983), p. 15

Barbara Rose, "Is It Art? Orlan and the Transgressive Act," *Art in America*, February 1993, p. 85

France Borel, *Le vêtement incarné: Les métaphorphoses du corps* (Paris: Calmann-Lévy, 1992).

De-Signing

Amédée Ozenfant, *Foundations of Modern Art*, trans. John Rodker (New York: Dover, 1952), p. 326

Mark Wigley, "White Out: Fashioning the Modern," *Architecture: In Fashion*, pp. 152–53

Charles Baudelaire, "The Painter of Modern Life," *The Painter of Modern Life and Other Essays*,
trans. Jonathan Mayne (New York: De Capo, 1964), p. 13

Adolf Loos, *Spoken into the Void: Collected Essays 1897–1900*, trans. Jane Newman and John Smith
(Cambridge: MIT Press, 1982), p. 102

Mark Wigley, "White-Out: Fashioning the Modern (Part 2)," *Assemblage* 22 (December 1993),
pp. 11, 13, 34–35

Le Corbusier, *Towards a New Architecture*, trans. Frederick Etchells
(New York: Dover Publications, 1986), pp. 35, 37

Søren Kierkegaard, *Fear and Trembling*, trans. Howard and Edna Hong
(Princeton: Princeton University Press, 1983), p. 82

Stuart Ewen, *All Consuming Images: The Politics of Style in Contemporary Culture*
(New York: Basic Books, 1988), p. 27

Fredric Jameson, *Postmodernism; or, The Cultural Logic of Late Capitalism*
(Durham: Duke University Press, 1991)

Robert Hughes, *The Shock of the New* (New York: Knopf, 1991), p. 43

Thomas Hine, *Populuxe* (New York: Knopf, 1986), p. 11

Gilles Lipovetsky, *The Empire of Fashion: Dressing Modern Democracy*, trans. Catherine Porter

(Princeton: Princeton University Press, 1994), p. 90

Clement Greenberg, *The Collected Essays and Criticism*, ed. John O'Brian

(Chicago: University of Chicago Press, 1986), vol. 1, pp. 11, 12

Andy Warhol, *The Philosophy of Andy Warhol* (New York: Harcourt Brace Jovanovich, 1975),

pp. 91, 92, 136

Jean Baudrillard, *Symbolic Exchange and Death*, trans. Iain Hamilton Grant

(London: SAGE Publications, 1993), p. 90

Roland Barthes, *The Fashion System*, trans. Matthew Ward and Richard Howard

(Berkeley: University of California Press, 1990), p. 273

G. W. F. Hegel, *Phenomenology of Spirit*, trans. A. V. Miller

(New York: Oxford University Press, 1977), p. 19;

Friedrich Nietzsche, *Thus Spoke Zarathustra*, trans. Marianne Cowan

(Chicago: Henry Regnery, 1957), p. 335.

GO FIGURE   Katherine Betts, "Body Language," *Vogue*, April 1994, pp. 345–47, 406

Suzy Menkes, "Fetish or Fashion?" *New York Times*, November 21, 1993

Shirley Lord, "Faking It," *Vogue*, September 1992, p. 423

"Body Language," *New York Times*, June 26, 1994

Tina Gaudoin, "The Devil Made Me Do It," The Fashions of the Times, *New York Times*, Spring 1994.

FALLING APART AT THE SEEMS   Amy Spindler, "Coming Apart," Styles of the Times, *New York Times*, July 25, 1993, pp. 1, 9

Katherin Betts, "La Mode Destroy," *Vogue*, May 1992, 108–10

Hamish Bowles, "Fashion's Visionary," *Vogue*, March 1993, pp. 344, 426

Holly Brubach, "Style," *New York Times Magazine*, April 2, 1995, p. 67.

FASHIONABLE RELIGION   Julia Szabo, "Fashion's New Crusade," *Harper's Bazaar*, September 1993, pp. 99–102

Henry Alford, "Simply Divine," *Vogue*, August 1993, pp. 131–36

Amy Spindler, "Piety on Parade: Fashion Seeks Inspiration," *New York Times*, September 5, 1993.

WEARING THIN   Jody Shields, "The Return of the Gamine," *Vogue*, January 1993, pp. 138–41.

THE TRANSPARENCY   Julia Reed, "Bare Truths," *Vogue*, March 1994, pp. 154, 158.
OF FASHION

WHAT'S IN?/ WHAT'S OUT   Paul Rudnick, "Lingerie," *Vogue*, April 1992, pp. 189–208.

DISDRESSING   Grace Coddington, "Grunge & Glory," *Vogue*, December 1992, pp. 254–60

Janet Siroto, "Punk Rocks Again," *Vogue*, September 1993, pp. 248, 258, 266

Eve Babitz, "Hippie Revival," *Vogue*, October 1992, pp. 296.

IN VESTMENTS Jennifer Steinhauer, "A Golden Moment at the Oscars," *New York Times*, April 2, 1995.

JEANETIC ENGINEERING "Levi Strauss & Co. Introduces Personal Pair Custom Fit Jeans for Women," Levi Strauss & Co. News, news release, November 8, 1994.

MAKING IT UP *Vogue*, April 1994, pp. 199–200
Vogue, September 1993, p. 285
Vogue, May 1993, p. 204
Vogue, December 1991, p. 19
Vogue, May 1992, p. 21
Vogue, March 1993, p. 33
Ladies' Home Journal, November 1994, p. 36.

MODELING REALITY Katherine Betts, "Getting Real," *Vogue*, June 1993, pp. 52–53; 60
Vogue, February 1991.

NET EFFECTS Camilla Nickerson, "Net Effects," *Vogue*, March 1993, pp. 388–94
Carlyne Cerf de Dudzeele, "Black of Night," *Vogue*, February 1993, pp. 202–9.

CYBERCHIC William Gibson, *Virtual Light* (New York: Bantam Books, 1993), p. 48
Janet Siroto, "Future Chic," *Vogue*, March 1994, p. 184
Rudy Rucker, R. U. Sirius & Queen Mu, *Mondo 2000: A User's Guide to the New Edge* (New York: HarperCollins, 1992), pp. 106–12
Amy Spindler, "Dressed to Thrill," *New York Times*, March 13, 1994.

TRENDY NOMADS Janet Siroto, "Future Chic," *Vogue*, March 1994, pp. 172–84
Katherine Betts, "Radical Chic," *Vogue*, July 1992, pp. 102–9.

STRIPPING FASHION Amy Spindler, "Learning from Las Vegas and Show World," *New York Times*, November 5, 1994.

Ground Zero

Jacques Derrida, *Glas*, trans. John Leavy Jr. and Richard Rand
(Lincoln: University of Nebraska Press, 1986), p. 40
Edgar Allan Poe, "Eureka," in *Poetry and Tales*, pp. 1291, 1277–78, 1355
G. W. F. Hegel, *Hegel's Philosophy of Subjective Spirit*, trans. M. J. Petry
(Boston: D. Reidel Publishing Co.), vol. 3, p. 177
Jacques Derrida, "The Pit and the Pyramid: Introduction to Hegel's Semiology," in *Margins*

of Philosophy, trans. Alan Bass (Chicago: University of Chicago Press, 1982), pp. 71–72, 82–83

Edgar Allan Poe, "Ms. Found in a Bottle," in *Poetry and Tales*, p. 198

G. W. F. Hegel, *Phenomenology of Spirit*, trans. A. V. Miller

(New York: Oxford University Press, 1977), p. 286

Georges Bataille, "The Obelisk," in *Visions of Excess: Selected Writings 1927–1939*, ed. Allan Stoekel

(Minneapolis: University of Minnesota Press, 1985), pp. 216, 215, 220, 222.

Avital Ronell, *The Telephone Book*, (Lincoln: University of Nebraska Press, 1989), p. 295

Konrad Wachsmann, *The Turning Point of Building: Structure and Design*

(New York: New York University Press, 1979), p. 31

Robert Smithson, *The Writings of Robert Smithson*, ed. Nancy Holt

(New York: New York University Press, 1979), pp. 43–44

Elihu Vedder, *Digressions* (New York: Houghton Mifflin Co., 1810), p. 451

Michael Heizer: Sculpture in Reverse, ed. Julia Brown

(Los Angeles: The Museum of Contemporary Art, 1984), p. 34.

Douglas Trumbull, unpublished "Corporate Overview";

audio tape for Luxor Hotel exhibition

Robert Venturi et al., *Learning from Las Vegas: The Forgotten Symbolism of Architectural Form*

(Cambridge: MIT Press, 1988), pp. 13, 18, 8–9

David Harvey, *The Condition of Postmodernity* (Cambridge: Basil Blackwell, 1989), p. 153

Paul Virilio, "The Third Window," in *Global Television*, ed. Cynthia Scheider and Brian Wallis

(Cambridge: MIT Press, 1988), p. 194

Margaret Crawford, "The World in a Shopping Mall," in *Variations on a Theme Park: The New American City and the End of Public Space*, ed. Michael Sorkin (New York: Hill and Wang, 1992), p. 3.

"Bernard Tschumi, "The Pleasure of Architecture," *Architectural Design* 3 (1977), p. 217

Bernard Tschumi, *The Manhattan Transcripts* (London: Architectural Design, 1981), p. 2

Bernard Tschumi, *Architecture and Disjunction* (Cambridge: MIT Press, 1994), pp. 234, 49

Bernard Tschumi and Isoaki Arata, "Architecture in a Non-linear Age: The Unceasing Flow of Change," *InterCommunication*, 1995, p. 83

Tschumi, *Architecture and Disjunction*, p. 248

Tschumi, "Ten Points, Ten Examples," in *Electrotecture: Architecture and the Electronic Future*,

ANY, no. 3 (November/December, 1993), p. 41

Tschumi, *Architecture and Disjunction*, pp. 116, 222

Tschumi, *The Manhattan Transcripts*, p. 8

Tschumi, *Cinégramme folie: La Parc de LaVillette*

(Princeton: Princeton Architectural Press, n.d.), p. 12

Tschumi, *Architecture and Disjunction*, p. 163

Tschumi, *Cinégramme folie*, p. vi

Tschumi, *La CaseVide* (London: Architectural Association, 1985)

Tschumi, *Cinégramme folie*, p. viii

Tschumi, "Ten Points, Ten Examples," pp. 42, 43

Tschumi, *Event-Cities* (Cambridge: MIT Press, 1994), p. 367

Tschumi, "Ten Points, Ten Examples," p. 43

Tschumi, "Architecture in a Non-linear Age," p. 86.

Interfacing

Barrie Sherman and Phil Judkins, *Glimpses of Heaven, Visions of Hell:*

Virtual Reality and Its Implications (London: Coronet Books, 1992), pp. 20, 63

Paul Virilio, *The Vision Machine* (Bloomington: Indiana University Press, 1994), p. 62

Howard Rheingold, *Virtual Reality* (New York: Summit Books, 1991), pp. 13 – 14, 128

Myron Kreuger, *Artificial Reality*, vols. 1 – 2 (Reading, MA: Addison-Wesley, 1991)

Jerry Garcia, *Rolling Stone*, November 30, 1989

"Virtual Reality: An Interview with Jaron Lanier," *Whole Earth Review*, Fall 1989, pp. 115 – 16

Friedrich Nietzsche, *The Gay Science*, trans. Walter Kaufmann

(New York: Random House, 1974), p. 181

Immanuel Kant, *The Critique of Judgment*, trans. James Meredith

(New York: Oxford University Press, 1973), p. 21

Friedrich Schiller, *Letters on the Aesthetic Education of Man*, trans. Reginald Snell

(New York: Frederick Ungar, 1977), pp. 27, 137

G. W. F. Hegel, *Science of Logic*, trans. A. V. Miller

(New York: Oxford University Press, 1969), pp. 747 – 48

Friedrich Nietzsche, *Beyond Good and Evil*, trans. Walter Kaufmann

(New York: Random House, 1966), pp. 50, 159

Friedrich Nietzsche, *Will to Power*, trans. Walter Kaufmann

(New York: Random House, 1968), pp. 302, 305, 306

Friedrich Nietzsche, *The Birth of Tragedy*, trans. Francis Golffing

(New York: Doubleday, 1956), pp. 42, 9 – 10

Clement Greenberg, "Abstract and Representational," *Affirmations and Refusals*, 1950 – 1956,

ed. John O'Brian (Chicago: University of Chicago Press, 1993), p. 191

Jean Baudrillard, "The Precession of Simulacra," in *Simulations*, trans. Paul Foss, Paul Patton, and

Philip Beitchman (New York: Semiotext[e], 1983), p. 2

Andy Warhol, *The Philosophy of Andy Warhol* (New York: Harcourt Brace Jovanovich, 1975), p. 182

Emil Zola, *The Ladies' Paradise* (Berkeley: University of California Press, 1992), p. 6

Michael B. Miller, *The Bon Marché: Bourgeois Culture and the Department Store*, 1869 – 1920

(Princeton: Princeton University Press, 1981)

Christoph Asendorf, *Batteries of Life: On the History of Things and Their Perception in Modernity*, trans. Don Reneau (Berkeley: University of California Press, 1993), p. 46

D. Sternberger, *Panorama of the Nineteenth Century*, trans. Joachim Neugroschel

(New York: Urizen, 1977)

Helmut and Alison Gersheim, *L. J. M. Daguerre:The History of the Diorama and the Daguerreotype*

(New York: Dover Publications, 1968)

Alfred Chapius and Edmond Droz, *Automata:A Historical and Technological Study*, trans. Alec Reid

(New York: Central Book Co., 1958)

Jack Burnham, *Beyond Modern Sculpture* (New York: George Brazillier, n.d.), pp. 199 – 200

David Freedman, "Bringing Up RoboBaby," *Wired* 2, no. 12 (December 1994), p. 74

Steven Levy, *Artificial Life:A Report from the Frontier Where Computers Meet Biology*

(New York: Random House, 1992)

K. Eric Drexler, *Engines of Creation:The Coming Era of Nanotechnology* (New York: Doubleday, 1987)

David H. Freedman, *Brainmakers: How Scientists Are Moving beyond Computers to Create a Rival to the Human Brain*

(New York: Simon and Schuster, 1994)

Gina Kolata, "Novel Kind of Computing: Calculation with DNA," *New York Times*, November 22, 1994

Gina Kolata, "A Vat of DNA May Become Fast Computer of the Future,"

New York Times, April 11, 1995

Daniel Dennett, *Consciousness Explained* (New York: Little, Brown and Co., 1991), pp. 253 – 54

J. M. McCelland, D. E. Rumelhart, and G. E. Hinton, "The Appeal of Parallel Distributed Processing,"

in *Parallel Distributed Processing:Explorations in the Microstructure of Cognition*,

ed. James L. McClelland and David E. Rumelhart (Cambridge: MIT Press, 1987), p. 10

Michael I. Posner and Marcus E. Raichle, *Images of Mind*

(New York: Scientific American Library, 1994), p. 13

Roger Penrose, *Shadows of the Mind:A Search for the Missing Science of Consciousness*

(New York: Oxford University Press, 1994), p. 216

Donna Haraway, Simians, *Cyborgs, and Women:The Reinvention of Nature*

(New York: Routledge, 1991), pp. 211 – 12, 218

Irun Cohen, "The Self, the World, and Autoimmunity," *Scientific American*, April 1988, p. 52.

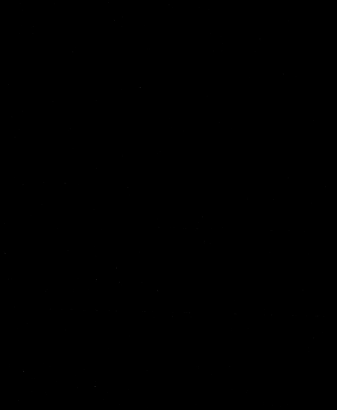

Image Credits

The sources for the images in each
chapter are listed below in the order
in which the images appear for the first time.

Skinsc(r)apes

Photo by Mark C. Taylor.

Cross-section of skin from William Montagna, Albert M. Kligman, and Kay S. Carlisle,
Atlas of Normal Skin (New York: Springer-Verlag, 1992), p. 5.

19th-century diagram from John Davies, *Phrenology: Fad and Science*
(New Haven: Yale University Press, 1955), p. 6.

Advertisement from CKS Partners, Inc.

Photo from C. Lombroso and G. Ferrero, *La Femme Criminelle et La Prostituée* (Paris: Félix Alcan, 1896).

C. Lombroso, *L'Homme Criminel* (Paris: Ancienne Librarie Germer Baillière et Félix Alcan, 1897).

Distributed to medical school dermatology programs by Glaxo, Inc., 1994.

Distributed to medical school dermatology programs by Sandoz company.

Francis Galton, *Inquires into Human Faculty and Its Development* (New York: Macmillan, 1883), p. 356.

C. Lombroso, *L'Homme Criminel.*

Francis Galton, *Inquiry into Human Faculty and Its Development.*

Francis Galton, *Specimens of Composite Portraiture.*

Nancy Burson, *Warhead I,* copyright 1982, Nancy Burson with Richard Carling and David Kramlich.

19th-century drawings from Edgar Alan Poe, *The Narrative of Arthur Gordon Pym, Poe: Poetry and Tales,*
Patrick F. Quinn, ed. (New York: The American Library, 1984).

Drawings from Paul Auster, *The New York Trilogy,* New York: Penguin Books, 1986).

By permission of the author.

Nancy Burson, *The Age Machine* copyright 1982, Nancy Burson with
Richard Carling and David Kramlich.

Nancy Burson, *1st and 2nd Beauty Composites,* copyright 1982, Nancy Burson
with Richard Carling and David Kramlich.

Cover of *Time* magazine.

Photo by Noel A. Taylor.

Photo by Mark C. Taylor.

Dermagraphics

Admiral Scotty, world's most tattooed man. *Tattootime,* no. 5, 1991, p. 128.

Utagawa Toyokuni III, "Hinotama-Kozo Oni Keisuke." Arnold Rubin, ed.,
The Marks of Civilization (Los Angeles: The Museum of Cultural History, 1988), p. 122.

Dr. Katsunari Fukushi. *Tattootime,* no. 4, 1986, p. 78.

Advertisement by permission of Guess Jeans.

Piercing Fans International Quarterly.

Tabwa woman. Arnold Rubin, ed. *The Marks of Civilization,* p. 42.

Jill Purce, *The Mystic Spiral*, Avon Books. *Tattootime*, no. 4, 1986, p. 14.

Coptic Tattoos. *Tattootime*, no. 2, 1983, pp. 8-9.

Arnold Rubin, *The Marks of Civilization*, p. 150.

An inhabitant of the Island of Nukahiwa, *Tattootime*, no. 5, 1990, p. 86.

Von den Steinen, 1925. *Tattootime*, no. 5, 1990, p. 97.

Tattootime, no. 5, 1990, p. 94.

Von den Steinen, 1925. *Tattootime*, no. 5, 1990, p. 99.

Lady Viola. *Tattootime*, no. 5, 1990, p. 14.

After discharge from Army, 1946. *Tattootime*, no. 5, 1990, p. 8.

Erasmus Neilssin, Tattooed by Brooklyn Joe Lieber (ca. 1930s). *Sailor Jerry Collins:*

American Tattoo Master, ed. Donald Edward Hardy, (Honolulu: Hardy Marks Publication, 1994), p. 45.

Tattootime, no. 5, 1990, p. 19.

Vito Acconci, *Trademarks*. By permission of the artist.

Chris Burden, *Trans-Fixed*, Venice, California, April 23, 1974. By permission of the artist.

Cliff Raven, Arnold Rubin, *The Marks of Civilization*, p. 239.

Leo Zuluerta, 1989. *Tattootime*, no. 5, 1990, p. 121.

Fred Corbin, 1988. *Tattootime*, no. 5, 1990, p. 117.

Jill Jordan, 1990. *Tattootime*, no. 5, 1990, p. 113.

Don Ed Hardy, 1986. By permission of the artist.

Laura Vida, 1990. *Tattootime*, no. 5, 1990, p. 116.

Coleman Tattooing, Norfolk, VA 1940s. *Tattootime*, 1988, no. 1, p. 40.

Fakir Musafar. Photo by Charles Gatewood. By permission of the photographer.

Michael Wilson, the "Tattoo Man." Photo by William Gibson and Martha Swope.

By permission of AP/Wide World Photos.

Stelarc, *Obsolete Body/Suspension/Stelarc*, J. Paffrath Publications.

Stelarc, courtesy of *High Performance*.

Orlan. By permission of the artist.

Cliff Raven. Arnold Rubin, *The Marks of Civilization*, p. 239.

De-Signing

Vogue, March 1994, p. 335.

Comme des Garçons. By permission of Peter L. Gould, Image Pictures, Inc.

Vogue, August 1993, p. 130.

Harper's Bazaar, April 1995, p. 181.

Dolce and Gabbana, Daryl K., and Karl Lagerfeld.

Vogue, March 1995, p. 63.

Vogue, December 1992, p. 255.

The New York Times, April 23, 1995. Courtesy of American Express Travel Related Services.

Detour, November 1995, p. 35.

Vogue, December 1992, p. 259.

Vanity Fair, October 1996, p. 51.

W, February 1996, p. 168.

Sportswear International, no. 6, 1995, p. 96.

W, April 1996, p. 180.

Sportswear International, no. 6, 1995, p. 70.

Ground Zero

Photo by permission of Las Vegas News Bureau.

Drawings from Edgar Alan Poe, "Eureka," *Poetry and Tales*, Patrick F. Quinn,

ed. (New York: The American Library, 1984).

Drawing by Albrecht Dürer.

Alexander Graham Bell with his tetragonal lattice kites. Photo from Robert Smithson,

The Writings of Robert Smithson, Nancy Holt, ed. (New York: New York University Press, 1979).

Alexander Graham Bell in his outdoor observation station. Photo from Robert Smithson,

The Writings of Robert Smithson.

Elihu Vedder, *The Questioner of the Sphinx*, 1863, oil on canvas, 36 x 41 3/4 inches.

Bequest of Mrs. Martin Brimmer. Courtesy, Museum of Fine Arts, Boston.

Mark Tansey, *Secret of the Sphinx (Homage to Elihu Vedder)*, 1984, oil on canvas, 60 x 65 inches,

Private Collection; Courtesy Curt Marcus Gallery, New York. Copyright Mark Tansey, 1985.

Alexander Graham Bell. Photo from Konrad Wachsmann, *The Turning Point of Building*

(New York: Van Nostrand Reinhold Publishing).

Don Ed Hardy, *Le Petit Chapeau*. Collection of Masami Teraoka and Lynda Hess.

By permission of the artist.

Mark C. Taylor, "Losing Your Head."

One Dollar Bill.

Alexander Graham Bell. Photo from Konrad Wachsmann, *The Turning Point of Building*.

Photo by Dietrich Christian Lammerts.

Photos courtesy of the Luxor Hotel.

Photos by Dietrich Christian Lammerts.

Photos courtesy of MGM Grand Hotel, Inc.

Photos by José Márquez.

Photos courtesy of Bernard Tschumi Architects.

Photo by José Márquez.

Photos courtesy of Bernard Tschumi Architects.

Photo by Dietrich Christian Lammerts.

Photo courtesy of Bernard Tschumi Architects.

Photo by José Márquez.

Photo courtesy of Bernard Tschumi Architects.

Photo courtesy of MGM Grand Hotel, Inc.

Photo courtesy of the Mirage Hotel.

Photo courtesy of Bernard Tschumi Architects.

Photo courtesy of the Mirage Hotel.

Photo by José Márquez.

Interfacing

Jaquet-Droz, "La Musicienne." Photo from Alfred Chapuis and Edouard Gélis,
Le Monde des Automates: Étude Historique et Technique (Geneva: Editions Slktkine, 1984).

Philon de Byzanne, "Oiseau;" Héron d'Alexandrie, "Oiseau." Photo from Alfred Chapuis and
Edouard Gélis, *Le Monde des Automates: Étude Historique et Technique.*

Teleoperator System designed and developed by Sarcos Research Corporation under a contract
with the U.S. Navy.

Advertisement courtesy of Dana Perfumes.

Ivan Sutherland. Photo by permission of the Department of Computer Science
at the University of Utah.

Raoul Hausmann, *Tatlin at Home*, 1920. Photo courtesy of Moderna Museet, Stockholm.

Laszlo Moholy-Nagy, *Light-Space Modulator*, 1923-30. Kinetic sculpture of steel, plastic, wood
and other materials with electric motor. 151.1 x 69.9 cm. Courtesy of the Busch-Reisinger Museum,
Harvard University Art Museums. Gift of Sibyl Moholy-Nagy.

Advertisement courtesy of AGFA.

Barbara Krueger, "I Shop, Therefore I Am." Photo courtesy of Mary Boone Gallery, New York.

Photo courtesy of *Popular Mechanics*, November, 1994.

Paul van Hoeydonck, *CYB, Head and Arm*, 1969.

Fortune-teller (after A-W. Gamage). Photo from Alfred Chapius and Edouard Gélis,
Le Monde des Automates: Étude Historique et Technique.

"Méchanisme du Coq," 1354. Photo from Alfred Chapius and Gélis, *Le Monde des Automates:
Étude Historique et Technique.*

Paul van Hoeydonck, *Robot*, 1968.

Cindy Sherman. Courtesy of Metro Pictures and the artist.

Nam June Paik, "Global Encoder." Courtesy Carl Solway Gallery, Cincinnati, Ohio.

Photographers: Tom Allison and Chris Gomlen.

P. Jaquet-Droz, "L'Écrivain." Photo from Alfred Chapius and Edouard Gélis, *Le Monde des Automates: Étude Historique et Technique.*

Reprinted by permission of 7th Level, Inc. and Python (Month) Pictures Ltd.

Photo from *Images of Mind* by Posner and Raichle. Copyright (c) 1994 by Scientific American Library. Used with permission of W. H. Freeman and Company.

P. Jaquet-Droz, "L'Écrivain." Photo from Alfred Chapius and Edouard Gélis, *Le Monde des Automates: Étude Historique et Technique.*

Photo by permission of Chip Simons Photography.

Cindy Sherman. Courtesy of Metro Pictures and the artist.

Hiding was designed and produced by Michael Rock, Susan Sellers, and Chin-Lien Chen of 2x4 in collaboration with the author. The serif fonts are Joanna, Bodoni Antiqua, and Didot. The sans serif font is News Gothic. Printed in Hong Kong by C & C Offset Printing Company, Ltd.